£25.00

DATE DUE

Micro-Sociological Theory
Perspectives on Sociological Theory
Volume 2

Micro-Sociological Theory
Perspectives on Sociological Theory
Volume 2

Edited by
H.J. Helle and S.N. Eisenstadt

 SAGE Studies in International Sociology 34
sponsored by the International Sociological Association/ISA

For information address

SAGE Publications Ltd
28 Banner Street
London EC1Y 8QE

SAGE Publications Inc
275 South Beverly Drive
Beverly Hills, California 90212

SAGE Publications India Pvt Ltd
C-236 Defence Colony
New Delhi 110 024

British Library Cataloguing in Publication Data

Perspectives on sociological theory, – (Sage studies in international sociology; v.
    33–34)
    1. Sociology
    I. Eisenstadt, S.N.   II. Helle, H.J.
    301'.01   HM24

Library of Congress Catalog Card Number 85–050094

ISBN 0–8039–9714–0 (V.2)

ISBN 0–8039–9715–9 (V.2) Pbk

Printed by J.W. Arrowsmith Ltd., Bristol, UK.

Contents

Table of Contents of
Macro-Sociological Theory

General introduction
to perspectives on sociological theory

S.N. Eisenstadt and H.J. Helle

The essays on macro- and micro-sociological analysis collected in these two volumes — most of which were presented at the symposia on Macro- and Micro-Sociological Analysis at the Tenth World Congress of Sociology in Mexico, in August 1983 — present from different vantage points some of the major dimensions of theoretical controversy in sociology in general.

These controversies — and the papers presented here — have several major, closely interconnected thrusts which cut across macro- and micro-sociological analysis alike. First, they indicate an important shift from concerns that were dominant in the 1950s and early 1960s, especially under the influence of the structural-functional school and the way in which it was accepted in the sociological community. This shift implied that no institutional order or any structure of social interactions in general, is any longer taken as given, nor explained by its needs and configurations as shaped, above all, by the extent of its differentiation; nor its functioning analysed according to the contribution of its different parts. Instead there developed a strong emphasis on the process of construction of such order.

Institutional orders and situations of interaction are more and more seen as being constructed by the activities of different actors — groups and individuals in different social areas and situations. Hence there also took place a shift to the analysis of the processes and mechanisms through which the different aspects of social order of macro- and micro-situations alike are being constructed by such activities.

Second, and closely connected with this shift to the analysis of the construction of patterns of social institutions and of institutional order, there has taken place another shift — namely the emphasis on the autonomy of the major social actors. Individual social actors are seen as being of crucial importance in the very process of the construction of social roles, structures and orders and it is stressed that they cannot be subsumed under these roles or structures. Indeed, potentially they are also creators of roles, of their meanings, of the definitions of situations. Hence, a major problem here is to identify the different levels and types of such structures — or counter-structures.

Third, also of special importance in this context has been the strong emphasis on the dimension of power and of the symbolic construction of reality in the shaping of situations of interaction and institutional orders.

The studies presented in these two volumes bring out these major theoretical themes in a great variety of ways and from different points of view — but they do indicate that these problems are common to all areas of sociological endeavour — above all to macro- and micro-sociological analysis alike.

Margaret Archer, Ralph Turner, Jef Verhoeven and others spell out in their chapters that macro- and micro-theory show promising signs of convergence after too many decades of senseless separation. It will be the task of historians of sociology to retrace the curious steps the field has taken in theory formation during the century from about 1850 to 1950. Here we can but sketch how a one-sided selection from the pioneering work of Comte, Spencer, Marx, Durkheim, Simmel and Weber caused unnecessary narrowness in the continuity of sociological theory, and how partisanship resulted in separating the field into camps whose members looked at each other with, at least, suspicion. One of the fissions that in retrospect seem particularly strange is the separation of macro- and micro-theory.

The classical sociologists, all of whom were born and received their academic training during the nineteenth century, have been very sensitive to problems of epistemology. Given the sound philosophical background — which Marx and Simmel of course had as trained philosophers, and which Comte, Spencer, Durkheim and Weber acquired before they started writing sociology — none of them could ignore the problem that what reveals itself to superficial sensual perception is certainly not all there is to know in the context of social reality. Faced with the dilemma that, in many respects, what could be known reliably was not very relevant, and what seemed of great importance was impossible to find out with sufficient precision, the great pioneers of our field did therefore not react with naïveté, but instead were prepared to make conscious decisions.

No matter which direction their decisions would take, the classical sociologists remained conscious of the dilemma that Plato had already captured in his parable of the cave, but their successors tended to misrepresent as a clean solution to an epistemological problem what from Comte to Weber was taken to be just the lesser of two evils. And this was probably the beginning of methodological cleavages of the kind that this volume is designed to overcome. Various brands of Marxism have thrived, but Marx is quoted as not wanting to be counted among the Marxists. Comte coined the concept of the positive stage in the evolution of human knowledge. He, as well as Spencer, was a follower of Francis Bacon in the desire to collect data on nature in order to gain control of nature, but with their incredibly rich studies in history and comparative culture, neither of them would fit the strict rules of modern behaviouristic positivism.

Durkheim wanted to draw a sharp line between sociology and psychology; to him the whole had a reality of its own that could not be explained in terms of individual parts that formed it. In his books of 1893 to 1897 he does lay the foundation for modern functionalism, but in 1912, in his great study on religion, he shows that the origin of the sacred cannot be nature as wind and lightning, nor as the sun, the moon or the planets, that it cannot be the dreams and hallucinations of individual sorcerers. Instead, Durkheim claims nothing less than that the sacred is generated and maintained in the interaction of the human cult. And Max Weber could be used selectively by almost anyone in support of his version of theory as long as Weber's indebtedness to Simmel was ignored, and as long as Simmel was reduced to being the founder of formal sociology.

Fortunately, the field of sociological theory has moved beyond these misrepresentations, and as partisan, selective and one-sided readings of the classics become obsolete, many of the schisms grow to be part of the less pleasant aspects of the history of the discipline. The cleavage between different methodological schools, and certainly the confrontation between micro- and macro-theory belong to the past, and the following pages are designed to help us recognize that in our future projects as students of sociology.

Introduction to micro-sociological theory

H.J. Helle

It is the objective of this volume on micro-sociology to contribute to the stock-taking and comparison of the most significant modern approaches to micro-theory and social psychology, and to demonstrate the numerous trends towards convergence with macro-theoretical paradigms. Since the 1960s sociology in general has passed through a phase of new beginnings and experimentation with novel approaches. The time has now come to take another look from a more distanced viewpoint in order to bring about a comparative appraisal with the intention of deciding what seems useful enough to be retained and developed further, and what ought to be abandoned. However, it is *not* the objective of these following chapters to take any such decision *for* the reader.

Georg Simmel's classical formulations of the principle of inter-relatedness (*Wechselwirkung*), of the I–you relationship as the foundation for '*verstehen*', and of his basic epistemological premises spelled out in his book, *The Problems of the Philosophy of History* (1892), are taken as a point of departure. Simmel is presented as an author in whose work macro- and micro-sociological paradigms are indissolubly interwoven, who contributed significantly to the establishment of the Chicago school, mediated by the teaching of Albion Small, Robert Park, Everett Hughes and others, and whose methodological premises coincide largely with those of Wilhelm Dilthey, Wilhelm Wundt, William James, Max Weber and George H. Mead. Simmel can also legitimately be seen as a precursor of role theory (compare his essay 'Zur Philosophie des Schauspielers'/ Towards a Philosophy of the Actor, 1908).

The modern state of the art in role theory is discussed by Ralph H. Turner. He demonstrates that several of the most fundamental interactionist assumptions remain in sharp contrast to structuralist assumptions: that the fundamental character of role behaviour is the effort to construct and execute a meaningful and rewarding complement of behaviour in a system of social relationships; that roles are gestalts rather than collections of discrete behaviours; that the allocation of persons to roles is a matter of continuing negotiation in even the most rigid organizational context; that these and other questions remain unanswered, but that there has been a remarkable convergence between the structuralist and the interactionist role paradigms.

Yet, Turner suggests further modifications of structuralist role theory from an interactionist point of view. To arrive at an adequate level of performance through the combined mainstreams of role theory, Turner proposes these requirements: (1) the concept of role must add something to the substance of the theory rather than be just a superfluous magical device; (2) it must be equally effective in dealing with valued (non-deviant) as with disvalued (deviant) roles; (3) it must be equally suitable for dealing with roles in organizational structures (positions) as with roles that are defined in terms of values (the hero, the saint); (4) the approach must be able to deal with role change; (5) it must include the concept of creativity in role playing. In his concluding remarks the author mentions an article by Charles Powers of 1981, which Turner considers to be 'one of the most constructive efforts to move towards a more adequate convergence' between structuralist and interactionist role theories.

In his 'historical reconstruction of the development of role theory' Hans Joas departs from George H. Mead, whom he regards as having been 'the most important source for the emergence and development of role theory'. He points to Mead's basic principles of human communication on the basis of the 'significant symbol' which implies people's ability:

> to react to their own gestures and utterances in a way that is anticipatory and thus inwardly represents their fellow actors' possible responses. This makes it possible for their own behaviour to be oriented towards the potential reactions of other actors. As these actors too, are principally in possession of this ability, common collective action oriented towards a common binding pattern of mutual behavioural expectations becomes a possibility.

Following his attempt to reconstruct the history of its development, Joas turns to defining the status of role theory 'as a metatheoretical scheme for the conceptual structuring of an area of study within the social sciences'. It is a part of the general theory of action and 'has its roots in the phylogenetic emergence of the prerequisites for all human history and sociality'. On this basis Joas finds himself confronted with two conflicting definitions of the role concept: (1) the structuralist definition: 'social roles are clusters of normative behavioural expectations directed at the behaviour of position-holders', and (2) the interactionist position, which Joas ties to Mead as well as to 'critical' role theory, which stresses the 'need ... for role-taking in the sense of situationally specific anticipation of *alter*'s behaviour'. Joas undertakes the task of closing the gap between these two definitions by introducing the concept of the situation. Role thus becomes 'the normative expectation of situationally specific meaningful behaviour'.

In his discussion of socialization research, Joas points out that aside from research on organizations this is 'the main field of empirical application of role theory'. He criticizes 'the naïve kind of role theory research' for reducing the process of role acquisition to learning how to fill a position.

G. David Johnson and J. Steven Picou address a recent controversy about Herbert Blumer's interpretation of philosophical pragmatism. In their chapter 'The foundations of symbolic interaction reconsidered' they 'attempt to document the philosophical foundations of the American social psychology represented in the works of Herbert Blumer, Erving Goffman and others'. Most authors relate this school of thought to George H. Mead and to William James. But a new, revisionist interpretation of Mead's work would make it appear based on doctrines of social and philosophical realism. If this reading of Mead should prove correct, 'Blumer's (1969) interpretative methodology cannot be the legitimate heir to this new revised Mead'.

This is precisely what Lewis and Smith (1980) claim to have shown. 'James and Dewey are said to have advanced nominalist philosophies, whereas Peirce's and Mead's philosophies are interpreted as realist.' Johnson and Picou very carefully read and present to their reader the texts by James and Mead. They demonstrate how 'Mead emphasizes that the world's order is in part constituted by our actions'. They go on to explain the misunderstanding by the fact that James, Dewey and Mead had developed an epistemological position beyond the dichotomy of nominalism versus realism. 'Both James and Mead contend that we cannot arbitrarily construct the world. Although both stress this world texture, neither James nor Mead are naïve realists.'

Working closely with the original texts, as Johnson and Picou do, opens up a number of interesting relationships of indebtedness. When Mead writes 'Nature ... is a perspective' (1932: 172) he echoes the very dictum by Kant on which Simmel based *The Problems of the Philosophy of History*. 'James also introduced the "I–Me" dichotomy developed by Mead (1934)', which in turn resembles Simmel's 'I–you' concept.

> Mead introduces the categories of self and society, and stimulus and response, in order to address the social psychological problem that James ignores. This introduction, however, does not constitute a metaphysical break. Mead, instead, extends the Jamesian metaphysics to a previously uncharted problem.

On the consensus in epistemology between James and Mead, the

authors show that 'both advocate the pragmatist criteria for truth —
an idea is true if it works in our experience'. But where there are
differences, those are documented also: 'For James, truth is known
through advantageous "connexions" in experience. For Mead, truth
is a process and is grounded in human activity.' But,

> Mead (1929–30: 386) became dissatisfied with James's reliance on the
> criteria of satisfaction as the test of truth. Mead aims to remove this
> private criterion of truth from his pragmatism and replace it with a
> greater degree of objectivity. In grasping this disagreement, they [Lewis
> and Smith] proclaim Mead a social realist and James a subjective
> nominalist. They contend that this difference overwhelms whatever
> continuities that exist in the two philosophers' work. Their analysis,
> however, tends to exaggerate these differences.

Johnson and Picou refer to D.L. Miller's interpretation of Mead,
and again stress Mead's relational position in connection with the
concept of the 'hypothetical perspective', that sounds very much
like Simmel's 'hypothetical you': 'the organism, in effect, makes a
proposal to its environment. If it works in the organism's own
system it is true.'

In their conclusion the authors again emphasize the fundamental
importance of James's two volumes *The Principles of Psychology*
(1980a, b), which in their opinion not only strongly influenced Mead
(via Dewey), but of which they say, 'In our view, one of the tremors
of that eruption destroyed the monolith of dualistic social psychology. From the ruins, Mead and the symbolic interactionists were
able to construct a processive, non-dualistic, that is Jamesian,
replacement.'

Jef Verhoeven's chapter, 'Goffman's frame analysis and modern
micro-sociological paradigms', starts out with an impressive review
of Goffman's numerous works to show that central concepts and the
basic approach of *Frame Analysis* were present in them and
developed out of them. Verhoeven then demonstrates 'the differences and similarities between Goffman's frame analysis on the one
hand, and Blumer's symbolic interaction, Schutz's phenomenological sociology, and Garfinkel's ethnomethodology on the other
hand'. He undertakes this ambitious project because several
one-sided readings of frame analysis have tended to confuse
Goffman's paradigm with one or several of those other approaches.
Thus, frame analysis is considered to be a formal sociology
(Jameson, 1976), a symbolic interactionist approach (Littlejohn,
1977; Glaser, 1976), ethnomethodological and semiotic (Jameson,
1976), and structuralist (Gonos, 1977)'. Verhoeven spells out the
originality of Goffman, his own creativity in theory construction,
and proves that frame analysis cannot be forced into any one of the
other paradigms.

Very systematically, Goffman as well as the other three authors (Blumer, Schutz and Garfinkel) are then as it were 'interviewed' by Verhoeven as to their concepts of reality, and their ideas of people and of society as the two most important aspects of (1) the world-view of the researcher. Further variables for comparison are: (2) how do Goffman and the other authors perceive the subject matter of sociology?; and (3) what are their methodological principles in (a) scientific reasoning, (b) their understanding of theory, (c) concept formation, and (d) data collection techniques? Among the list of conclusions is Verhoeven's statement that frame analysis 'delivers a brilliant description of the structure of our experience. This approach is important because it puts structural analysis back into the study of small groups'. This summary by Verhoeven implies a concept of structure which in itself is a step towards closer integration of micro- and macro-theory in sociology.

Arthur W. Frank develops a new sociological epistemology *out of ethnomethodology* in order to find a way *out of ethnomethodology*. His chapter is a striking exercise in theory creation. Nobody having read it would describe its content as theory *construction* because of its *deconstructing* impetus which is self-proclaimed as well as convincingly performed. Frank starts out with a sentence from a book review by Douglas W. Maynard that deals with the difficulties in explaining the basic concept of ethnomethodology (EM): 'These concepts have been defined and illustrated in as many ways as there are secondary sources on ethnomethodology, but I suspect they remain inaccessible to the untutored reader.'

Frank analyses this brief text using EM procedure and, by supplementing other short quotations from the same book review, demonstrates that EM gives oral communication priority over reading written texts. An interesting change of perspective that occurs during the chapter brings its topic closer to the reader by letting him or her look at it from different vantage points. Thus Frank first takes EM's perspective 'that certain difficulties of learning through texts are surmounted when learning takes place in person'. He then identifies this perference for talk over text as an issue not 'of pedagogy but one of epistemology' that 'suggests an essential limitation in the present formulation of EM'.

Frank's own epistemological position comes to the foreground of the argument when he confesses his conviction of 'the irremediable uncertainty of interpretation'. EM undercuts this insight by constructing a hierarchy that suggests infallibility: texts are open to interpretation, in any case of doubt there is recourse to the tape-recording of the conversation, and finally the 'tutored' interpreter can appeal to the actual speech situation as a source of certainty that is defined by EM as infallible as it is in fact —

according to Frank — inaccessible to the social scientist. This is made quite plausible in the passages on conversation analysis (CA). Frank is indebted to Jacques Derrida and his concepts of phenomenology. Applying those to his line of reasoning leads to the startling result that what first appeared to be a weakness of EM now turns out to be an epistemological defect of sociology in general.

Frank confirms his premise that 'the sign is always uncertain' and praises 'early EM' for having known this. 'In later EM, however, the centrality of irremediable uncertainty got lost'. Since then it has no advantage over other branches of sociology, because there too the basic problem of interpretation is obscured 'by rhetorically constructing "the data" as the unmediated presence of the world, the possibility of direct knowledge'. Frank does not leave his reader with frustrating problems to which there seem to be no solutions. Rather he suggests 'to decentre sociology between text and world. Eventually, text and world must be understood as mutually constitutive'. This is the resurrection of the relational epistemology of Georg Simmel whose main critique — as implicitly Frank's — has been directed against reification of relationships.

The problem of revisions and relations among modern paradigms in the tradition of ethnomethodology is also discussed in the chapter by Paul Atkinson. He describes 'ethnography' and 'conversational analysis' as two directions in contemporary micro-sociology which many commentators treat as mutually incompatible. Under the heading 'Talk and identity: some convergences in micro-sociology' Atkinson argues against such a polarization and for a systematic rapprochement between these two strands of methodology. The argument is illustrated primarily from recent British work on organizational settings (medical, educational and legal), and includes a detailed treatment of a sequence of talk from a higher education seminar.

In opposition to the programme of EM, Atkinson argues that the fundamental distinction between 'topics' and 'resources' 'has been rendered in terms which are too rigid and absolute'. But he wants to develop further than abandon 'ethnography'. He undertakes this in the tradition of Simmel, Mead, Schutz and Goffman, all of whom he mentions in his text.

> The logic of interactionist ethnography is predicated on the homology between the social action as observed, and participant observation as social action: that is, the identity of the social actor as known object and as knowing subject. This is, after all, central to Mead's theory of knowledge as well as implicit in the empirical investigations of interactionist researchers.

The '"traditional", interactionist ethnographer' has paid too little attention to language, given his confessed interest in matters of identity and moral careers of 'selves'. Therefore, Atkinson demonstrates 'that close attention to the organization of talk can directly inform an ethnographic interest in the social production and display of "selves" and "identities"'. A brief but convincing 'data extract' shows that 'the recipient design of conversational talk provides one way in which identity-relevant work may get done through the social organization of talk itself'. Language, then, to Atkinson and probably most of his readers, is 'constitutive of social selves and social order'. The paper supports Goffman's insistence on the interdependence of 'ritual' and 'system' constraints in the accomplishment of face-to-face encounters.

Steven L. Gordon in his chapter 'Micro-sociological theories of emotions' widens the theoretical scope in order to examine the socio-cultural sources of emotional experience and expression. He draws upon such diverse paradigms as behavioural exchange theory, conflict theory and symbolic interactionism. These he applies to four different problem areas of the sociology of emotions: (1) *Differentiation* — how does emotion become available in qualitatively distinct kinds or types? (2) *Socialization* — through what learning processes do people acquire understandings about meanings, expressions and consequences of emotions? (3) *Normative management* — how do societies and groups induce their members to intensify, reduce and otherwise manage their emotional experiences and expressions? (4) *Link to macro-structure* — what is the nature of the connection between large-scale societal structures and the everyday emotional experiences of individuals? Gordon refers to Arlie Hochschild and Randall Collins to show the 'important linkages between emotional experience and the larger social structure'.

In the final chapter of this volume, Joseph Berger, David G. Wagner and Morris Zelditch present 'Theoretical and metatheoretic themes in expectations states theory'. Their point of departure is problem-solving interaction in 'small, initially undifferentiated' groups. This type of interaction then 'gives rise to differences in under-lying, unobservable expectations for future performance'. The authors suggest a flexible concept of theory that is not to be confused with 'a "paradigm" in Kuhn's sense'. Through continual testing in empirical research theories are developed in scope and precision.

There is a common core to the wide variety of contributions to the 'expectation states programme': (1) there is a common set of terms and assumptions; (2) there are 'common metatheoretical directives'; and (3) there are 'common methods of observation and inference'. Although no reference is made to classic (W.I. Thomas) or contemporary (H.P. Buba) authors who would most likely concur, the central unit of theory formation 'is the situation (not the group, organization or society)'. The key concept is defined like this: 'expectation states are stable relational structures, their stability is relative to specific features of the interactive situation. The same actor can hold any one of an almost infinite number of expectation states, depending on the situation.' The 'translation' of such a state into empirical observable behaviour is described along three variables, using the 'power-prestige-theory' as an example: the 'expectation advantage' or disadvantage of an interactant is mutually interdependent with his chances to (1) perform, (2) communicate 'positive or negative evaluations', and (3) accept or resist 'influence by another'.

The authors remind the reader, that 'expectation states are not observable' and they implicitly at least conform to Max Weber's concept of the ideal type when they use the term 'ideal generalizations'. There is one reference to 'all interactionist theory', of which this approach appears to be a part, and there is the compelling distinction between theoretical research (in the laboratory situation) and applied research (in 'natural settings'). To the authors, 'expectation states theories cut across the "micro-macro" distinction that is so common in sociological theory', but they do in fact 'rest on individual level social psychological principles'.

References

Buba, Hans Peter (1980) *Situation*. Berlin: Duncker und Humblot.
Helle, Horst J.(ed.) (1982) *Kultur und Institution*. Berlin: Duncker und Humblot.
Simmel, Georg (1908) 'Zur Philosophie des Schauspielers', *Morgen*, 2: 1685–9.

For further references see the following chapters.

1

The classical foundations of micro-sociological paradigms

H.J. Helle

Neo-Kantianism and sociology

Kantian philosophical methodology either explicitly or implicitly became the background against which the method of *'verstehen'* as well as symbolic interactionism were developed. Among the historical sources of this type of theory were the works of Georg Simmel which contain the methodological foundations of the search for meaning. Additionally, the American thinkers chiefly associated with the philosophy of pragmatism followed in the tradition of Kant. William James dealt with the problems of epistemology in terms somewhat different from Simmel's. James stressed that it was necessary to differentiate between the content of perception on one side, and the reality status attributed to it by the perceiver on the other. Perception is, thus, not to be separated from the evaluation of what is perceived. It is at this juncture that individuals are seen as having the ability to ascribe significance and meaning to a particular appearance. For Erving Goffman it later became one of the purposes of 'frame analysis' to reconstruct that process of ascription (Goffman, 1974: 2–3).

Interactionist methodology will be shown to be associated with the *'verstehen'* approach that has commonly been credited to Max Weber. While this view is not incorrect in so far as it takes into account the significant contributions Weber made towards improving this approach, it is incomplete because it tends to underrate the influence that Simmel had on Max Weber as well as on the Chicago school of sociology and probably on George H. Mead who, like Simmel, studied in Berlin with Wilhelm Dilthey. The list of American scholars who studied at the University of Berlin at the time when Simmel was there also includes the names of Albion W. Small and Robert E. Park.

The circle of friends with whom the philosopher and sociologist Simmel had frequent contacts included Heinrich Rickert, Edmund Husserl and Max Weber. In his philosophical and sociological thought, Simmel was not so much a representative of neo-Kantianism as he was a prominent autonomous authority on the work of Kant. One may consider Simmel as a mediator between Kant and Max Weber: the intensive familiarity of Simmel with the writings of Kant, as well as the familiarity of Max Weber with the writings of Simmel, are well documented (Simmel, 1904; Weber, 1905). Simmel's essay on historical materialism (Simmel, 1977: 185) has been strangely ignored.

Simmel probably exerted considerable influence on the thoughts of philosophers and sociologists at the University of Chicago. It is striking in the biography of George H. Mead (1863–1931) that from 1889 until 1891 he studied at the University of Berlin, and previously had studied at the University of Leipzig (1888–9). The question of a possible personal contact between Mead and Simmel would be of great interest, but so far it appears to have been neglected. However, documents prove that Mead intended to write a dissertation in Berlin under the supervision of Wilhelm Dilthey; it was to have dealt with Kant's concept of space (*Raum*). Mead's Berlin dissertation was never concluded, however, because he hurriedly left Europe in 1891 in response to an opportunity to take a position in the US (Joas, 1978: 12).

Irrespective of this, we know from Simmel's biography that he entered Berlin University as a first-year student in 1876 to study there for five years. The thesis on the basis of which his doctor's degree was conferred was entitled 'Darstellung und Beurteilung von Kants verschiedenen Ansichten über das Wesen der Materie' (Description and Evaluation of Kant's Different Perspectives of the Essence of Matter). Simmel's '*Habilitationsschrift*' again was concerned with Kant's philosophy, now centring on Kant's theory of space and time. After much difficulty and criticism by faculty members, which was overcome only because of Dilthey's intervention on the part of Simmel, he passed the '*Habilitation*' and became '*Privatdozent*' in 1884, five years prior to Mead's arrival in Berlin. It is quite improbable that Mead, undertaking a similar dissertation project under Dilthey, would have failed to take account of Simmel's works.

Besides, by the time Mead arrived in Berlin, Simmel had gained prominence through his lectures inside and outside the University, and opponents of his unconventional style criticized the fact that so many women and foreigners attended his remarkable lectures. Mead was probably one of those foreigners.[1]

While the influence of Simmel on Mead has not yet been established with sufficient clarity, Simmel's influence on Weber has been acknowledged by Weber himself. Weber cited Simmel in his methodological writings:

The most developed logical account of a theory of 'verstehen' may be found in the second edition of Simmel's 'The Problems of the Philosophy of History' (Probleme der Geschichtsphilosophie: 1905, pp. 27–62) ... Simmel should first of all receive all the credit for establishing within the wide range of possible contents of the word 'verstehen' ... a clear distinction between objectively 'understanding' the meaning of a message and subjectively 'interpreting' the motives of the (talking or acting) person (Weber, 1922: 92–3).

There are numerous other references to Simmel in Weber's publications. Indeed, Simmel spelled out the concept of *'verstehen'* on the basis of Kant's philosophy and — prior to Weber (Tenbruck, 1958: 604–7) — constructed it on the assumption that there are two independently given types of reality: the reality of objects and the reality of meaning. Friedrich H. Tenbruck pointed out as early as 1958 that Simmel had written his sociological texts between 1890 and 1900, after which time he devoted his attention to philosophy, while Max Weber, originally a historian of law, did not start his sociological writings until 1904. This means that *as sociologists*, Simmel and Weber were *not* contemporaries, Donald N. Levine had made a significant contribution to the problem of the relationship between Simmel and Weber by publishing in 1971 a previously unknown manuscript by Max Weber on 'Georg Simmel as Sociologist' (Levine, 1972).

Verstehen as synthesis

In this chapter the term *'verstehen'* is used in the special context of the recognition of meaning as an attempt to solve — in a methodologically valid manner — the ancient problem of the division on one side between subject and object, and on the other side, between essence and appearance.

> The structure of every 'verstehen' is, from the beginning, intrinsically a synthesis between two separate elements. Given is a factual appearance, which as such is not yet understood. And added to it is from inside the subject, to whom this appearance is given, something else, which either emerges directly from this subject or is taken over and applied by it: the recognition of meaning [*verstehender Gedanke*], which in a way penetrates the initially given factual appearance and transforms it into something that is 'understood' [*verstanden*]. (Simmel, 1918: 4)

With this assertion, Simmel was, of course, interested in how the subject attains the recognition of meaning. According to Plato, the subject's soul had a chance to familiarize itself with the recognizable 'essence' qualities in the realm of ideas, where the soul was present and capable of making pre-natal experiences prior to becoming incarnated into a living human being. Later in inner-worldly life the subject 'remembers' what Platonic ideas he or she had seen prior to birth. Plato developed this concept of recognition of meaning as

'Anamnesis' in his dialogue 'Phaidon'. Simmel explicitly developed his methodology in the continuity of Plato's approach (Simmel, 1911: 104).

Kant distinguishes between '*verstand*' or intelligence, which operates on the basis of experience, and '*vernunft*' or reason, which 'contains in itself the foundation of ideas' (Kant, n.d.: Par. 40, 70). Reason is not, as with Plato, the memory of a mythical pre-natal form of being. Rather, it is provoked by discontent with the imperfection and narrowness of the senses in searching for 'noumena' that transcend experience. With this reasoning Kant took a decisive step towards what much later became the concept of 'the social construction of reality'. The philosophical foundation for the concept of '*verstehen*' as a synthesis of elements from experience and from reason is explained in Kant's words:

> If, however, '*vernunft*', cannot be fully content with any application of the rules of empirical perception ... intelligence is driven outside of its proper circles of activity: it will henceforth imagine objects of experience that expand far beyond the reach of any empirical perception, or it will even (for the sake of perfection) search 'Noumena' to which to tie the chain of thought in order finally for once to become independent of the conditions of experience and nevertheless to be able to produce an attitude of having arrived at a solution.' (Kant, n.d.: Par. 45, 75)

From the foundation of this teaching came Simmel, Mead and others, who searched for the source of the recognition of meaning of '*verstehen*' within the context of interaction. Even in Mead's methodology, 'reality per se' ... as Simmel had already asserted, cannot be experienced: it is [just as the "subject of perception"] socially organized. As such, reality can only be experienced from the perspectives of various standpoints and interactional contexts.' (Bühl, 1972: 58.) Simmel explicitly referred to Kant and pointed to the problem that Kant has dealt with: that a complete image of nature can emerge only as the result of an autonomous achievement of that reason which is carefully applied by the observer.

In the continuity of this Kantian teaching, Simmel also believed that the unity of society is not objectively given but rather a mental construct which is based on the recognition of meaning. This 'social construction of reality' Simmel already saw as the result of a process of interaction. In his widest read book, *Soziologie*, he dealt with the 'a priori' of society by asking 'How is Society Possible?' (Simmel, 1922: 21–30). In his first 'a priori' he anticipated what later was to become a fundamental category in Mead's social psychology: the concept of the 'generalized other' (Schnabel, 1976: 299). According to Simmel:

we see the other not simply as an individual, but rather as colleague, or comrade, or member of our political party, in short: as fellow citizen of the same particular world; and this inevitable prerequisite that operates automatically is one of the means of formating one's personality and reality in the other's perception according to the quality required by his place in society. (Simmel 1922: 25)

These words show the close methodological ties between the concept of '*verstehen*' and the interactionist approach.

But Max Weber too was fully aware of the work Simmel had based upon Kant, and Weber placed it in the centre of his concept of meaningful action, which contains the notion of a synthesis between the two types of reality: the appearance of the objective elements of action and the meaning to be recognized in an operation called '*verstehen*'.[2]

According to Weber, the synthesis of appearance and meaning is accomplished in the process of action. The objectifications or culture objects that are produced in the action process can then be understood: their meaning can be recognized if the researcher succeeds in reconstructing the process by which meaning has been imparted in action. As with Simmel, Weber also saw society from the perspective of its culture. He asserted that two inseparably intertwined levels, that of the material object and that of meaning, enter into culture, and he defined culture accordingly: '"Culture" is a finite segment of the meaningless infinity of world events that man has selected from his perspective, and that he has thoughtfully created as meaningful.' (Weber, 1922: 180.) Upon cursory examination, the sum total of 'world events' appears to be unending and meaningless. Nevertheless, mankind has the potential for endowing activities with significance and meaning, and 'culture' arises from these collective evaluations.

In Volume 1 of his collected essays on the sociology of religion Weber reflects on the difficulty of summing up one's life as something relatively complete. He writes about the pre-industrial peasant who was firmly imbedded in his regional culture, that he could die 'full of years' like Abraham. The same was true for the feudal lord and knightly hero. To Weber these are personages who were capable of fulfilling, as he puts it, 'a circle of being beyond which they did not reach. Thus, in their way they could achieve an innerworldly perfection that followed from the fact that the meaning of their lives was naïvely unambiguous.' (Weber, 1920: 570.) By contrast, modern 'cultured' people, who through progressive individualization leave behind structured contexts of interaction, distance themselves more and more from any concrete regional culture, and are left with the unending task of rational self-perfection.

On the frustrations involved in this task Weber writes: 'And the more the cultural goods and goals of self-perfection become differentiated and multiplied, the smaller becomes the fraction thereof, which the individual can span in his lifetime, be it passively as recipient or actively as co-creator.' (Weber, 1920: 570.) This frustration is the fate of the isolated individual of modern rational culture, who, unlike Abraham, does not terminate his or her life full of years but rather full of tears.

Weber paints the image of modern rational culture in dark colours. Much of what he has to say sounds strangely up-to-date, although he wrote these passages more than sixty years ago. He describes what in his day were essentially the difficulties of the intellectual population, of which he of course was a leading member. But since in the past decades the intellectual has more and more become the image in which people want to create themselves, Weber's analysis of over-individualization has grown to be valid for an increasing percentage of the population.

> The world has become a place of imperfection, injustice, suffering, sin, and transience, a place for a culture burdened down with inevitable guilt which becomes more and more meaningless as it unfolds and differentiates further and further: in all of these instances the world had to appear, from a purely ethical point of view, equally fragile and devalued given the religious postulate of a divine meaning of its existence.

There is hardly room for brotherly closeness in a culture organized purely on the basis of occupational work. About such a culture Weber writes: 'To lead the life of Buddha, Jesus or Saint Francis under the technical and social conditions of a rational culture is condemned to failure for purely external reasons alone.' (Weber, 1920: 571.)

Over-rationalization and over-individualization dissolve the webs of social coherence with their potential to support stable contexts of interaction. Weber's analysis returns to its point of departure: the mystical content of coherent patterns of meaning does not endure the process of rational analysis. Instead, such a process dissolves it and deprives it of its very essence. On the level of concrete individual experience, the man or woman concerned is torn between the demand for rational self-sufficiency on the one hand and the religious command for brotherly solidarity. Guilt and loneliness are the qualities of this experience of conflicting goals, and Weber leaves his research on the sociology of religions with the doctrine that religion cannot be kept alive by the isolated individual, but only by a collectivity united round the consensus on the importance of something rational analysis cannot grasp (Helle 1982b: 113–18).

For Simmel, the structure of all recognition of meaning through '*verstehen*' is synthesis. For Weber, every '*verstehen*'–synthesis reflects the structure of a synthesis already completed in action. Object and meaning become joined in the action, and this union is also implied in the process of '*verstehen*'.

The relationship of one mind to another

The point of departure for the method of '*verstehen*' is the question of the very possibility of individuals understanding each other, which in turn represents a fundamental problem in human existence. The I–You relation is inseparable from it, as Simmel has brilliantly shown (Simmel, 1918: 9–13): whether I find once more my own subjective quality reflected in the other person, or whether the other appears to me merely as a largely incomprehensible object, is decisive both for the success or failure of '*verstehen*' and for the quality of interaction. For Simmel, '*verstehen*' is 'the relationship of one mind to another', and a 'fundamental event of human life' (Simmel, 1918: 3). In his view it comes about as a synthesis of the empirically given fact 'which as such is not yet understood' (Simmel, 1918: 4), and the recognition of meaning as a mental element, which identifies the essence of an appearance.

Granting to 'alter' the quality of an autonomous subject does not mean, however, making him an echo of one's own self. Simmel rejects the notion that only those things can be understood in 'alter' which previously have been experienced by 'ego' in his own biography: 'For nobody can deny his ability of sensing feelings in someone else, which he has never felt himself, nor his ability to untie knots of inner fates with others, that he never had to live through himself.' (Simmel, 1918: 9.) Max Weber later echoed this same insight when he wrote: 'As has often been said, one does "not have to be Caesar to understand Caesar".' (Weber, 1922: 404.) Thus, Simmel constructed the method of '*verstehen*' on the basis of the assumption that the derivation of the You from the I is not acceptable, and that the person who wants to understand by recognizing meaning does not have the option of simply incorporating his own mind into the You facing him. Accordingly, those sociologists who want to work in the tradition of Simmel are bound by his principle 'that the You is rather an independent fundamental phenomenon, just like the I' (Simmel, 1918: 10–11).

To follow the rules of '*verstehen*' as Simmel described them, 'ego' must not duplicate his I in order to project it into 'alter' and then have a dialogue with himself rather than with his You: instead, the I does not even emerge until a You turns to it in interaction. Simmel clearly anticipates Mead's 'significant other' in pointing to the contribution of the You to the formation of the I. Simmel sums up his theory of '*verstehen*' in the surprising sentence: 'The You and '*verstehen*' are simply the same, as it were, once expressed as substance and once as function' (Simmel, 1918: 13). Our fellows may neither become an object nor a duplicate of our ego's I: Simmel demands that he be a You to us.

If the method of '*verstehen*' is to become a widely accepted procedure in attaining scientific knowledge, it must be capable of both execution and verification. Because, according to Simmel, the You and '*verstehen*' are the same, it is possible to describe the operation '*verstehen*' by describing the You that serves as the source of the perspective of interpretation. In the context of '*verstehen*' in historical research Simmel called the You, that was to be applied, a 'simulated subject', and he also spoke of the 'methodological subject' as a 'hypothetical construct', which allows the researcher to interpret behaviour from the perspective of a concrete You. The social scientist's achievement that can be described and tested, is his selection or construction of that particular You which is appropriate and adequate given the phenomenon to be studied. This means that the sociologist should strive towards congruence between his 'simulated subject' as the methodological You applied by him and the actual You that the actors being researched wanted to relate to in interaction. Thus, he can reconstruct the meaning which they wanted their interaction to have.

The human being is the one creature which has the ability to present himself as a 'problem' to himself. Thus, his own 'I' can appear to him as something estranged. The search for meaning and for an understanding of his own thoughts may therefore motivate him towards gaining clarification of his own identity. At the University of Michigan, Charles H. Cooley engaged in the problem of the determination of the self. There is a striking similarity between Simmel's I and You and Cooley's model of the Looking-glass Self: we like to look in a mirror, because there we can perceive how the others perceive us. We are able to see, then, the perception of who we are in the consciousness of our fellow human beings. Cooley's Looking-glass Self, as Simmel's I, cannot take any concrete shape until Cooley's others or Simmel's You reflect it. To both of them the exchange of meaning in interaction is a prerequisite for the formation of individual identity. The Looking-glass Self is the I that came into being through interaction with the You.

Of course, everything becomes dependent upon which You is

chosen to reflect ourselves, Mead conceived of the You as a 'significant other', which consists of parents and those persons who engender within the child a sense of identity, as the child sees himself reflected in their perceptions of him. Additionally, we are indebted to Mead for his introduction of the concept of the perspective as that point of view, which the I takes over from his or her 'significant other'. Mead is often quoted as having discussed 'taking the role of the other', but his concept of role taking really means adopting the perspective of the other. There is a passage in Simmel's methodological study, from which Weber took the concept of '*verstehen*', in which Simmel wrote: 'we must be able to "occupy or inhabit the mind of the other person". The understanding of an utterance entails that the mental processes of the speaker — processes which the words of the utterance express — are also reproduced in the listener by means of the utterance.' (Simmel, 1977: 64.) This passage sounds very Meadian; it anticipates role taking as well as the 'significant symbol', and it shows the basic concern for '*verstehen*' as the recognition of meaning in interpretation.

With the transition from the behaviour associated with 'play' to that of a 'game', the child gradually learns to conceive of abstract forms of association, and thus to identify with the 'generalized other'. The successful cooperation of the individual in team sports establishes his capacity to perceive himself from the standpoints of the other positions, which operate under the rules of the game. The contribution of the young person becomes standardized into a role; e.g., in the role of quarterback. He must, in order to succeed in his role, see through the eyes of every other teammate. Through repetition of this experience, he learns gradually to see himself from the perspective of every other participant, and this Mead called the perspective of the 'generalized other'. The 'individualist' perspective, therefore, becomes supplanted by a perspective which entails the relevance of the perspections of the entire group.

The equivalent of Simmel's You is, with Cooley, a mirror from which the Looking-glass Self (or I) becomes engendered. It becomes, with Mead, expanded to a plurality, to the group, which introduces the I to a 'generalized' You and hence to a group perspective. This perspective then conditions the I in such a way as to fit the situation in which the group interacts. Regardless of whether the You operates as individual other or as reference group, according to Simmel it must never become the screen on which to project the I, but it must always by the mirror in which the I can find its own identity. Cooley placed more stress upon the notion of the interchange of the content of consciousness, while Mead placed more stress upon the actors, the I, the other and the group, but they were both in agreement with Simmel that 'self' and 'other' lie on the same plane of experience, and that each becomes the medium through which the other is perceived. It is the one stream of consciousness that carries them both: the I and the You. It would take us too far afield here to compare Simmel's concepts of I and You with Mead's concepts of I and me.

For Max Weber, the notion of '*verstehen*' revolves round the concept of social action. If the I orients its activity towards the You, this becomes social action by definition. The investigation of social reality requires '*verstehen*' as a method, which assists in rendering intelligibility to action. In the action process, material phenomena, the surfaces of which are easily accessible, become joined to the intended context of meaning, like the two parts of a zip when it is pulled shut. Thus, Weber differentiates between various types of social action, according to their meaning for the actor. Weber solves this task by constructing 'ideal types', which he describes like this: 'As far as their content goes, these constructs have a utopian quality, and they are theoretically created by emphasizing certain elements of reality.' (Weber, 1922: 190.) Because, as we have seen in Kant's terminology, the intellect can register only empirical details, reason must be aided through the establishment of 'ideal types', which show an obvious affinity to the Platonic realm of ideas.

In his typology of authority, Weber differentiated with great care the three forms of authority. In the beginning of his study he demonstrated how on the level of micro-analysis the immediate personal interests or habits of the people concerned may be interesting enough as motives for the maintenance of a relationship of dominance and submission, but in order to explain the stability of authority in various cultures, this approach would be far too shallow (Weber, 1956: 151). Accordingly, Weber based his type-construction on alternative notions of values on the level of macro-analysis. Three different notions of value make authority seem legitimate, and each corresponds to a different culture type. Thus, Weber's ideal types are culture-specific perspectives, used as methodological tools just as Simmel's 'hypothetical constructs' were intended to be used.

While Mead assigned a specific perspective to both the individual You (significant other) and the group You (generalized other), which the I can take over in interaction, Weber constructed culture-specific perspectives without, however, admitting the empirical presence of a supportive collective. Thus, as the concept of the perspective is widened to the macro-level, the concept of the 'methodological You' is lost in the process, because although Weber did work with value-ideas as perspectives, he would have rejected the thought as sheer metaphysics to name a corresponding subject. It seems, therefore, that Simmel's methodology opened more opportunities for elaborating the *'verstehen'* approach than either Mead or Weber have used.

Ever since Tamotsu Shibutani published his article, 'Reference groups as perspectives' (Shibutani, 1955), and since Anselm Strauss's book *Mirror and Masks* became widely read (Strauss, 1959), the fruitful application of Simmel's *'verstehen'* concept to micro-theory was potentially extended to macro-research. Shibutani used the Meadian tool of 'perspective' while avoiding the implicit weaknesses of Weber's 'ideal types'. In the absence of supportive collectives Weber's type constructions are in danger of becoming metaphysical entities. Shibutani remedies this by tying them to reference groups, thus giving them an empirical foundation. Strauss sets out explicitly to break the barrier between micro- and macro-theory, and to open, as it were, the fence of social psychology that for decades kept the Meadian tradition from spreading to wider territories. Strauss, of course, quotes Simmel but, irrespective of that, the Chicago school kept the teaching of Simmel very much alive: Albion Small translated Simmel's early methodological articles for the *American Journal of Sociology*, Robert E. Park was himself a student of Simmel (Park, 1931) and Everett C. Hughes incorporated much of Simmel's theory of *'verstehen'* in his teaching. While obviously being the promulgator of Mead's teachings, Herbert G. Blumer also considers himself a student of Robert E. Park (Blumer and Helle, 1983: 202).

Notes

1. Simmel did not mind the foreigners, but the women distracted him. In a letter to Rickert of 15 August 1898 Simmel writes:

> I cannot say that I am very happy with the large percentage of female students: they disturb the uniformity of the auditorium. Since I do not really speak to the listeners but rather to myself, I like for the audience to be as colourless and indifferent as possible. The duality of the form of appearance and the colourful dresses disturb me. (Gassen and Landmann, 1958: 96)

2. Additionally, 'meaning' also is associated with Weber's concept of 'value', because without reference to culturally defined values, meaning to him would not be possible.

References

Blumer, H.G. and H.J. Helle (1983) 'Una conversazione tra Herbert G. Blumer e Horst J. Helle', *Sociologia della communicazione*, II (3): 199–215.

Bühl, W.L. (1972) 'Einleitung: Die alte und die neue Verstehende Soziologie', pp. 7–76 in W.L. Bühl (ed.), *Verstehende Soziologie: Grundzüge und Entwicklungstendenzen*. München: Nymphenburger.

Gassen, K. and M. Landmann (1958) *Buch des Dankes an Georg Simmel: Briefe, Erinnerungen, Bibliographie*. Berlin: Duncker und Humblot.

Goffman, E. (1974) *Frame Analysis: An Essay on the Organization of Experience*. Cambridge, Mass.: Harvard University Press.

Helle, H.J. (1982a) 'Chancen und Mängel in der Rezeption Max Webers' pp. 11–24 in H.J. Helle (ed.) *Kultur und Institution*. Berlin: Duncker und Humblot.

Helle, H.J. (1982b) 'Kultur und Staat bei Max Weber und Elman Service', pp.107–23 in J. Listl and H. Schambeck (eds) *Demokratie in Anfechtung und Bewährung. Festschrift für Johannes Broermann*. Berlin: Duncker und Humblot.

Joas, H. (1978) 'George Herbert Mead', pp. 7–39 in D. Käsler (ed.), *Klassiker des soziologischen Denkens* Vol. 2. München: C.H. Beck.

Kant, I. (n.d.) 'Prolegomena zu einer jeden künftigen Metaphysik, die als Wissenschaft wird auftreten können', pp. 1–122 in H. Renner (ed.), *Immanuel Kants Werke in acht Büchern: Ausgewählt und mit Einleitung versehen von Hugo Renner* Vol. 1, *Viertes Buch*. Berlin: A. Weichert. (References refer to number of paragraph 'Par.' and page)

Levine, D.N. (1972) '"Georg Simmel as Sociologist" by Max Weber', Introduction by Donald N. Levine, *Social Research* 39 (1): 155–63.

Park, R.E. (ed.) (1931) *Soziologische Vorlesungen von Georg Simmel: Gehalten an der Universität Berlin im Wintersemester 1899*. Society for Social Research, Series I, No. 1. Chicago: University of Chicago.

Schnabel, P.-E. (1976) 'Georg Simmel' in D. Käsler (ed.), *Klassiker des soziologischen Denkens* Vol. 1. München: C.H. Beck.

Shibutani, T. (1955) 'Reference Groups as Perspectives', *American Journal of Sociology* 60: 562–9.

Simmel, G. (1892) *Die Probleme der Geschichtsphilosophie: Eine erkenntnistheoretische Studie*. Leipzig: Duncker und Humblot.

Simmel, G. (1904) *Kant: 16 Vorlesungen, gehalten an der Berliner Universität*. Leipzig: Duncker und Humblot.

Simmel, G. (1911) *Hauptprobleme der Philosophie*. Leipzig: Göschen (1st edition, 1910).

Simmel, G. (1918) *Vom Wesen des historischen Verstehens*. Berlin: E.S. Mittler und Sohn. (Based on 'Die Probleme der Geschichtsphilosophie', 1st edition, 1892.)

Simmel, G. (1922) *Soziologie: Untersuchengen über die Formen der Vergesellschaftung*. München und Leipzig: Duncker und Humblot (1st edition, 1908).

Simmel, G. (1977) *The Problems of the Philosophy of History: An Epistemological Essay*. Translated, edited and with an Introduction by Guy Oakes. New York: Macmillan/Free Press. (Based on the 2nd edition of 1905.)

Strauss, A. (1959) *Mirrors and Masks: The Search for Identity*. Glencoe: Free Press.

Tenbruck, F.H. (1958) 'Georg Simmel', *Kölner Zeitschrift für Soziologie und Sozialpsychologie*, 10: 587–614.

Weber, M. (1904) 'Die Objektivität sozialwissenschaftlicher und sozialpolitischer Erkenntnis', *Archiv für Sozialwissenschaft und Sozialpolitik* 19: 22–87. (Reprinted in Weber, 1922: 146–214.)

Weber, M. (1905) 'Roscher und Knies und die logischen Probleme der historischen Nationalökonomie: II. Knies und das Irrationalitätsproblem', *Schmollers Jahrbuch für Gesetzgebung, Verwaltung und Vorlkswirtschaft* 29: 1323–84. (Reprinted in Weber 1922: 42–105.)

Weber, M. (1913) 'Über einige Kategorien der verstehenden Soziologie', *Logos: Internationale Zeitschrift für Philosophie der Kultur* 4: 253–94. (Reprinted in Weber, 1922: 403–50).

Weber, M. (1920) *Gesammelte Aufsätze zur Religionssoziologie* Vol. I. Tübingen: J.C.B. Mohr (Paul Siebeck). For an English translation of excerpts see: Gerth, H.H. and Mill C.W. (eds) (1964) *From Max Weber: Essays in Sociology*. New York: Oxford University Press, reprinted 1977: 353–7.

Weber, M. (1922) *Gesammelte Aufsätze zur Wissenschaftslehre*. Tübingen: J.C.B. Mohr (Paul Siebeck).

Weber, M. (1956) *Soziologie, Weltgeschichtliche Analysen, Politik*. Stuttgart: A. Kröner.

2

Unanswered questions in the convergence between structuralist and interactionist role theories

Ralph H. Turner

Two role theories from four

Role theory as we know it today has at least four important historical sources. Each source incorporates different objectives and assumptions. One source is the work of Robert E. Park (1926, 1927) and George Herbert Mead (1935) that has come to be incorporated into the symbolic interactionist approach. The objectives in using the concept of role were to find a way to conceive the relationship of the individual to society and a way to account for human intelligence. Among the assumptions was the view of human behaviour as creative and the use of social interaction as the crucial starting point for understanding larger social systems. Unfortunately, many authors today confuse symbolic interactionism with a more deterministic model. Of crucial significance in understanding this approach is Mead's distinction between *play*, as the less mature pattern, and the *game*, as a creative and mutually adaptive system of actions.

A second source is 'gestalt' theory, as it was introduced to American social psychology by Kurt Lewin (1948, 1951). The objective was to find a way to extend the insights of gestalt psychology from a purely individualistic kind of theory to a social psychology that stressed the structure and interrelationship of social settings that link human actors. The underlying assumption was that all human psychological processes take shape through the discovery and creation of integrating patterns, and that the creation of meanings in terms of gestalts is essential for human social behaviour.

A third source is the sociodrama, associated with the work of Jacob Moreno (1934). For Moreno, the concepts of role and role playing provided a way of bringing a person's system of interpersonal relationships into awareness so that therapy could be applied more effectively. Among Moreno's assumptions were that everyone is engaged in playing roles, and that these roles are highly individual creations.

The source for role theory that has been the most widely used by sociologists is the theory of culture, taken from anthropology and formulated by Ralph Linton (1936). Linton's objective was to refine a fundamentally behaviouristic and consensual concept of culture so as to take realistic account of the fact that not everyone subjected to a common culture behaved, thought and felt in the same way. Linton assumed that roles could be defined as sets of social norms, which were parts of the culture transmitted to interactants in any given situation.

Historically, the Lintonian concept caught on among sociologists for several reasons. It was most in accord with the strongly behaviouristic bias of psychology and sociology for several decades. Second, it gave social structure firm priority over individual behaviour. It accorded very nicely with the naïve bias of a generation of sociologists who felt it necessary to assert the priority of social structure in order to justify the existence of sociology as a social science distinct from psychology. Third, it fitted into a tendency for sociologists to conceive social structure as primarily a system of social norms, and to conceive social behaviour as primarily a manifestation of internalization and compliance with these norms.

Historically, some aspects of the gestalt approach merged with the Lintonian view and allowed the concept of social norms to be replaced by the concept of expectation, thus allowing for even more variation, and modifying the excessively static conception of institutionalized social norms. Other aspects of the gestalt approach, and perhaps its most fundamental assumptions, have tended to merge with the interactionist view. Interactionists stressed that role playing and role taking processes do not consist primarily of conforming to norms and expectations and of coping with obstacles to conformity. Instead, they are ways of finding meaning within which intelligent action can be framed. The idea of the role as a creative gestalt within which meaning is formulated is highly compatible with this view. The gestalt approach has consequently not persisted as an independent stream but has been merged into the two rather different main streams.

Sociodrama has remained separate because of its largely thera-peutic and utilitarian uses and a lack of interest on the part of its practitioners in formulating a coherent theoretical account of the processes involved. However, the assumption that role playing (which Moreno called role taking) is creative is highly compatible with the interactionist approach. It is also compatible with the aspect of the gestalt approach that has merged with interactionism. Consequently, symbolic interactionists have or can benefit by incorporating some of Moreno's insights into their own approach.

Consequently, the four earlier streams have evolved into two main streams, commonly known as the structural and interactionist approaches to role theory. Most published research has followed the structural pattern, though theorists who use the symbolic interactionist approach in psychology find many aspects of the structural approach unacceptable.

In an early statement, I posed the challenge of interactionist theory to structural theory in black and white terms in order to encourage efforts to work towards a more adequate form of role theory than either stream could provide on its own (Turner, 1962).

More recently Warren Handel (1979) has made a penetrating case for the view that refinements, primarily in the structural approach, have led to considerable convergence between the two main streams of role theory, with the result that most of the interactionists' criticism of role theory have been met. In making this case, Handel relied heavily on the refinements in the tradition of Gross, Mason and MacEachern (1958), Merton (1957) and Kahn et al. (1964). These investigators have rejected the oversimplified assumption of role consensus and substituted the concept of expectation for the concept of norm in talking about roles. They have also focused attention on the processes by which a role incumbent deals with the receipt of incompatible expectations from the incumbents of the alter roles with which ego is legitimately engaged in interaction. Handel's conclusion has been widely accepted among role theorists and was treated as non-controversial in the most recent comprehensive statement of role theory by Heiss (1981).

Handel's specific contentions concerning the refinements of structural role theory have much validity. In this paper, however, I wish to call attention to the limitations of the convergence and to stress more than Handel and Heiss have done those aspects of an interactional viewpoint that are neither understood nor adequately incorporated into contemporary studies in role theory.

Critical questions for role theory

As a first step, I shall offer a set of critical questions that must be answered positively if a theory of roles is to be sufficiently realistic to be acceptable for use in sociology and social psychology. These critical questions constitute a way of stating some underlying assumptions that transcend either a structural or an interactionist approach, though they may be least satisfactorily answered by unrefined versions of structural theory.

First, does the use of the concept role add something to the substance of the theory that is not otherwise derivative from such component concepts as norm, expected behaviour, etc.? Many studies seem to incorporate the concept of role as a magical device, when in fact nothing about the investigation or the theory is any different than it would have been had the concept of role not been used. For example, there are papers on the resolution of role conflict that could just as well have been phrased as statements on the resolution of conflict, because no distinctive implications are introduced by the use of the concept 'role'. The exhaustive and otherwise excellent volume on role theory by Biddle (1979) is often subject to this criticism. The bulk of the book is taken up with discussing various kinds of social psychological theory which are in no way altered by the fact that they are used in connection with the discussion of roles. Lengthy discussions of the circumstances under which role behaviour conforms to role expectations are usually indistinguishable from discussions of the extent to which an individual conforms to the expectations of others. If introduction of the concept of role is merely an excuse for the restatement of theories already well established without the use of the concept of role, we would be better off dropping the concept so as to reduce redundancy and obscurantism in our discipline.

Second, can the approach deal equally effectively with valued and disvalued roles? Is the theory as suitable for analysing deviant roles as non-deviant roles? Any theory that uses compliance with expectation as the dynamic process in the enactment of roles runs into difficulty, particularly if the principle of positive reinforcement is the mechanism through which conformity to expectations is achieved. Some investigators deal with this problem by lodging deviant roles in deviant subcultures, so that the deviant is indeed conforming to expectations and receiving positive reinforcement from others in the deviant subsociety. There is considerable merit to this approach, but there are also dramatic limitations. In many instances deviant roles are developed and played out when the deviant has very little in the way of obvious relationships with a deviant subgroup and when the disapproval from other groups is more salient than subgroup approvals.

Third, can the approach deal equally well with roles that are legitimately defined within an organizational structure and roles that are legitimately defined in terms of values rather than positions? We should not overlook the importance of roles such as the hero role or the saint role as very significant facts of social life. A Mexican baseball player with the Los Angeles Dodgers who became 'Rookie of the Year' and Cy Young award winner, provoked an outburst of disapproval because he absented himself from a local victory parade after his team had won the national championship in 1981. The reason for the disapproval was that Valenzuela had become a symbol to the large Mexican-American community in southern California and was now cast in the role of ethnic hero. By failing to appear prominently so as to demonstrate appreciation for the adulation of his admirers and contribute symbolically to the prestige of the Mexican-American community he seriously violated the role of ethnic hero. An earlier period produced sad accounts of the great difficulties some American astronauts experienced because they, too, were expected to change their lifestyles in order to play out the roles of national heroes. In some cases they did not understand what was expected of them. In other cases, what was expected of them was incompatible with their personal dispositions and their life situations. A theory of roles must deal as convincingly with these roles that do not correspond to explicitly and legitimately defined positions in the social structure as it does with roles that correspond with precisely specified statuses.

Fourth, can the approach deal readily with role change and particularly with the kind of role change that forces organizational role definers to accede to those changes? In recent years we have witnessed secretaries rising up as a group and refusing to make coffee and to perform other menial services for their employers, on the grounds that these tasks are not properly part of the role of a secretary. How have secretaries taken it upon themselves to redefine the role of the secretary in this authoritative fashion? Nothing in the formal organizational structure in which they operate grants them this right. Secretaries are employees and subordinates. They occupy positions in well-defined organizational charts that clearly specify the lines of authority. Yet the secretaries have had considerable success in forcing their superiors in the formal structure to accede to their redefinitions of the secretary's role. Events of this sort are not unusual but take place continuously, so that role definitions are continuously modified. Legitimate role definers are constantly forced to negotiate role definitions in a way that is inconsistent with the formal structure in which the roles are lodged.

Fifth, can the approach deal with creativity in role playing? Again, the view of role enactment as an unimaginative, uncreative process of conforming to expectations, in which the only scope for creativity arises out of the necessity for dealing with incompatible expectations, is quite inadequate.

Unresolved issues
In the remainder of this paper I shall suggest several ways in which I believe that even the carefully defined versions of structural role

theory must be further modified in order to take account of the most critical aspects of interactionists' observations.

Construction of meaningful relationships versus conformity to expectations

The first modification addresses the assumption that the dynamic process in role enactment is best formulated as the effort to conform to expectations. Heiss (1981: 99) comments: 'In sum, it seems clear that there is little validity to the oft-repeated contention that structuralists see interaction as the simple playing out of internalized social norms.' Heiss in this statement has simply missed the point of the interactionist critique. The issue is not whether or not interaction is the playing out of internalized social norms. The issue is whether role interaction can best be understood as dealing with the norm of conformity to expectation, or not. All of the modifications in Merton's (1957) scheme and Kahn's (1964) scheme are based on that assumption. The interactionist contention is that the more fundamental character of role behaviour is the effort to construct and to execute a meaningful and rewarding complement of behaviour in a system of social relations.

Empirically, I believe that common experience will confirm that conformity or scheming non-conformity to expectations is merely the 'safe' or 'fall-back' way to conceive and deal with this process. It is prevalent when opportunities for creative role making are minimal, when the potential balance of satisfaction is negative, or when the role incumbent is insecure about role capability. In short, this model of role behaviour is derived from observing interaction in relatively pathological situations rather than in normal and positive forms of interaction. It is not in a thriving marriage but in a stagnating or deteriorating marriage that interaction becomes primarily focused on dealing with the other's expectations. Similarly, the image of role enactment centring round conformity or scheming non-conformity to expectations applies to the rigid and stagnant bureaucracy rather than to the expanding and productive concern. It applies most to the roles of the 'little people' who are rendered passive by a tragic awareness of their powerlessness in large organizations.

Positively, we assign highest role adequacy ratings to role incumbents who do the unexpected rather than to those who do the expected. When we think of our great military heroes, for example, we do not think of officers who performed in precisely the expected fashion. We think rather of a General Patton, who did outrageous things. We think of an Admiral Halsey whose behaviour as a fleet commander was constantly upsetting and surprising. Another example to illustrate this point is provided by a series that was popular for many years in the *Reader's Digest* magazine. The series was entitled 'The Most Unforgettable Character I Ever Met'. It consisted of vignettes, each of which described someone who was strikingly out of the ordinary, someone who did entirely unexpected things which were greatly appreciated by the persons who came into contact with him or her.

This issue is an application of Mead's distinction between play and the game. In play the child is merely conforming to expectations. In the game the individual understands the vantage points of the other participants well enough to improvise a role that will interact effectively with the roles that are simultaneously being improvised by others. The result should be to maximize the overall effectiveness of the team's performance. The advance from play to the game is what makes possible creative intelligence in human beings. The issue is between a view of role enactment as conformity or scheming non-conformity to expectation and a view of role enactment as role making in relation to 'alters' who are capable of appreciating role performance for its consistency with the values and roles round which the role is organized, even when the specific course of action is unexpected or even surprising.

Gestalt versus behavioural inventory
A second contrast can be drawn between viewing a role as a behavioural inventory and viewing it as a gestalt. Heiss (1981: 96) again takes note of the interactionist perspective but rejects it in this respect, saying 'We are not taught gestalts; we are taught specific behaviours, or, at best, low level principles'. It is hard to imagine a statement that is more contradicted by everything we know about human socialization. We know that while individuals learn from specific experiences, they learn by assigning meanings to those experiences as they occur. What they learn, then, are the meanings rather than specific behaviours. There are exceptions in the learning of mechanical habits or in cases of military drill in which very specific behaviours are required. These are only incompletely social and relatively unintelligent forms of learning and cannot appropriately be used as the model for significant social behaviour.

An illustration of this observation comes from research into the understanding of earthquake warnings issued in southern California throughout 1976. A survey conducted one year after a ten-month period of warnings found that a relatively small proportion of the population remembered or grasped details of the specific warning notices that had been given and widely advertised on television, radio and in the newspapers. But most of them had grasped the general message that there was going to be a serious earthquake in southern California fairly soon. The detailed communications were not retained, but the general meaning was learned (Turner et al., 1979). The observation that people learned gestalts rather than specific behaviours is merely an extension of the principle underlying this example.

The reconceptualization of role introduced by Robert Merton (1957) and applied in different ways by Bates and Harvey (1975) and by Nye and his associates (1976) does particular violence to the idea of role as a meaningful whole or gestalt. Merton proposed that we think of the role as only that pattern of behaviour which is geared to the expectation of a particular alter role: thus, Linton's more comprehensive status-role is broken down into several roles, depending upon the legitimate alter roles with which the incumbent must deal. The new approach is not a particularly satisfactory solution to the problem that the role incumbent is subject to contradictory expectations, because it assumes that the expectations from any particular set of role alters are consistent. When we acknowledge that the expectations that parents bring to the teacher are often just as diverse as the average difference between the expectations of parents and the school superintendent towards the teacher, much of the utility of atomizing the concept of role as Merton has done is lost. In effect, the implications of recognizing heterogeneous expectations have been followed only part way to their logical conclusion. The role consensus assumption which Gross (1958) criticized at such great length has been enshrined once again at a different level.

Nye and associates (1976) have added further confusion by breaking the role down into parts, but not according to alter roles but according to the functions performed in the role. Only a quick glance at their investigation will make evident that their partitioning of the role into functions is quite arbitrary and that another group of investigators would surely have come up with a somewhat different list of functions. Since the specific roles produced by this process do not correspond to the conceptions in terms of which people organize their relations with each other, they have limited merit as social analytic concepts.

If the gestalt assumption is taken seriously, the comprehensive view of the role is the critical one in assigning meaning to component acts. When we think of the role of marriage partner and the role of parent and their sometimes conflicting expectations we do not think of each component apart from the other. We do think in terms of the meaning of the whole set and we shall be in a much better position to understand behaviour if we maintain that orientation.

In practice the attempt to distinguish between different roles by comparing behavioural inventories does not work well. There is too much overlap, and there is too much vagueness in the behavioural items. My associates and I have attempted to prepare such inventories as a step towards measuring degrees of role overlap or extent of differentiation between roles. In every instance, it has become clear that in strictly behavioural terms there is extensive overlap between roles that are quite clearly differentiated as social entities and as personal identities. Even the development of an inventory requires that we rely on vague terms and assign to those vague terms unrealistically precise meanings in order to make the technique usable.

It is an underlying assumption of the interactionist approach that in common understanding roles are not defined primarily as specific inventories of behaviour. Such behavioural inventories are a product either of the attempts to bring roles into much more rigid control in bureaucratic organizations, or efforts of behaviouristically oriented social scientists to conceive roles in terms that are more susceptible of measurement than the concepts that organize human behaviour. It is not at all uncommon for members of a profession to conduct investigations or hold seminars with the object of attempting to define their professional roles. Police departments have paid out large sums of money in support of a project that was supposed to answer the question, 'What is the police role?' (American Justice Institute, 1971) more precisely than the authorities were able to do. Nurses have asked collectively 'What is the role, or what is the true role, of the nurse?' It is just because roles are not normally understood as inventories of behaviour that this kind of problem besets the responsible role definers.

In one of our own investigations we set out to demonstrate the interchangeability of roles, drawing upon the extent to which the same behaviour was assigned quite different meanings depending upon how the observer was led to identify the role that the behaviour expressed (Turner and Shosid, 1976). Roles that convey diametrically opposed evaluations and meanings are often expressed through behaviours that are objectively indistinguishable. In the same investigation we also called attention to role ambiguity, the difficulty of assigning meaning to specific behaviours when the nature of the role is not understood. The most reasonable conclusion seems to be that the sense of precision we have about the behaviours associated with different roles arises from the confidence we have in categorizing behaviours on the basis of prior knowledge of the roles which they are supposed to be expressing.

In unpublished research we have asked people identified with or concerned about particular roles to give us capsule descriptions of the roles, or to state what they consider to be the essence of the roles in question. The answers usually come back as statements of sentiments, values and non-specific normative principles rather than specific behaviours. For example, a mother loves and looks after her child; an attorney looks out for the interests of the clients; a teacher understands students. The meaningful gestalt rather than the behavioural inventory is the key to understanding roles.

Negotiated versus fixed role allocations
The third contrast between interactionist assumptions and structural role assumptions is between negotiated and fixed role allocations. Structural analyses take for granted that identities in the interaction are given and proceed from there. For example, in the classroom everyone knows who is the professor and who is the student, so all that is problematic is how the professor and teacher play out their roles.

In many situations, however, roles are not pre-determined and the allocation of roles is negotiated in the course of interaction and even continuously renegotiated. The question is whether these situations should be considered aberrant and situations in which the allocation is fixed should be treated as the fundamental pattern, or the reverse. I propose that we should consider the case of predetermined role allocation the limiting case rather than the prototype situation. I propose to take this position because even in the pre-determined role situation the question of whether or not the role allocation is appropriate is often raised. For example, the student may say, 'He's no teacher, he knows less about the subject than I do!' As a result of this questioning of the appropriateness of the allocation the student abandons many aspects of the traditional student role and the teacher is unable to play many features of the teacher role. Typically, in this kind of situation, interaction proceeds at two levels. The minimally unavoidable attention to appearances is maintained, while role interaction is constructed from one side according to an assumed different role allocation. In practice this is very common and should not be regarded as an aberration. We should recognize that the appropriateness of the formal role allocation is constantly under question in any organization, even though that questioning does not usually become manifest in the relations between the questioner and the person whose role tenure is being questioned. In an extreme instance the phenomenon of *role appropriation* has been demonstrated in a crisis situation. In role appropriation the child takes over the parent's role and altercasts the parent to the child's role in a crisis (Perry et al.,

1956) or the enlisted man appropriates the officer role and casts the officer in the enlisted role during a combat crisis.

The implications of this argument go beyond role allocation to the entire process of role making and role enactment. Handel (1979: 866) states that the role making process 'is recognized to be consequential in only certain kinds of situations and to be only one value of a continuum of ways in which actors can be involved in role behaviour, each way particular to, and constrained by, the structural context of interaction'. Others have gone further than Handel in treating role making as a relatively rare phenomenon that appears only when the social structure is inadequate, so that the structural view of role processes is the correct one for describing a normal role phenomenon.

In the interactionist view, role making and the whole creative process associated with it are constantly in operation, even in the most rigidly defined situation. That is why students of formal organizations were forced decades ago to talk about the formal organization *and* the informal organization of the factory or military organization or other unit. The informal organization within the formal organization represents the role making process and is a continuation of the same dynamic processes that apply in situations when roles are not clearly defined formally.

In attempts to analyse the police role and other quite formally defined roles we have found it most useful to employ the concept of *working role*, which is always at considerable variance from the formally conceived role as it is described in connection with the organizational chart. The functionality and tenability principles that I have described elsewhere (Turner, 1980) in attempting to offer the beginnings of a theory concerning the dynamics of roles must be used in attempting to explain the emergence and continual evolution of a working role in connection with every formally defined structural role. Furthermore, the formal conception of the role is subject to periodic revision because of the nature of the working role.

Symmetry versus asymmetry in role relations
A fourth challenge to the refined versions of structural role theory is to incorporate adequately the symmetry in role interaction. The standard treatments assume an asymmetry in which alter is role sender and ego is forced to cope. Weinstein and Deutschberger's (1963) conception of altercasting is more realistic in recognizing that ego is not only responding to a role sender but attempting to recast the sender into a more acceptable role. The central idea that roles are negotiated (Strauss, 1978) implies that all parties to the role

negotiation are both sending and receiving. We have not begun to formulate a theory of role interaction that replaces the simple role sender conception with an adequate view of role negotiation.

Role interaction goes well beyond sending and receiving. According to the interactionist view the central problem is one of discerning and making sense of the character or meaning of the interaction. Questions like 'What is he up to?' or 'Who does she think she is?' are more than tangential aspects of the interaction. They get to the heart of an attempt to arrive at a way of conceiving the interaction in terms of roles that will permit it to proceed as a meaningful exchange.

Socialization: role learning versus rule internalization
The final contrast has to do with the incorporation of socialization processes into role theory without modification from other sources, in contrast to the search for a distinctive role-theoretic view of socialization. Orville Brim (1960), in his classical statement on role socialization, made a thoughtful beginning. But little has been done to carry the analysis further. Standard treatments merely apply some currently fashionable psychological theory of learning to the component elements that make up a role. But the distinctive aspect of role socialization is how the socializee learns the gestalt, how the idea of a whole for which specific behaviours are but manifestations is acquired. A derivative problem is how the learner thereby comes to appreciate certain innovative behaviours as expressions of the role and to rule out others as not being expressions of the role. The question is, further, how learning takes place in such a way that the role incumbent may decide that certain of what are accepted as standard features of the role are not really part of the role.

An even more important question is how the insight that all socialization takes place in particular role relationships enables one to understand the whole process of socialization. The psychological principles of learning are well documented and need not be challenged or rejected. However, their application takes place in patterned contexts, and role theory is critical to understanding the patterning of those contexts. For example, one need not question the validity and utility of notions of positive and negative reinforcement. However, outside the laboratory experiment, reinforcement takes place in the course of a complex exchange in which what is being reinforced is not in the least obvious. The meanings attached to interaction are critical in determining what aspect of behaviour is being reinforced in a given situation.

One obvious lead to understanding the implication of roles for socialization theories is the prevalence of hypocrisy. Hypocrisy is a disturbing problem in many socialization theories. If social learning is a matter of internalizing norms, values, expectations, etc., allowance can be made for incomplete internalization. But it is hard to reconcile this interpretation with the hypocrisy in which the individual fails to apply values in his own behaviour which he asserts aggressively in communication to other people. Role theory invites the plausible explanation that one learns behaviours and attitudes only in the contexts of the roles in which they are learned. One does not internalize norms or values, so much as one learns a norm or a value as an aspect or a resource in connection with a particular role. The same norm or value is then learned as a quite different phenomenon in the context of different roles. The implications of this thinking have been further explored elsewhere and may provide a useful lead towards developing a more genuinely role theoretic formulation of socialization processes (Turner, 1974).

Conclusion
I conclude by reaffirming my agreement with Handel (1979) that structural role theory has made great strides from its initial formulation by Ralph Linton. Formulations such as Merton's theory of the role set (1957) have been quite fruitful and will continue to be useful in research. However, I seriously doubt that convergence has proceeded as far as Handel contends. Both Handel and Heiss (1981) have viewed this convergence primarily from the perspective of structural role theory and have not therefore addressed themselves to the critical assumptions of interactionist theory, most of which still remain unsatisfied by structural role formulations.

One of the most constructive efforts to move towards a more adequate convergence has been made by Powers (1981) who recognizes that interactionist processes are in operation in even the most rigidly constrained structures. He assumes that both the processes as structuralists conceive them and the processes as interactionists conceive them are in operation simultaneously, but that the relative scope for one or the other set of processes varies according to a number of circumstances. He proposes a series of interesting and plausible propositions to identify the circumstances under which either interactionist dynamics or structural dynamics will gain at the expense of the other. Further work in this direction and a fuller consideration of the unmet interactionist assumptions should enable us to approach a formulation of role theory that more accurately describes social interaction as human behaviour, and less as the programmed performance of bureaucratic robots whose circuits sometimes get overloaded and which behave in aberrant fashion when contradictory messages are relayed to their control boxes.

References

American Justice Institute (1971) *Systems and Training Analysis of Requirements for Criminal Justice Participants*. Sacramento, Ca.: American Justice Institute.

Bates, Frederick and Clyde Harvey (1975) *The Structure of Social Systems*. New York: Gardner Press.

Biddle, Bruce (1979) *Role Theory: Expectations, Identities, and Behaviors*. New York: Academic Press.

Brim, Orville (1960) 'Personality Development as Role-learning', pp. 127–59 in Ira Iscoe and Harold W. Stevenson (eds), *Personality Development in Children*. Austin: University of Texas Press.

Gross, Neal, Ward S. Mason and Alexander W. MacEachern (1953) *Explorations in Role Analysis*. New York: John Wiley.

Handel, Warren (1979) 'Normative Expectations and the Emergence of Meaning as Solutions to Problems: Convergence of Structural and Interactionist Views', *American Journal of Sociology*, 84: 855–81.

Heiss, Jerold (1981) 'Social Roles', pp. 94–132 in Morris Rosenberg and Ralph H. Turner (eds), *Social Psychology: Sociological Perspectives*. New York: Basic Books.

Kahn, Robert L,; Donald M. Wolfe; Robert P. Quinn and J. Diedrick Snoek (1964) *Organizational Stress*. New York: John Wiley.

Lewin, Kurt (1948) *Resolving Social Conflicts*, Gertrude Weiss Lewin (ed.), New York: Harper and Brothers.

Lewin, Kurt (1951) *Field Theory in Social Science*, Dorwin Cartwright (ed.), New York: Harper and Brothers.

Linton, Ralph (1936) *The Study of Man*. New York: D. Appleton-Century.

Mead, George Herbert (1934) *Mind, Self and Society*. Chicago: University of Chicago Press.

Merton, Robert K. (1957) 'Role Set: Problems in Sociological Theory', *British Journal of Sociology*, 8: 106–20.

Moreno, Jacob (1934) *Who Shall Survive?* Washington, DC: Nervous and Mental Disease Publishing Co.

Nye, F. Ivan (1976) *Role Structure and Analysis of the Family*. Beverly Hills, Ca.: Sage Publications.

Park, Robert E. (1926) 'Behind Our Masks', *Survey Graphic*, 56 (May): 135–9.

Park, Robert E. (1927) 'Human Nature and Collective Behavior', *American Journal of Sociology*, 32: 695–703.

Perry, Stewart E., Earle Silber and Donald A. Bloch (1956) *The Child and His Family in Disaster: A Study of the 1953 Vicksburg Tornado*. Washington, DC: National Academy of Science — National Research Council.

Powers, Charles (1981) 'Role-Imposition or Role-Improvisation: Some Theoretical Principles', *Economic and Social Review*, 12: 287–99.

Strauss, Anselm (1978) *Negotiations: Varieties, Contexts, Processes and Social Order*. San Francisco: Jossey-Bass.

Turner, Ralph H. (1962) 'Role Taking: Process Versus Conformity', pp. 20–40 in Arnold M. Rose (ed.), *Human Behavior and Social Processes*. Boston: Houghton-Mifflin.

Turner, Ralph H. (1974) 'Rule Learning as Role Learning: What an Interactive Theory of Roles Adds to the Theory of Social Norms', *International Journal of Critical Sociology*, 1: 52–73.

Turner, Ralph H. (1980) 'Strategy for Developing an Integrated Role Theory', *Humboldt Journal of Social Relations*, 7: 123–39.

Turner, Ralph H., Joanne M. Nigg, Denise H. Paz and Barbara Shaw Young, (1979) *Earthquake Threat: The Human Response in Southern California*. Los Angeles: Institute for Social Science Research, University of California.

Turner, Ralph H. and Norma Shosid (1976) 'Ambiguity and Interchangeability in Role Attribution: The Effect of Alter's Response', *American Sociological Review*, 41: 993–1006.

Weinstein, Eugene A. and Paul Deutschberger (1963) 'Some Dimensions of Altercasting', *Sociometry*, 26: 454–66.

3

Role theories and socialization research*

Hans Joas

It has become commonplace to begin papers on role theory with a reference not only to the frequent use in the social sciences of role theory concepts but also to their confusing ambiguity. This seems to indicate that purely definitive attempts at clarification as well as global attacks on role theory have not been particularly successful up to now. Behind the disparate and disputed terminology there seems to be a social reality that presses to be treated in role theory terms. But what exactly is the nature of this theory? Does it actually encompass certain basic anthropological structures of social action, or is it just the ideological expression of historical facts in capitalist society, or do we have in it simply an efficient instrument with which to formulate sociopsychological laws? What is meant by a clarification and definition of role theory depends on how this question is answered. The order of the day is, in the first case, the shaping of role theory within an over-arching anthropological theory of human action competence and intersubjectivity; in the second, the improvement of the ideologically critical evidence of its historical roots; and, in the third case, the scientific clarification of role theory propositions as a preliminary to the transparent formation of hypotheses. In this debate it seems inappropriate to proceed simply by taking an a priori decision before discussing the different positions. As a result, the history of the development of role theory will be reconstructed in brief to prepare the ground for a reasoned definition of the key concepts. The particularly interesting question as to the position of role theory in socialization research can only be dealt with summarily in the following section since various phases in the development of the child and the adolescent and the inner structure of all socializatory stages are accessible to treatment in role theory terms. Consequently, only one dimension — the development of role-taking ability — will be singled out for detailed treatment as it does not represent a mere application of role theory but discusses the verification by socialization theory of the key concept of role-taking itself. This is also an appropriate way of showing that role theory — whether it wants to or not — emerges at a point at which the grounding of socialization research in social theory and the relationship between individuality and sociality have become problematical.

A brief historical reconstruction of the development of role theory
The works of George Herbert Mead (1934, 1964) have, undeniably, been the most important source for the emergence and development of role theory. Mead introduces the concepts of 'role' and 'role-taking' within the framework of an anthropological theory of a specifically human form of communication. Human communication is, according to Mead, principally superior to animal forms of communication in that it operates through 'significant symbols'. By this is meant that people are able to react to their own gestures and utterances in a way that is anticipatory and thus inwardly represents their fellow actors' possible responses. This makes it possible for their own behaviour to be oriented towards the potential reactions of other actors. As these actors, too, are principally in possession of this ability, common collective action oriented towards a common binding pattern of mutual behaviour expectations becomes a possibility. Mead believes that he has, with his theory of communication, revealed the fundamental feature of human sociality. In human society, individual, non-naturalistically determined behaviour develops and is integrated into a group activity via mutual behaviour expectations. As a pattern of sociality, this differs fundamentally from that of a system of strict division of labour guaranteed through biological specialization in anatomical structure or the differentiation of hereditary patterns of behaviour. The regulation of communal life through rigid instinctive forms of behaviour that only the acquisition of status in a unilinear dominance hierarchy can modify is another principle of the vertebrate world that has been overcome in human beings. Although *traditions* occur in social groups of primates, they remain severely limited due to the fact that they do not become objectified. The motive for the anthropological elaboration of a pattern of sociality based on the idea of an identity of meaning constituted collectively and through action, can be found in Mead's theoretical and political biography as a radical democratic intellectual. The concept of role is introduced by Mead in a model of practical communication and collective self-determination and describes expectations towards a fellow actor's behaviour in an interactive context; 'taking the role of the other' is the anticipation of alter's behaviour in a specific situation.

It is not necessary to describe the fundamental lines of Mead's theory to an American public. It has to be emphasized, however, that the sense in which Mead uses the concept of role taking has major ramifications for a theory of socialization and, by extension, for theories of ethics and politics. Role taking involves not only a delineable sector of the communicative abilities but is related by Mead to general cognitive, to motivational and to moral development. The development of communicative abilities becomes a condition for cognitive progress in as much as it is the development of role taking ability that allows an actor to assume a reflexive attitude towards him or herself and substantial cognitive achievements presuppose just such an attitude. Mead's elaboration of this idea, particularly the problem of the constitution of the permanent object, is contained in works that are little known and poorly understood. He puts forward a theory of the social constitution of the development of general intelligence (Joas, 1980: 180ff.). Its ethical implications are expounded at the individual level as universal role taking ability and performance and, at the societal level, in a concept of an ideal society with a universal capacity for communication. While all this frequently has a speculative and fragmentary quality and is in parts incomplete, Mead has provided future role theory and research into the development of role taking ability with a sociophilosophical framework and daring hypotheses. This should be remembered along with the elementary version of role taking as a precondition for the use of significant symbols and, consequently, for all typically human communication.

Talcott Parsons combined Mead's idea of the reciprocity of expectations with other ideas in his attempt to integrate socialization theory into a comprehensive social theory. It is not possible to describe his solutions here. As an examination of his reception of Mead shows, the critical element in his scheme is the question of the autonomy and uniformity of a society's value system. This question arose during the period of Parsonian domination in American sociology, chiefly in the light of empirical reseach into role conflict (Handel, 1979). By this was meant inter-role conflict, i.e. a conflict in the individual's orientation towards two simultaneously occurring, possibly contradictory, roles. The Parsons school initially assumed that conflicts of this kind have to be solved by a clear-cut decision for one of the roles. Merton's (1957) list of mechanisms with which such inter-role conflicts can be handled represented a significant differentiation. He had in mind a clear-cut spatial and temporal separation of the modes of behaviour demanded by the various roles, or the sequentialization of mutually exclusive roles. While inter-role conflicts involved the problems of the individual in coming to terms with his or her various roles, the topicalization of *intra*-role conflicts posed an even greater threat to the construct of Parsonian theory. The assumption of a normative consensus as a prerequisite for the successful functioning and stability of the social system was threatened if it was not only possible for various roles to be in situational contradiction but if one and the same role could itself contain this contradiction. Merton also suggested a number of mechanisms for the resolution of this type of role conflict, which consists of the contradiction in the expectations towards one and the same role as a result of alter's varying roles. The varying sanctional power available to those in the ascribed roles, the limiting of reference to these and similar features produce societal mechanisms for dealing with role conflict. One immediately notices that Merton's conception was only a liberalization of Parsons's theory and not a fundamental transformation. It was precisely the dimension of the individual actor's action competence that was not yet attained with an examination of the mechanisms provided by society — i.e. structurally — for dealing with role conflict. Questioning the normative consensus in no way indicated another medium for the integration of social systems. It was only logical for Merton to demand just a toning-down of Parsons's claim to theoretical comprehensiveness and the acceptance of theories of middle-range. However, this lost sight of Parsons's highly fertile ambition — the systematic incorporation of socialization into a theory of society — and left the door wide open for the concept of role and a few associated concepts, such as role conflict and role taking, to be used in isolation from all theories of society, as well as the danger that they would become uncritically accepted sociological jargon.

It was in this diluted form, far removed from Mead and Parsons, that role theory terminology reached Germany. Dahrendorf's *Homo Sociologicus* (1959) represented an attempt to catch up with developments in American sociology from which Germany had been cut off through fascism and war. What Dahrendorf did, however, was to present a catalogue of role theory concepts without the underlying theory. In its place came a superficially speculative discussion of the theatrical metaphor and the question of human freedom given the universality of roles. There was no mention of the question of the systemic structure of society — this being a co-determinant of the expectations towards the individual actor — nor of needs and motivation as a basis of action. In their place came the statics of a mesh of positions and the abstraction of a universal motivation towards the avoidance of sanctions.

Dahrendorf's book triggered off a host of contributions to a debate that is still not quite over. Contemporary replies particularly worth mentioning came from Bahrdt, Claessens and Tenbruck. While Bahrdt (1961) quite rightly insisted on the necessity of creative performance on the part of the individual actor (something that had disappeared in Dahrendorf's model of conformity), Claessens (1963) did the same for the dimension of rational justification. Tenbruck (1961) alone criticized Dahrendorf's approach extensively from his knowledge and understanding of Parsons and pointed out his total neglect of the fields of internalization and the formation of a systemically adequate personality structure. In doing so, his position was that of orthodox Parsonianism.

Role theory developed along other paths. In the United States, criticism of the form in which role theory had become established drew mainly on Mead. In two perceptive essays (1955, 1962) Ralph Turner, one of the leading representatives of the symbolic interactionist school, criticized conventional role theory's assumptions on interaction and personality theory. His concept of 'role standpoint' allowed a clear distinction to be made between cognitive role taking and an identification with the identities and intentions of other actors: anticipating alter's behaviour does not imply a readiness to behave conformistically. Turner's concept of 'role making' is even more important. Its principal meaning is the active definition of social relations through mutual consideration of the claims and expectations actors have towards each other. Turner, like Mead, sees this situation of the interactive emergence of common meanings and a process of flexible interaction not as a problematic limiting-case of extreme instability but as a feature of all routine interaction that never completely disappears from even the most formalized and highly institutionalized social organizations. Social relations are not to be thought of as immutably stabilized patterns of expectations, nor role enactment merely as the practical realization of prescriptions; the definition of the relation and the development of the action plan themselves call for active and creative efforts for interpretation and design.

Another dimension that could only with the greatest difficulty be given a place in dominant role theory was developed by Erving Goffman, an author loosely connected with symbolic interactionism. Goffman (1961) elaborated the phenomenon of 'role distance', with which he described two things. On the one hand he meant public signalization by the actor of a differentiation between himself and his role with the aim of articulating the difference between his image of himself and his implied role identity, and, on the other hand, a 'sovereign' distancing demanded by the role itself from its obligations. What these two definitions had in common was that they obviously did not assume, as did Parsons, 'unconscious' conformity with role expectations as a result of actors' prior internalization of the associated value orientations, but rather the possibility of distance as a structural component of the role or as the actor's own creation. Goffman's blurring of the difference between the two meanings shows that he did not unequivocally belong either to the structural-analytical or to the interactionist camp, and that he did not clarify the relationship between the two approaches. Gouldner, who presented a third, influential critique (1960), demonstrated that Parsons had failed to distinguish sufficiently between the complementarity of behavioural expectations and the reciprocity of gratifications. If this distinction is introduced it can be seen that general norm-conformity in no way guarantees the equal distribution of gratification. This would apply only if authority was not a factor in the determination of norms. Consequently, the question of the unequal satisfaction of needs can again be discussed within a theory of society.

In postulates that were as concise as they were precise, Jürgen Habermas (1973, written 1968) drew together these various strands of criticism. His postulates attained an extraordinary influence in German socialization research and educational thinking and were the subject of much debate, no doubt because they were seen as formulating a concept of emancipation that could be utilized pedagogically. Drawing on Gouldner he put forward a repression theorem in place of the integration theorem in Parsons's theory of motivation; drawing on Goffman, a distance theorem in place of the conformity theorem; and drawing on Turner, a discrepancy theorem in place of the identity theorem with its assertion of a congruence of role definition and role interpretation. These three theorems formulate

> three dimensions of possible degrees of freedom of action ... We can introduce the three neglected dimensions in order to distinguish institutions (role system) according to the degree of their repressivity, the degrees of their rigidity and the nature of the behavioural control imposed by them. As we interpret the primary socialization process as the acquisition of basic role-playing qualifications, at the personality structure level the same dimensions can serve to express basic qualifications not covered by the normal concept of role learning. (Habermas, 1973: 127f.)

And Habermas develops the basic qualifications of frustration tolerance, controlled self-presentation and the flexible superego formation and brings them together in a concept of ego identity signifying the capacity actively to restructure one's own ego.

Krappmann (1971) took Habermas's suggestions a comprehensive step further. Habermas himself returned to role theory mainly in connection with his attempts to work out a logic of the development of moral consciousness and role competence and to present it as an ontogenetic counterpart to a social theory of evolution (Habermas, 1976). Dreitzel (1972) put forward his own extensive model of a 'critical' role theory. He also referred to the American developments mentioned by Habermas, placed particular stress on the dimension of needs and their repression and saw it as a preliminary to an analysis of the sociogenesis of behavioural maladjustment. Its shortcomings are the lack of clarity of its conceptual borrowing from Alfred Schütz's phenomenological sociology and the fact that, influenced by Plessner's anthropology (1974), it sees only a balance between individuation and sociality, unlike Mead and Habermas who take the radical view that individuation is itself a product of socialization.

Definition of the role concept

This brings us to the question of role theory's status, a question that can be answered now that we have reconstructed the history of role theory. Role theory should not be interpreted as a theory in the sense of a systematic body of hypotheses on empirical regularities; it therefore does not contain ready answers on the processes of socialization. Rather, it should be regarded as a metatheoretical scheme for the conceptual structuring of an area of study within the social sciences. As such its job is to provide a conceptual framework for the formulation of fields of empirical research. However, the choice of this metatheoretical scheme cannot be a random one; the scheme itself requires empirical, i.e. anthropological, justification. Role theory and the general theory of action, of which it is a part, should thus be seen as a reconstruction of the basic features of the interaction and action competence of actors and of the basic features of interactive systems of action (Joas, 1973: 91ff.; Döbert, Habermas and Nunner-Winkler, 1977: 27f.). Anthropological justification does not mean the premature dehistorization of historically specific contexts but has its roots in the phylogenetic emergence of the prerequisites for all human history and sociality. This is the view to be found in Mead but not in Parsons, who took his concepts mainly from Max Weber as opposed to the American forerunners of a naturalistic concept of action; and Weber was not concerned about the anthropological justification of his basic sociological categories.

On the basis of the above definition of the status of role theory we can now move on to the question of an appropriate definition of the role concept. The problem here is as follows: on the one hand, a kind of minimal consensus has developed among the competing schools of thought summed up by the often-heard formula: 'Social roles are clusters of normative behavioural expectations directed at the behaviour of position-holders'. On the other hand, it has been shown that Mead, symbolic interactionism and all 'critical' role theory take a more fundamental approach, namely the need — in any interaction — for role taking in the sense of situationally specific anticipation of alter's behaviour. How can the two definitions be linked in a way that is consistent?

A first step towards closing the gap is the introduction of the concept of situation and with it the need for norms to be interpreted. Roles then become *situationally specific* normative expectations toward position-holders. The problem, however, is the concept of position. The questionableness of Parsons's interaction model would, in a way, just go through a terminological shift if the strict concept of position, rooted as it is in structures, were to be weakened and generalized on to all interactive situations. For this reason, a reverse introduction of the concept from the unstructured interactive situation itself is to be recommended. Turner (1955–6: 317) interprets role as a 'meaningful unit of behaviour', although he, too, maintains the reference to a vague concept of position. Waller (1978: 57) very convincingly describes roles as 'meaning categories of social action ... through which social situations, persons, patterns of action and their underlying motive structures are placed in normative relation to one another'. In this definition of role there is no reference to positions and yet no confusion between role and mere expectation of particular features or modes of behaviour. *Role is thus the normative expectation of situationally specific meaningful behaviour.*

This expectation can become reflexive in two ways. First, the individual acquires the ability to see a situation not only in his or her own immediate perspective, and not only, through role taking, in alter's perspective but to adopt a third perspective in which the context of both actors is reconstructed as an objective one. This is what Mead had in mind with his idea of taking on the role of the 'generalized other'. Second, the extent to which interaction is structured through predefined expectations towards actors can be such that they act as if they were under a quasi-causal constraint that is independent of their intentions. This state of the value system becoming autonomous in formalized, e.g. bureaucratic, institutions is what Parsons had in mind. The question is not so much whether or not this actually occurs but how norms and values that have become autonomous react to problematization and to attempts at change by the individuals subsumed under them. Shibutani (1961: 47) is quite clear on this point:

Some social psychologists have spoken of behaviour as being 'determined by roles, as if the latter existed independently of human conduct and forced men into some mould. Roles, however, exist only in the behaviour of men, and the patterns become discernible only in their regularized interaction. Roles are models of conduct which constitute the desired contribution of those participating in group activity. But even in stable societies men are not automatons, blindly acting out conventional roles. The very fact that deviation is possible indicates that such models do not 'cause' behaviour.

This is the only way that a non-subject-free concept of transpersonal action structures can be introduced analytically and normatively.

The Meadian concept of role taking has come to be of crucial importance in this definition of the role concept. This being so, a number of widespread misconceptions needs to be dealt with. In a useful clarification, Lauer and Boardman (1970–71) systematize these misconceptions and point out a genetic connection between role taking in the strict sense and other meanings. They distinguish three dimensions that role taking can exhibit. It can (1) be reflexive or not. This preserves Mead's reference to direct complementary reactions in gestural communication and introduces the concept of role before the higher level of cognitive development at which role taking is already reflexive. Role taking can (2) be appropriative or not, that is to say it can or cannot lead to an adoption of alter's standpoint, which ego has understood cognitively. It is in this dimension that the distinction between identification, imitation and role taking is located. Finally, role taking can (3) be synesic[1] or not. By this Lauer and Boardman mean aesthetic, therapeutic and emotional-expressive forms of behaviour. Role taking as such is not identical with affective empathy, nor even with emotional sympathy and is not to be confused with mimetic 'playing-at-a-role' (Coutu, 1951). These are demarcations of definition. Investigation of the relations between the phenomena thus distinguished, and of their development, is an important theoretical and empirical task.[2]

Role theory in socialization research

Stimulations and achievements. Socialization research is, with the sociology of organizations, the main field of empirical application of role theory. It achieved this key position following the passing of the hegemony of psychoanalytical/cultural anthropological and behaviouristic/learning theory approaches.

As there is not enough room here to outline the findings of the various schools and currents within role theory in the numerous divisions of socialization research, only a few essential details will be mentioned.

There is no theory of socialization as such associated with role theory in its reduced form, e.g. as in Dahrendorf. Dahrendorf's assumptions in fact replace the question of the development of specific motivations and cognitive abilities. Where Dahrendorf's ideological overtones are missing, a number of fields do indeed become accessible. Topics frequently discussed include the acquisition of the fundamental gender and age roles, the structure of anticipatory socialization, the inner social structure of basic institutions of socialization such as the family and the school class and the personality structure of socialization agents (synopsis in Sewell, 1970). However, there are two obvious problems here. First, the naïve kind of role theory research tends to simplify the acquisition of roles in a way that gravitates towards positions. This means that what is examined is not the development of role taking ability itself, but solely the development of the discrimination of positionally specific characteristics and the formation of stereotype, role-conforming modes of behaviour.

This ignores the problems involved in the transformation of such stereotypes into situationally specific behaviour (see also Waller, 1978: 40ff.). Second, the link-up with a comprehensive theory of socialization in the Parsonian sense is often rather tenuous. Though in no way able to match Parsons's distinctions, Brim's model is often cited as a point of reference. In it socialization is seen as role learning in a sense that makes personality seem to be merely a 'learned repertoire of roles' (Brim, 1960: 141) and trans-situational consistence in behaviour to be insufficient flexibility and thus deficient socialization. What we encounter here in its crude form is also a critical question in Parsons. He, too, as Geulen (1977: 156) aptly puts it, 'does not see socialization as a societally mediated genesis, formulated in psychological categories, of the subject itself but as societal programming of the action decisions of a subject otherwise assumed to be complete.' Mead's crucial dimension of the formation of the self as the core of the socialization process is, therefore, not reflected in Parsons's model of socialization, a deficiency that remains even after a later, explicit examination of this question (Parsons, 1977).

The Meadian tradition of role-theoretical socialization research can point to its achievements in four fields. The social genesis of the self (1) constitutes a major topic. This requires the inclusion of motivation theory and sections of the psychoanalytical tradition as well as Parsons's work, but also a reference to dimensions of cognitive development, to an examination of the development of communicative abilities and to the relations between these dimensions. (2) Consideration of the open and process-like character of interaction has led to a different analysis of the inner structure of socialization agencies. Attention is focused more on the dynamics of mutual processes of definition than on static structural factors. (3) Through a loosening of the reference to an irrevocably complete personality structure, socialization research has been extended beyond the fields of childhood and adolescence to (4) an investigation of professional socialization and life-long personality changes. Vital pioneer work was undertaken here by symbolic interactionists (Becker, Strauss and Hughes). It cannot be denied that these new lines of research have not yet taken on the categorical solidity of Parsons's work and that the models of the development of the action competence of the subject are often insufficiently grounded in theories of society.

Theories and research on the development of role-taking ability. Conceived as a specifically anthropological feature by Mead, role-taking ability is at least mentioned in other role theories. A discussion of its development is of more fundamental importance than the question of the contribution of role theory approaches to our understanding of specific problems. In a certain sense this makes the core of role theory itself accessible to empirical validation in spite of its 'metatheoretical' status. Furthermore, a clear distinction between role-taking ability and the stages of its development means that a distinction is made, at least in principle, between levels of competence and performance as far as social learning is concerned even though this poses a number of difficult problems. Finally, a discussion of this kind inevitably produces a more precise statement of views on the relationship between cognitive and communicative development.

It will be obvious that those currents within role theory that give only very implicit consideration to active communicative performance have little to contribute to the genesis of role-taking ability. It will be less obvious why the symbolic interactionist school provided so few impulses for research of this kind when Mead's original model decidedly pursued a genetic explanatory strategy. While the reasons for this are many, the fact that the approach has not spread particularly far is only one of them, and it was not as if authors had not been soon aware of the problem (Cottrell, 1950). Certain conceptual reinterpretations of Mead's initial conception played a part as a contemporary, self-critical retrospective in the symbolic interactionist tradition shows (Sherohman, 1977). The subject of the majority of studies was not role taking ability but accuracy, which meant that anthropological themes were hurriedly translated not into universalistic questions of developmental psychology but into questions of differential psychology. The results of accuracy surveys were frequently interpreted as indicating ability levels, an inadmissible step because of the countless components of substantive nature in the index of accuracy — actors' common culture, for example — which as such have nothing to do with role taking competence. Role taking ability is just one of several sources of the accuracy of role taking. Another misleading operationalization is the investigation of only the anticipation of certain attitudes in another actor and not of role taking ability. This type of operationalization dissolves the context of a shared situation that practically forces actors to co-ordinate their behaviour and replaces this role-taking situation by test situations in which individuals are questioned about their context-free assessments of fictitious alters.

Other schools of experimental psychology are also characterized by these deficiencies of symbolic interactionist work. A decisive change did not occur until the meeting of the Meadian and Piagetian traditions, something that did not apply to Piaget himself. It is a well-known fact that in his lifetime of work Piaget neglected the dimension of the child's early social behaviour. This neglect resulted in a tendency to operationalize role taking with regard to the co-ordination of perspectives towards non-social contexts. Apart from forerunners such as Feffer and parallel developments such as that of Kerckhoff, the pioneer work in empirical research was done by Flavell and colleagues (1968). Flavell introduces his own research programme with an interesting critique of Mead, whom he accuses of not giving sufficient consideration, in his concept of communication, to the problems of inter-individual heterogeneity.

> The two-year-old who looks at his mother, points to the household pet, and says 'Doggie' has met at least the minimal requirements for Mead's acquisition. The ten-year-old who can picture to himself how an object in front of him appears to a friend standing on the opposite side of it, and who simplifies his message when explaining something to his three-year-old brother — he is well on the way to acquiring the kind of skills we have in mind. Mead defines a significant symbol as a gesture which arouses the same response in both A and B; what he does not deal with is how A acquires the ability to discern B's qualities as a respondent generally, and in particular how he acquires the ability to select those gestures which will, in fact, arouse the same response in B. (Flavell, 1968: 16)

It is ironic that Flavell's step towards a treatment of this question and his quite justified pointer to the general character of Mead's comments should be marked by a profound lack of understanding of Mead's conception of language. What Flavell says about egocentric communication (Flavell, 1975: 45 ff.) shows that his starting point is an initially non-social inner language that only secondarily becomes socially oriented for communicative purposes. But in doing so he destroys the continuity that can be seen in the Meadian tradition between the earliest form of role taking and subsequent communicative and co-operative ability. The importance of the dimension of cognitive development is then emphasized instead of this continuity, and this is what characterizes Flavell's operationalizations. His test situations favour linguistic communication to the detriment of mime or gesture and ignore the possibility of emotional involvement in the set tasks (cf. Köstlin-Gloger's introduction to Flavell, 1975).

Flavell's pioneer work was taken considerably further by Selman (1971 a and b, 1977). The merits of Selman's work are that the form of interactive game is indeed made the method of research and that, drawing on Kohlberg, the development of role taking ability is related not only to cognitive but to moral development in particular. His differentiated models of phases of development in early and middle childhood should also be mentioned. However, his dating of early childhood (beginning at the age of three) shows that he, too, feels there can be no meaningful discussion of the child's social interaction at a considerably earlier age in terms of the theory of role taking. The focal question in Selman's studies has been brilliantly defined by Keller (1976: 65) as the genetic priority of cognitive operations. While not assuming a determinative connection between cognitive and social abilities, Selman does refer to the cognitive dimension as a necessary if not sufficient prerequisite for the development of social abilities. This precludes any reverse effect.

Habermas, Döbert and Nunner-Winkler, who draw on Piaget but above all on Kohlberg and Selman, are surprisingly uncritical as regards internal problems in the works and theoretical approaches of these three authors. In fact, they absorb the problems in question unaltered, increasing the claim to general validity even further. Keller (1976) and Waller (1978), both excellent pieces of work, are the two most important critical contributions and relatively extensive models. Keller identifies the principle shortcomings in previous analyses,

> obviously, in all these previous operationalizations of role taking, abstract formal thought processes are demanded which are alien to the child's world in as much as relations or identification with those acting

are not available. The child is therefore expected to supply a trans-situational generalization. Role taking would then be acquired in a particular experiential situation highly motivational in content and could be performed initially in similar situations as an 'act of social-cognitive achievement'. It is only later that this ability is separated from the context of its genesis by means of generalizing abstraction and becomes available regardless of situation. (Keller, 1976: 152f.)

Her emphasis is on the social background to the development of role taking ability and primarily on parent-child interaction. Waller, who bases his argument on other theoretical traditions, comes to the similar conclusion that social-cognitive structures have to be deduced from social experience. Though his concept of role taking is not as profound as Mead's, which is the one adopted by Keller, he does place greater stress on interaction between children.

There are signs of a convergence between various schools of thought in socialization theory and developmental psychology in the emphasis on the social dimension of development. With Keller's and Waller's work in the narrower field of role theory and with several other contributions on the development of social cognition in children (Edelstein and Keller, 1982), suitable approaches seem to be emerging for an empirically and conceptually precise treatment of the problem of the development of social and communicative abilities, approaches that will not turn this field into a new version of the sociolinguistically outmoded 'deficit hypothesis' as a result of an over-estimation of the cognitive-linguistic dimension and a neglect of cultural and subcultural typicalities. Premature talk of grades of competence in role taking ability may be the product of inadequate 'role taking' where other cultures and classes are involved. Unconsciously imported prejudice must not be allowed to turn the illuminatory conceptual strength of role theory into the merely ideological expression of a society in a particular historical state.

Notes

* This text is a partially abridged, partially elaborated version of my 1980 German handbook article 'Rollen- und Interaktionstheorien in der Sozialisationsforschung', pp. 147–60 in Hurrelmann and Ulich (eds), *Handbuch der Sozialisationsforschung*. Weinheim: Beltz. This had been written on the background of my books on role theory (Joas, 1973) and on George Herbert Mead (Joas, 1980). The text was translated by Steven Minner, who died the day after finishing this work. I want to dedicate the article to him and his young widow.

1. This expression is explained (Lauer and Boardman, 1970–71: 147, note 8): 'From the Greek "synesin", which means a running or flowing together; the faculty of comprehension, insight, understanding'.

2. Hilbert (1981) sees roles merely as legitimatory devices for action; he could not explain how an actor is able to follow a rule without explicitly knowing it.

References

Bahrdt, H.P. (1961) 'Zur Frage des Menschenbildes in der Soziologie', *Europäisches Archiv für Soziologie*, 2: 1–17.

Brim, O.G. (1960) 'Personality Development as Role-Learning', pp. 127–59 in J. Iscoe, J. and H.W. Stevenson (eds), *Personality Development in Children*. Austin, Tex.: University of Texas Press.

Cicourel, A.V. (1970) 'Basic and Normative Rules in the Negotiation of Status and Role', pp. 4–45 in H.P. Dreitzel (ed.), *Recent Sociology No. 2, Patterns of Communicative Behavior*. London: Macmillan.

Claessens, D. (1963) 'Rolle und Verantwortung', *Soziale Welt*, 14: 1–13.

Claessens, D. (1970) *Rolle und Macht*. München: Juventa.

Cottrell, L.S. (1950) 'Some Neglected Problems in Social Psychology', *American Sociological Review*, 15: 705–12.

Coutu, W. (1951) 'Role-Playing vs. Role-Taking', *American Sociological Review*, 16: 180–87.

Dahrendorf, R. (1959) *Homo Sociologicus. Ein Versuch zur Geschichte, Bedeutung und Kritik der Kategorie der sozialen Rolle*. Köln/Opladen: Westdeutscher Verlag.

Döbert, R., J. Habermas and G. Nunner-Winkler, (1977) 'Zur Einführung', pp. 9–30 in Döbert, Habermas and Nunner-Winkler (eds), *Entwicklung des Ichs*. Köln: Kiepenheuer und Witsch.

Dreitzel, H.P. (1972) *Die gesellschaftlichen Leiden und das Leiden an der Gesellschaft. Vorstudien zu einer Pathologie des Rollenverhaltens*. Stuttgart: Enke.

Edelstein, W. and M. Keller, (eds) (1982) *Perspektivität und Interpretation*. Frankfurt-am-Main: Suhrkamp.

Flavell, J.H. et al. (1968) *The Development of Role-Taking and Communication Skills in Children*. New York: Wiley.

Geulen, D. (1977) *Das vergesellschaftete Subjekt. Zur Grundlegung der Sozialisations-theorie*. Frankfurt-am-Main: Suhrkamp.

Geulen, D.(ed.) (1982) *Perspektivenübernahme und soziales Handeln*. Frankfurt-am-Main: Suhrkamp.

Goffman, E. (1961) 'Role-Distance', pp. 85–152 in E. Goffman, *Encounters. Two Studies in the Sociology of Interaction*. Indianapolis: Bobbs-Merrill.

Gouldner, A. (1960) 'The Norm of Reciprocity. A Preliminary Statement', *American Sociological Review*, 25: 161–78.

Gross, N. (1966) 'Role Conflict and Its Resolution', pp. 287–96, in B.J. Biddle and E.J. Thomas (eds), *Role Theory. Concepts and Research*. New York: John Wiley.

Habermas, J. (1973), 'Stichworte zur Theorie der Sozialisation', pp. 118–94 in J. Habermas, *Kultur und Kritik*. Frankfurt-am-Main: Suhrkamp.

Habermas, J. (1976) 'Moralentwicklung und Ich-Identität', pp. 63–91, in J. Habermas, *Zur Rekonstruktion des Historischen Materialismus*. Frankfurt-am-Main: Suhrkamp.

Handel, W., (1979) 'Normative Expectations and the Emergence of Meaning as Solutions to Problems: Convergence of Structural and Interactionist Views', *American Journal of Sociology*, 84: 855–81.

Heiss, J. (1981) 'Social Roles', pp. 94–129, in M. Rosenberg and R. Turner (eds), *Social Psychology*. New York: Basic Books.

Hilbert, R. (1981) 'Toward an Improved Understanding of "Role"', *Theory and Society*, 10: 207–25.

Jackson, J.A. (ed.) (1972) *Role*. Cambridge: Cambridge University Press.

Joas, H. (1973) *Die gegenwärtige Lage der soziologischen Rollentheorie*. Wiesbaden: Akademische Verlagsgesellschaft.

Joas, H. (1980) *Praktische Intersubjekivität. Die Entwicklung des Werks von G.H. Mead*. Frankfurt-am-Main: Suhrkamp.

Joas, H. (1981) 'G.H. Mead and the "Division of Labor": Macro-sociological Implications of Mead's Social Psychology', *Symbolic Interaction*, 4: 177–90.

Keller, M. (1976) *Kognitive Entwicklung und soziale Kompetenz. Zur Entstehung der Rollenübernahme in der Familie und ihrer Bedeutung für den Schulerfolg*. Stuttgart: Klett.

Keller, M. (1976a) 'Development of Role-Taking Ability', *Human Development*, 19:120–132.

Kerckhoff, C.C. (1969) 'Early Antecedents of Role-Taking and Role-Playing Ability', *Merrill-Palmer Quarterly*, 15: 229–47.

Krappmann, L. (1971) *Soziologische Dimensionen der Identität. Strukturelle Bedingungen für die Teilnahme an Interaktionsprozessen*. Stuttgart: Klett.

Lauer, R.H. and L. Boardman (1970–71) 'Role-Taking: Theory, Typology and Propositions', *Sociology and Social Research*, 55: 137–48.

Maccoby, E. (1959) 'Role-Taking in Childhood and Its Consequences for Social Learning', *Child Development*, 30: 239–52.

Mead, G.H. (1934) *Mind, Self and Society*. Chicago: University of Chicago Press.

Mead. G.H. (1964) *Selected Writings*, A. Reck (ed.), Indianapolis: Bobbs-Merrill.

Merton, R.K. (1957) *Social Theory and Social Structure*. Glencoe: Free Press.

Parsons, T. (1951) *The Social System*. London: Routledge and Kegan Paul.

Parsons, T. (1977) 'Der Stellenwert des Identitätsbegriffs in der allgemeinen Handlungstheorie', pp. 68–88 in R. Döbert et al. (eds.), *Entwicklung des Ichs*. Köln: Kiepenheuer und Witsch.

Parsons, T. and R.F. Bales (1955) *Family, Socialization and Interaction Process*. Glencoe: Free Press.

Parsons, T. and E.A. Shils (eds) (1951) *Toward a General Theory of Action*. New York: Harper.

Plessner, H. (1974), 'Soziale Rolle und menschliche Natur', pp. 23–35 in H. Plessner, *Diesseits der Utopie. Beiträge zur Kultursoziologie*. Frankfurt-am-Main: Suhrkamp.

Popitz, H. (1967) *Der Begriff der sozialen Rolle als Element der soziologischen Theorie*. Tübingen: Mohr.

Selman, R. (1971a) 'Taking Another's Perspective. Role-Taking Development in Early Childhood', *Child Development*, 42: 1721–34.

Selman, R. (1971b) 'The Relation of Role-Taking to the Development of Moral Judgement in Children', *Child Development*, 42: 79–91.

Selman, R. and D. Byrne (1977) 'Stufen der Rollenübernahme in der mittleren Kindheit – eine entwicklungslogische Analyse', pp. 109–14, in R. Döbert et al. (eds), *Entwicklung des Ichs*. Köln: Kiepenheuer und Witsch.

Sewell, W.H. (1970) 'Some Recent Developments in Socialization Theory and Research', pp. 566–83, in G.P. Stone and H.A. Farberman (eds), *Social Psychology through Symbolic Interaction*. Waltham, Mass.: Xerox College Publishing.

Sherohman, J. (1977) 'Conceptual and Methodological Issues in the Study of Role-Taking Accuracy', *Symbolic Interaction*, 1: 121–31.

Shibutani, T. (1961) *Society and Personality. An Interactionist Approach to Social Psychology*. Englewood Cliffs, NJ: Prentice-Hall.

Tenbruck, F.H. (1961) 'Zur deutschen Rezeption der Rollentheorie', *Kölner Zeitschrift für Soziologie und Sozialpsychologie*, 13: 1–40.

Turner, R.H. (1955–6) 'Role-Taking, Role-Standpoint and Reference-Group Behavior', *American Journal of Sociology*, 61: 316–28.

Turner, R.H. (1962) 'Role-Taking: Process Versus Conformity', pp. 20–40, in A.M. Rose (ed.), *Human Behavior and Social Processes*. Boston: Houghton-Mifflin.

Turner, R.H. (1975–6) 'The Real Self: From Institution to Impulse', *American Journal of Sociology*, 81: 989–1016.

Turner, R.H. (1978–9) 'The Role and the Person', *American Journal of Sociology*, 84: 1–23.

Waller, M. (1978) *Soziales Lernen und Interaktionskompetenz. Die Ausbildung von Verhaltenserwartungen und die Konstruktion von Regeln interpersonalen Verhaltens beim Kinde*. Stuttgart: Klett.

4

The foundations of symbolic interactionism reconsidered*

G. David Johnson and J. Steven Picou

A number of recent commentaries present a new, revisionist interpretation of the work of George H. Mead. These commentaries, including those of Lewis and Smith (1980), McPhail and Rexroat (1979) and Lewis (1976), present what we call the objectivist reading of Mead (Johnson and Shifflett, 1981). The revised Mead is said to have authored doctrines of social and philosophical realism (Lewis and Smith, 1980) and advanced elaborately detailed positions on the methods and techniques of objective scientific methodology (McPhail and Rexroat, 1979). This reading of Mead would quite clearly require the rejection of the orthodox account of the origins of symbolic interactionism — Blumer's (1969) interpretative methodology cannot be the legitimate heir to this new revised Mead. Indeed, the objectivists argue that Mead's influence on sociology was actually minimal and that Blumer was thereby able to disseminate his misinterpretation of Mead (Lewis and Smith, 1980).

The objectivist reading, of course, has not gone unchallenged. Blumer (1977, 1980), in particular, denies the validity of both Lewis's (1976), and McPhail and Rexoat's (1979) arguments. Johnson (1983) and Johnson and Shifflett (1981) offer an extended critique of many of the objectivists' claims. The controversy, none the less, is not yet settled. Lewis and Smith's (1980) intellectual history of Mead and interactionism, in particular, requires a more fundamental rebuttal. In this chapter, we enter the controversy at its core — the problem of the philosophical underpinnings of Mead's social psychology.

Lewis and Smith in their *American Sociology and Pragmatism* (1980) argue that a fundamental cleavage separates the American pragmatist philosophers. James and Dewey are said to have advanced nominalist philosophies, whereas Peirce's and Mead's philosophies are interpreted as realist. Philosophical nominalism, according to Lewis and Smith, denies independent reality status to universals. Social nominalism similarly denies the reality of social universals. Philosophical and social realism affirm the reality of both sets of universals. Essentially, Lewis and Smith read Mead's philosophy and social psychology in terms of Peirce's purportedly realist categories. They emphasize Mead's concern with objectivity, as revealed in the use of behaviourism in social psychology and in the doctrine of the objectivity of perspectives, along with the concern with the role of society in both his epistemology and social psychology. This Peircian reading of Mead is not altogether unattractive. It is true, for instance, that Mead, certainly more than James and perhaps more than Dewey, was interested in the analysis of the scientific act and in the problem of the interrelations of society with personality. The relevant question, however, focuses on the degree of the differences between the American philosophers. Do these differences constitute what Lewis and Smith call a metaphysical break, a break that not only separates Mead from James and Dewey, but also from Blumer? We will argue that no such break exists. In support of this answer we offer a Jamesian, and implicitly a Deweyian,[1] reading of Mead in contrast to the Peircian approach of Lewis and Smith.[2] If sustained, that is, if Mead can be meaningfully interpreted as a member of a continuous tradition of classical American philosophy (McDermott, 1978), including at least James and Dewey in addition to Mead, then the objectivist reading will be cast into doubt. The objectivist interpretation makes sense only if Mead did, indeed, author a realist metaphysics. We will argue that Mead's positions on objectivity and sociality should be viewed from a Jamesian perspective, a perspective compatible with Blumer's symbolic interactionism.

Other histories of symbolic interactionism
In the present work, we attempt to document the philosophical foundations of the American social psychology represented in the works of Herbert Blumer, Erving Goffman and others.[3] Overlooking for the moment Lewis and Smith's (1980) questionable historical reconstruction of Mead's influence on sociology (Johnson and Shifflett, 1981), all accounts identify Mead as the fountainhead of the tradition (Blumer, 1969; Manis and Meltzer, 1978; Meltzer, Petras and Reynolds, 1975). A number of historical commentators also contend that William James made substantial social psychological contributions (Karpf, 1932; Petras, 1966; Blumer, 1969). Unlike Mead, however, James's contributions are not easily available nor widely understood by sociologists. In summing up James's role in social psychology, the extant histories specify his development of a few concepts, most notably the concepts of impulse, habit and the social self (Karpf, 1932; Petras, 1966). These concepts, however, constitute a very insignificant aspect of James's

work. Given James's prominence in the intellectual community of the early 1900s (Perry, 1948), it is much more likely that a wider range of James's thought, including his metaphysics, influenced American social psychology via Mead.

In their philosophical comparison, Lewis and Smith divide American philosophy and Chicago sociology into nominalist and realist camps. Our argument poses no such metaphysical or social ontological disjunction. The argument for continuity was anticipated by Martindale (1960: 354):

> Just as James had taken pure experience as a starting point, treating subject and object as distinctions arising within it, so Mead proposed to start analysis with an observable activity, the dynamic on-going social process, and the social acts which are its component elements, and then to treat the mind and society as arising as discriminations within this process.

We argue along much the same lines: James's radically original metaphysics is amazingly continuous with Mead's theory of the self. Martindale's highly suggestive, but clearly underdeveloped, comment requires detailed support. The discussion that follows develops and elaborates the argument assumed by Martindale.

Our position requires a comparison of the essential tenets of James's philosophy with those of Mead. We will compare the two philosophies on a number of key aspects, including metaphysics, epistemology, and the conception of the social aspects of experience. We begin with the fundamental continuity between the philosophies: the rejection of dualist metaphysics.

The rejection of dualism

In their division of American philosophy and sociology into realist and nominalist camps, Lewis and Smith (1980) fail to appreciate the most basic feature of James's, Dewey's and Mead's thought. All reject the dualistic world-view that the nominalist/realist distinction requires. For classical American philosophy, and its social science derivatives, reality cannot be said accurately to lie within either organism or environment exclusively. Reality is, instead, located in their interrelations. This relational conception of the world, so prominent in American philosophy, can be traced at least to James's *The Principles of Psychology* (1890).

In the *Principles*, James struggles with the problem of dualism. Explicitly, James (1890a:vi) posits a dualism of knower and known; and yet, implicitly, James hints strongly that this dualism cannot be sustained. He (1948:467) writes that his work constitutes 'a psychology particularly fragile, and into which the waters of metaphysical criticism leak at every joint'. James's struggle with dualism is revealed in his account of perception. James (1890a: 284–5) writes,

> Out of what is in itself an undistinguishable swarming *continuum*, devoid of distinction or emphasis, our senses make for us, by attending to this motion and ignoring that, a world full of contrasts, of sharp accents, of abrupt changes, or picturesque light and shade.

James contends that outside of the mind's selective apparatus, the world is an 'infinite chaos of movement'. For the world to become sensible, so that we may act within it, the mind must actively engage the world. The world does not present itself to a passive mind. Rather, the mind must actively seek out the world and supply order. The world can be known only from a perspective that is never complete. The world is known relative to one's interests: 'as I am always classing [a thing] under one aspect or another, I am always unjust, always partial, always exclusive' (James, 1890b: 333).

Mead's metaphysics advocates a similar doctrine of selectivity in perception. Mead (1934: 128), for example, states:

> The appearance of the retinal elements has given the world colour; the development of the organs in the ear has given the world sound. We pick out an organized environment in relationship to our response, so that these attitudes, as such, not only represent our organized responses but they also represent what exists for us in the world.

For Mead, just as it is for James, the world is known only relative to experience. The order of the world, its colour and sound, are as much the product of our 'attitudes' (Mead, 1934: 128) as they are characteristic of the external world. Note Mead's use of 'given' in this text. That the eye's structure gives the world colour is far from any simple realism. For James and Mead, then, the doctrine of selectivity in perception calls into question the dualism that underlies both realism and nominalism.

James's emphasis on an active mind that selects an order out of the 'infinite chaos' constitutes an important epistemological achievement within American philosophy. This idea amounts to formulation of a dialectical epistemology, where mind and matter interact, each determining the other. James, however, had not embraced dialectical thinking fully in the *Principles*. Indeed, although eventually he made significant advances in developing the metaphysical implications of the world-view implicit in his early work, James never achieved a final systematic statement of his dialectical metaphysics. According to Seigfried (1978), James alternatively posed a world as infinitely chaotic, as above, or as occasionally ordered, as in the 'necessary truths' chapter in the *Principles*. James can be said to have struggled against the inadequacies of both philosophical realism and nominalism, to use Lewis and Smith's terms. In a resolution of James's problem, Seigfried (1978: 34) writes:

> James realized that the strength of his philosophical position depended on the denial of the extremes of asserting either the priority of arbitrary imposition of selective interest on a completely malleable manifold or the priority of immutable natures and intrinsic relations dictating to completely impressionable minds. In denying the one-sidedness of either position he tends to misleadingly overemphasize the contrary one.

Seigfried posits the 'true' Jamesian position through a reconciliation of these polar expressions of nominalism and realism. She suggests that for James, the world is a 'quasi-chaos', neither altogether chaotic nor altogether ordered. The world limits the activities of the mind; we are not totally free to believe as we see fit. On the other hand, one does not simply apprehend an already ordered universe. We must strive to find order.

James's dialectical metaphysics, with the world understood as quasi-chaos, is isomorphic with Mead's world-view. Mead explicitly notes the dialectic throughout his work. For example, from *Mind, Self and Society* (1934: 130), Mead contends,

> And since organism and environment determine each other and are mutually dependent for their existence, it follows that the life process, to be adequately understood, must be considered in terms of their interrelations.

Mead, then, is quite explicit: organism and environment determine one another.

Mead's formulation of the dialectic, moreover, is not limited to *Mind, Self and Society*.[4] In *The Philosophy of the Act* (1938), Mead articulates at several points what he argues is the pragmatist rejection of dualism (cf. 1938: 360–442). Mead (1938: 163–4) writes, for instance, defining 'perspective':

> The process by which the organism has arisen is, however, one in which the organism has determined its field by its susceptibilities and responses. There is a mutual interdependence of the two. This is expressed in the term 'perspective' ... The environment is a selection which is dependent upon the living form.

Mead's 'perspective', then, shares with James's 'quasi-chaos' a most fundamental metaphysical position — each rejects a dualistic image of the world.

On relations and process

The notion of relations functions as the heart of James's thought. In the *Principles* James broke from the atomism of the associationistic psychologists, including Hume and Locke, and advanced a relational psychology. Thought was not conceived as the addition of discrete sensations; instead, thought is like a bird's life. Like a bird, thought is a series of flights and perchings. When we hold a 'sensorial imagination' in mind, our thought 'perches' momentarily at rest. When moving from one 'perch' to another, the mind 'flies'. In an important breakthrough, James attests to the reality of our 'flights'. James insisted on the reality of felt relations. He contends, 'we ought to say a feeling of *and*, a feeling of *if*, a feeling of *but*, and a feeling of *by*, quite as readily as we say a feeling of *blue* or a feeling of *cold*' (1890b: 245–6). In emphasizing feelings of relations, James achieved a processive understanding of thought. This notion of process represents a radical departure for James from more conventional discrete philosophies and social theories. Following James's breakthrough in this 'doctrine of relations' (James, 1975b: 7), American philosophers, including Dewey and Mead, advanced process philosophies.

Mead's processive philosophy begins with the 'passage' of events. Passage 'involves simply happening, a coming into being and going out' (Mead, 1938: 331). In the experience of mere passage, the most basic experience possible according to Mead, endurance or sameness is not known. For instance, 'the sameness of the green of one event and of the green of the next event' (Mead, 1938: 332) are not realized at the level of passage. The experience of passage is the only experience available to other life forms and it grounds our own experience (Mead, 1938: 331–2; Miller, 1973: 28–9). With the concept 'process', such as the 'life process', Mead indicates a continuous interrelationship between events and acts. Unlike mere passage, the life process implies a particular meaning that holds across all parts of the process. The most important process in Mead's social psychology is the 'social process'. Mead writes, in a passage particularly reminiscent of Dewey's (1896) 'Reflex Arc' article, that the social process is a 'dynamic whole ... no part of which can be considered or understood by itself — a complex organic process implied by each stimulus and response involved in it' (Mead, 1934: 7). It is important to note that Mead's (1934) social psychology begins with this assumption of a social process. From the pre-human social interchange, human mind, selves and societies are said to emerge. Mead shares with James a rejection of an entity or discrete image of the world. For each, entities such as stimulus and response, or organism and environment, have meaning only within a single, complex process. James came to label the foundational process, 'pure experience'. For Mead, the organic of life process operates as first principle.

James's radical metaphysics

James's rejection of dualism becomes explicit in his *Essays in Radical Empiricism*,[5] where he advances the hypothesis of 'pure experience'. James argues that the world is best conceived not as a world of thoughts and things, nor as a world of objective realities and subjective sensations. Rather, prior to the distinction between sensation and object lies a primary reality that James calls pure experience. Mind and matter are not ontological categories: 'thoughts and things are absolutely homogeneous as to their material, and ... their opposition is only one of relation and function' (James, 1976a: 69).

This ambiguity of object and subject is especially revealed, for James, in affectional experiences. Our emotions are not merely in the mind; they are also in the body as the James–Lange theory attests (James, 1976a: 71). Motion, as well, is frequently attributed 'incorrectly' to bodies that are not 'actually' in motion. With these ambiguous experiences,

> In practical life no urgent need has yet arisen for deciding whether to treat them as rigorously mental or as rigorously physical facts. So they remain equivocal; and, as the world goes, their equivocality is one of their great conveniences. (James, 1976a: 73)

James believed that all of experience, all of reality, is like these ambiguous experiences. Experience is not dual; it is *initially* undifferentiated 'and the separation of it into consciousness and content comes, not by way of subtraction, but by way of addition' (James, 1976a: 7). The categories of consciousness and content are added to the pure experience.

James's doctrine of pure experience operates as a hypothesis that is intended to account for the world (Seigfried, 1978: 40). Using this hypothesis, James largely overcomes problems of conventional dualistic alternatives. Radical empiricism grew out of his earlier insights into the selective character of perception and of his naturalistic, functional psychology. The value of the approach lies in the continuity of these insights. James's thought remains centred on human activity — humans, experiencing their world, remain the 'given' in his work. All truth claims must be appealed to experience for James. James's own analysis of experience reveals that the 'given is "a simple that" — it is "pure"'. Pure experience is in continuous process, as humans are in continuous transaction with their worlds. The processive character of experience is maintained by naturally occurring relations. James writes that 'the relations between things, conjunctive as well as disjunctive' (1975b: 7) are real. Consequently, the universe 'possesses in its own right a concatenated or continuous structure' (James, 1975b: 7). Just as relations sustained the continuity of thought in the *Principles*, relations sustain the continuity of experience in the *Essays*.

In the *Essays*, James postulates a somewhat ordered and somewhat chaotic world. The world is to a large extent chaotic, but 'here and there' experiences 'intersect with one another in the shared perceptual world'; consequently, 'the chaos is not total but only partial' (Seigfried, 1978: 47). James's 'quasi-chaos', as Seigfried formulates it, stands midway between nominalism and realism. The mind constitutes the world as the idealists would have it, but we are not free to construct the world arbitrarily. The experiences of 'others', including the functioning physical world, bounds our experience, limiting us. And because of this limitation, our worlds are not altogether chaotic. Our experience 'makes sense' when in 'context' (Seigfried, 1978: 37).

Metaphysical continuities
Arguing against James and Dewey, Lewis and Smith (1980: 14) contend that philosophical nominalists approach ontology via epistemology; that is, 'how do we know?' is primary to 'what is there?' James's hypothesis of pure experience is clearly nominalistic in this sense. In the contention that pure experience is prior to the distinction between thought and thing, James begins his enquiry with the human experience and not with the assumption of some independent reality. Inference about a real world is just that — an inference.

In contrast to Lewis and Smith's arguments, however, we contend that Mead also elevates epistemology to a position prior to ontology. As we demonstrated above, Mead often contends that the organism 'determines' the environment. In this dialectical metaphysics, the organism's selections constitute its environment. What we label reality is dependent upon our knowledge and upon our interests. Epistemology precedes ontology for Mead as it does for James.

James's formulation of the world as a quasi-chaos seems to fit Mead's understanding, as well. With the dialectic, Mead emphasizes that the world's order is in part constituted by our actions. Mead like James, however, recognized the need for a world texture. For Mead, as for James, our constitution of the world is bounded. Mead expressed this understanding in the 'world that is there'. Defining this concept, David Miller writes, 'This is an expression he uses when he is defending the contention that there is a world that exists apart from our knowing that it exists and apart from our perception of it' (1973: 88). For Mead, the world is not available for our arbitrary manipulation. Against any particular problem, we must assume an unquestioned world that contexts our efforts. Mead writes, 'But it must not be forgotten that however wide the problematic area assumes, it is always surrounded by a universe that is simply there' (1983: 30). Mead rejects the idealistic claim that the mind constitutes the world totally. Rather, a universe that is simply there always restricts our efforts. James, of course, advocates a similar metaphysical position. In *Pragmatism* (first published in 1907), he writes, 'Woe to him whose beliefs play fast and loose with the order which realities follow in his experience; they will lead him nowhere or else make false connexions' (James, 1975a: 99). Both James and Mead contend that we cannot arbitrarily construct the world. Although both stress this world texture, neither James or Mead are naïve realists. As Miller interprets Mead, 'But that world is one that can be changed into another world, or it may be added to, because of emergent entities and active minds which give new meanings, new structures, to the world' (Miller, 1973: 89). The world, Miller argues, is altered by the actions of men and women. The world is understood only relative to our active minds. For Mead, we always act within the restrictions of a world that is there. Our knowledge of the world, however, is necessarily related to our perspective — the world is never known independent of our categories, interests and actions. For human purposes, Mead writes, 'Nature ... is a perspective' (1932: 172). In James's image, the world is a quasi-chaos, where the world is potentially ordered but requires our action to order it. Similarly, in Mead's system, the world answers our efforts to make sense of it (Miller, 1973: 98). Both James and Mead present a metaphysics that is in part realistic and in part nominalistic.

The problem of the social
James is often credited as having made contributions to social psychology, although the acknowledgement is typically merely honorific (Blumer, 1969; Manis and Meltzer, 1978). James's direct contributions are actually relatively minor. He developed notions of the 'social self' (1890a: 292), 'impulse' (1890b: 383–411) and 'habit' (1890a: 104–27), each of which proved to be of some consequence in social psychology (Petras, 1966; Karpf, 1932). James (1890) also introduced the 'I–Me' dichotomy developed by Mead (1934). The wealth of James's contribution, however, lies not in his explicit development of social themes. Rather, his thought 'boils over' with implications that were developed by other thinkers, particularly by Mead.

Mead's development of the social aspects of experience and

James's lack of concern for these aspects constitute the most important difference in their philosophies. None the less, this difference does not constitute a fundamental cleavage in the two men's philosophies. James's hypothesis of pure experience, it will be remembered, de-emphasized the categories of subject and object. Certainly, James does not attempt to *account* for self or society. Rather, James attempts to avoid all categories in the formulation of his metaphysics. In the *Essays*, he does not detail a self within pure experience, nor does he detail features of the environment, as in the social environment. He is committed, instead, to descriptive accuracy of concrete experience as it is undergone. He wants to give full attention to the thickness of life, without presupposing the character of experience. In his concrete description he accepts the world as it is, both in its conjunctions and disjunctions, its novelties and regularities, and in its intimacy and its distance. Consequently, although James's metaphysics is 'thick', it cannot support the *explanation* of events within the fabric of experience. Such an explanation requires the introduction of categories.

In contrast to James's pursuit of descriptive accuracy, the problem that begins Mead's enquiry is much more specific. Mead attempts to and, to a great extent, achieves an account of the human self and human society. Self and society are examples of the categories James chooses to avoid in his metaphysics. In overcoming dualism, James felt the need to pose a non-dualistic, non-substantive vocabulary. Consequently, James hypothesized a 'pure' experience, prior to categorical classification. Mead, in contrast, continued to use the categories of mind and society, categories that conventionally imply a dualism. As should be clear by now, however, Mead did not accept ontological dualism. Mead's dualism, like James's, is functional. For James, pure experience can function as object or subject; however, ontologically, it remains pure. Similarly, for Mead, we can conceive of self or society, but both self and society can be understood only in terms of the complex and organic social process. The core of the Jamesian metaphysics remains — Mead sustains process and the dialectical rejection of dualism. Mead introduces the categories of self and society, and stimulus and response, in order to address the social psychological problem that James ignores. This introduction, however, does not constitute a metaphysical break. Mead, instead, extends the Jamesian metaphysics to a previously uncharted problem.

Lewis and Smith (1980) argue that Mead is a social realist, that, like Durkheim, Mead assumes that a real, external, social reality exists prior to and determines human personality. This reading is, indeed, incompatible with a Jamesian metaphysics. Mead, however, is not a social realist in this sense. Quite obviously, Mead does not assume a *human* society that exists prior to the emergence of human minds and selves. Instead, Mead assumes an ongoing, pre-human, social process — essentially a group of interacting animals. As David Miller (1978: 1) has said, Mead assumes society 'at the biological level, not the human level'. With the emergence of the significant symbol, selves, generalized others, and human societies are possible. Mead's theory of the self, then, is also a theory of society. Read in this way, Mead's social psychology may fit a Jamesian metaphysics. The ongoing social process, like James's pure experience, is all that need be assumed.

Epistemology
Probably the most obvious, yet most misunderstood, continuity between the philosophies of James and Mead is epistemological. Both advocate the pragmatist criterion for truth — an idea is true if it works in our experience (James, 1975a: 28; Mead, 1964e: 342). This deceptively simple epistemology is frequently equated with subjective utilitarianism or solipsism, as if our beliefs may be true regardless of context or simply because we will them to be true. These misapprehensions can be overcome by grounding pragmatic epistemology in the metaphysics that we have identified as shared by James and Mead.

Given James's world-view, a conventional epistemology, for example a correspondence theory of truth, cannot be sustained. James's emphasis in *Pragmatism* on the practical is altogether consistent with his long-standing approach since the *Principles*. Humans acting in their environment are at the centre of the approach — this is James's starting point. In human action, he postulates pure experience, not mind/matter, as the primeval 'stuff' of the universe. With these as first principles, a rationalistic, dualistic conception of truth cannot be maintained. The world is known only through our experience of it; the world is always known from a *perspective*. The world, for James, is not separate from human experience. If we accept this Jamesian world, truth must exist within experience. In *Pragmatism*, James argues that truth is a kind of relation within experience:

> When a moment in our experience, of any kind whatsoever, inspires us with a thought that is true, that means sooner or later we dip by that thought's guidance into particulars of experience again and make advantageous connexion with them. (James, 1975a: 98-9)

For James, truth is known through advantageous 'connexions' in experience. Within experience, James writes, truth 'means this function of a leading that is worth while' (James, 1975a: 98). Truth is not a stagnant property; rather, truth is in process.

Mead's account closely parallels James's. For Mead, truth is a process and is grounded in human activity. Mead (1964e: 342) writes,

> The criterion of truth does not transcend experience, but simply regards the conditions of ongoing experience which has become problematic through the inhibitions of the natural processes of men. The solution of the problem lies entirely with experience.

For Mead, as for James, truth is a process within experience. Within this process of locating truths in experience, the process of verifying, James emphasized that we know truth when our idea works. If an idea 'leads' us in our conduct in a way that is worthwhile, then the idea is true (James, 1975a: 98). Mead's conception of truth is very similar to James's 'leading that is worthwhile'. For Mead, the pursuit of truth begins with the appearance of a problem within experience. A new meaning arises which confronts habitual ways of acting in a situation and, consequently, we are unable to act (Mead, 1964e: 327–8). The anomaly in our experience, whatever its source, has blocked our normal ways of acting and we are frustrated. We propose a new solution and we attempt to test it.

> The test of truth ... is the ongoing of conduct, which has been stopped by a conflict of meanings ... The test is the ability to act where action was formerly stopped. The action may be a very sorry affair and afflicted with gloom, but if the road now lies open to the meanings which had nullified each other, this road is the true road. (Mead, 1964e: 328)

Truth is known, for Mead, when conduct can start again after its frustration. For Mead and James, a true notion 'leads' us in our conduct. In these general terms, therefore, Mead's and James's epistemologies are compatible.

On objectivity
Beyond these fundamental agreements, however, Mead extended the pragmatist epistemology in a direction not developed by James. In particular, Mead (1964e: 386) became dissatisfied with James's reliance on the criterion of satisfaction as the test of truth.

Mead aims to remove this private criterion of truth from his pragmatism and replace it with a greater degree of objectivity. This attempt on the part of Mead to escape the private is the element of Mead's thought that Lewis and Smith (1980) grasp in their effort to drive a wedge between Mead and James. In grasping this disagreement, they proclaim Mead a social realist and James a subjective nominalist. They contend that this difference overwhelms whatever continuities that exist in the two philosophers' work. Their analysis, however, tends to exaggerate these differences. The agreements noted above between James and Mead on the most fundamental characteristics of their thought appear to temper Lewis and Smith's position. These fundamental agreements, which are surely not trivial, pertain to the issues of experience, dualism, the dialectic, process, human conduct, and pragmatic epistemology. In failing to consider these issues, Lewis and Smith fail to give fair treatment to the comparison of these philosophers. The continuities presented earlier illustrate the limitations of the realist and nominalist categories. These epistemological differences must be placed within a broader frame of analysis.

Our position with regard to Mead's objectivity and its relevance to symbolic interactionism has been presented elsewhere (Johnson and Shifflett, 1981). To temper the claims of the 'Illinois school' (Johnson and Shifflett, 1981), we present the argument's highlights. First, as noted above, objective reality does not exist 'out there', according to Mead, awaiting our discovery. Instead, environment and organism constitute a mutually dependent perspective. Second, truth is demonstrated when a hypothetical perspective, if you will, is sustained. The organism, in effect, makes a proposal to its environment. If it works in the organism's own system it is true (Miller, 1973: 211–12). Finally, Mead grounds truth in the social community. A proposal is successful in a community if it matches the 'whole act' of that community (Mead, 1964d: 318–19). Mead's objectivity, therefore, is not conventional. In contrast to McPhail and Rexroat's (1979) contentions, for example, what Mead meant by objective is not equivalent to the definition accepted by the contemporary sociological community. Mead (1938: 417) consciously rejects conventional scientific objectivity, for example, in the following passage from *The Philosophy of the Act*:

> As we look back over what has taken place, we can give ... the reasons that determine what has taken place. The only situation within which such a proposition holds is a mechanical one, which becomes perfect only when the world is reduced to physical particles, their velocities and accelerations ... such a world ... does not define the reality of a living being, for a living being acts. Its reason for movement lies within itself, and in that action, as we have seen, the living being determines its environment.

Given his rejection of 'mechanical' science, it is difficult to understand how Mead's epistemology could be identified with positivism or with philosophical realism.

Conclusion

In this research, we argue that the objectivist reading of Mead, as exemplified by Lewis and Smith (1980), cannot do justice to the foundations of his thought. We propose a reconstruction of Mead's intellectual genealogy, a genealogy more consistent with Blumer's (1969) claims. Our interpretation of Mead shares with James and Blumer a non-dualistic, processive metaphysics rooted in ongoing human experience. We conclude that Lewis and Smith's emphasis on Mead's realism can only have been overstated.

We have neither space nor intention to develop a complete history of the biographical connections between James and Mead. Our work merely demonstrates the plausibility of a Jamesian influence upon Mead. We can suggest, however, a most plausible historical connection. Although Mead studied at Harvard for a time and even lived in the James household, there is little evidence of James having influenced Mead directly (Miller, 1973). Mead certainly read the *Principles*, *Pragmatism* and several of James's essays including the essays on radical empiricism. Mead, for example, references each of these works on numerous occasions (cf. Mead, 1934, 1936, 1964e). More crucial, however, is James's influence via Dewey. Mead and Dewey were very close — Dewey served as Mead's closest intellectual confidant (Miller, 1973). Dewey's functionalism, as announced in the 'Reflex Arc' (1896) article, had great effect in shaping the direction of Mead's career (Cook, 1972). One may note, for example, crucial citations to Dewey in many of Mead's early articles (1964a: 6, 1964b: 36–59, 1964c: 79).[6]

Dewey, on the other hand, was greatly influenced by having read James (Dewey, 1973b: 51-52). Prior to the James influence, Dewey's thought was predominately Hegelian (Rucker, 1969: 57; McDermott, 1973: 98). After reading James, Dewey (1973 a, b) announced his functionalism in the Reflex Arc article. We argue, then, that the most probable line of influence went from James to Dewey to Mead. James unquestionably had great influence upon the thought of his time; indeed, Gardner Murphy (1949: 195) said that after the publication of the *Principles*, James's thought 'burst upon the world like a volcanic eruption'. In our view, one of the tremors of that eruption destroyed the monolith of dualistic social psychology. From the ruins, Mead and the symbolic interactionists were able to construct a processive, non-dualistic, that is Jamesian, replacement.

The ultimate purpose of our efforts in this chapter was to identify and clarify the intellectual foundations of symbolic interactionism. In particular, we suggest that Mead's social psychology was informed by an ambitious project. This project of classical

American philosophy aimed to frame a non-dualistic intellectual perspective, including a social science, that is grounded in human experience. The new objectivists would argue that Mead abandoned the project. Our arguments have attempted to show the opposite — Mead contributed greatly to the tradition exemplified by James.

Notes

* The authors gratefully acknowledge the helpful suggestions of Herbert Blumer, Mary Jo Deegan, Jerry Gaston, Charles Lemert, James Lemke, John McDermott, Jay Meddin, Bernard Meltzer, David Miller and Anselm Strauss. Appreciation is expressed for the typing assistance provided by Connie Alexander.

1. We accept, with Lewis and Smith (1980) that Dewey's metaphysics was essentially continuous with James's. Dewey's departures, including his emphasis on nature, were significant and, we would argue, were influential of Mead. None the less, the argument presented here assumes that the continuity from James to Mead would include Dewey with no major problems. A complete analysis, however, would have to deal with Dewey in more detail than is presented here.

2. Rochberg-Halton (1982, 1983), however, argues that even Lewis and Smith's interpretation of Peirce is flawed fundamentally. Lewis and Smith distort Peirce's realism, ironically presenting a position that Peirce would identify as nominalistic. For further details see Rochberg-Halton's (1982) excellent reappraisal of Peirce's work and its relevance to contemporary social theory.

3. In emphasizing intellectual continuity, we do not deny that important issues separate the various theorists of this tradition. Certainly, Goffman's later works, for example, diverge quite widely with Blumer's. We do emphasize, however, that a *fundamental metaphysical continuity* is sustained throughout the works in question.

4. Lewis and Smith (1980) reject *Mind, Self and Society* as not truly Mead's work and ultimately as inconsistent with his true intentions. They imply that a conspiracy of Mead's student-editors who compiled their lecture notes into the text resulted in its nominalistic arguments. Although we think this contention implausible, we none the less, offer evidence from the 'less questionable' examples of Mead's work.

5. The *Essays* were not published as a complete volume until 1912, two years after James's death. The individual essays, however, were published as journal articles during 1904 and 1905. The two most important essays are 'Does Consciousness Exist?' (1976b) and 'A World of Pure Experience' (1976c).

6. The importance of the biographical connection between Dewey and Mead to the latter's development is also documented in Coughlan (1975).

References

Ayer, A.J. (1978) 'Introduction', pp. vii–xxx in W. James (ed.), *Pragmatism and the Meaning of Truth*. Cambridge, Mass. : Harvard University Press.

Blumer, H. (1969) *Symbolic Interactionism: Perspective and Method*. Englewood Cliffs, N.J.: Prentice-Hall.

Blumer, H. (1977) 'Comment on Lewis's "The Classic American Pragmatists as Forerunners to Symbolic Interactionism"', *Sociological Quarterly*, 18: 285–9.

Blumer, H. (1980) 'Mead and Blumer: The Convergent Methodological Perspective of Social Behaviourism and Symbolic Interactionism', *American Sociological Review*, 45: 409–19.

Cook, G. (1972) 'G.H. Mead's Social Behaviorism', *Journal of the History of the Behavioral Sciences*, 13: 307–16.

Coughlan, N. (1975) *Young Man Dewey: An Essay in American Intellectual History*. Chicago: University of Chicago Press.

Dewey, J. (1973a) 'The Reflex Arc Concept in Psychology', pp. 136–44 in J. McDermott (ed.), *The Philosophy of John Dewey*. New York: Putnams.

Dewey, J. (1973b) 'The Development of American Pragmatism', pp. 41–57 in J. McDermott (ed.), *The Philosophy of John Dewey*. New York: Putnams.

James, W. (1890a) *The Principles of Psychology* Vol. 1. New York: Henry Holt.

James, W. (1890b) *The Principles of Psychology* Vol. 2. New York: Henry Holt.

James, W. (1948) *Psychology*. Cleveland: World Publishing.

James, W. (1976a) 'The Works of William James', *Essays in Radical Empiricism*. Cambridge, Mass.: Harvard University Press.

James, W. (1976b) 'Does Consciousness Exist?', pp. 3–19 in *Essays in Radical Empiricism*. Cambridge, Mass.: Harvard University Press (first published 1904).

James, W. (1976c) 'A World of Pure Experience', pp. 21–44 in *Essays in Radical Empiricism*. Cambridge, Mass.: Harvard University Press (first published 1904).

James, W. (1975a) *The Works of William James. Pragmatism: A New Name For Some Old Ways of Thinking*. Cambridge, Mass.: Harvard University Press (first published 1907).

James, W. (1975b) *The Works of William James. The Meaning of Truth*. Cambridge, Mass.: Harvard University Press.

Johnson, G.D. (1983) 'Mead as Positivist: A Review of American Sociology and Pragmatism', *Theory and Society*, 12(2): 273–7.

Johnson, G.D. and P.A. Shifflett (1981) 'George Herbert Who? A Critique of the Objectivist Reading of Mead', *Symbolic Interaction*, 4(2): 153–65.

Karpf, F.B. (1932) *American Social Psychology*. New York: McGraw-Hill.

Lewis, J.D. (1976) 'The Classic American Pragmatists as Forerunners to Symbolic Interactionism', *Sociological Quarterly*, 17: 347–59.

Lewis, J.D. and R. Smith (1980) *American Sociology and Pragmatism: Mead, Chicago, Sociology and Symbolic Interaction*. Chicago: University of Chicago Press.

McDermott, J.J. (ed.) (1973) *The Philosophy of John Dewey*, Vol. 1. New York: Putnam's.

McDermott, J.J. (1978) 'The Renascence of Classical American Philosophy', *American Studies International*, XVI (3): 5–17.

McPhail, C. and C. Rexroat (1979) 'Mead vs. Blumer: The Divergent Methodological Perspectives of Social Behaviorism and Symbolic Interactionism', *American Sociological Review*, 44: 449–67.

Manis, J.G. and B.N. Meltzer (1978) *Symbolic Interaction: A Reader in Social Psychology*. Boston: Allyn and Bacon.

Martindale, D. (1960) *The Nature and Types of Sociological Theory*. Boston: Houghton-Mifflin.

Mead, G.H. (1932) *The Philosophy of the Present*. Chicago: Open Court Publishing.

Mead, G.H. (1934) *Mind, Self and Society*, Chicago: University of Chicago Press.

Mead, G.H. (1936) *Movements of Thought in the Nineteenth Century*. Chicago: University of Chicago Press.

Mead, G.H. (1938) *The Philosophy of the Act*. Chicago: University of Chicago Press.

Mead, G.H. (1964a) 'Suggestions Toward a Theory of the Philosophical Disciplines', pp. 6–24 in A. Reck (ed.), *Selected Writings: George Herbert Mead*. Indianapolis: Bobbs-Merrill.

Mead, G.H. (1964b) 'The Definition of the Psychical', pp. 25–59 in A. Reck (ed.), *Selected Writings: George Herbert Mead*. Indianapolis: Bobbs-Merrill.

Mead, G.H. (1964c) 'Concerning Animal Perception', pp. 73–81 in A. Reck (ed.), *Selected Writings: George Herbert Mead*. Indianapolis: Bobbs-Merrill.

Mead, G.H. (1964d) 'The Objective Reality of Perspectives', pp. 306–19 in A. Reck (ed.), *Selected Writings: George Herbert Mead*. Indianapolis: Bobbs-Merrill.

Mead, G.H. (1964e) 'A Pragmatic Theory of Truth', pp. 320–54 in A. Reck (ed.), *Selected Writings: George Herbert Mead*. Indianapolis: Bobbs-Merrill.

Mead, G.H. (1964f) 'The Philosophies of Royce, James and Dewey in Their American Setting', pp. 371–91 in A. Reck (ed.), *Selected Writings: George Herbert Mead*. Indianapolis: Bobbs-Merrill.

Meltzer, B., J. Petras and L. Reynolds (1975) *Symbolic Interactionism, Genesis, Varieties and Criticism*. London: Routledge and Kegan Paul.

Miller, D.L. (1973) *George Herbert Mead: Self-Language and the World*. Austin, Tex.: University of Texas Press.

Miller, D.L. (1978) 'A Conversation on the Philosophy of G.H. Mead with Dr D. Miller, 3 November, 1978, Austin, Texas', transcription of a personal conversation.

Murphy, G. (1949) *Historical Introduction to Modern Psychology*. New York: Harcourt Brace and World.

Perry, R.B. (1935) *The Thought and Character of William James*, Vols. I and II. Boston: Little, Brown.

Perry, R.B. (1948) 'Introduction', pp. vii–ix in W. James, *Psychology*. Cleveland: World Publishing.

Petras, J. (1966) 'The Genesis and Development of Symbolic Interactionism in American Sociology' (unpublished dissertation). Storrs, Conn.: University of Connecticut.

Petras, J. (1968a) 'Psychological Antecedents of Sociological Theory in America: William James and James Mark Baldwin', *Journal of the History of the Behavioral Sciences*, 4: 132–42.

Petras, J. (1968b) 'John Dewey and the Rise of Interactionism in American Social Theory', *Journal of the History of the Behavioral Sciences*, 4: 18–27.

Rochberg-Halton, E. (1982) 'Situation, Structure and the Context of Meaning', *Sociological Quarterly*, 23: 455–76.

Rochberg-Halton, E. (1983) 'The Real Nature of Pragmatism and Chicago Sociology', *Symbolic Interaction* 6(1): 139–54.

Rucker, D. (1969) *The Chicago Pragmatists*. Minneapolis: University of Minnesota Press.

Seigfried, C. (1978) *Chaos and Context: A Study of William James*. Athens, Ohio: Ohio University Press.

5

Goffman's frame analysis and modern micro-sociological paradigms*

Jef Verhoeven

Few contemporary sociologists are as creative as Erving Goffman. One product of this creativity is frame analysis (Goffman, 1974), a method that is both admired and neglected. Comparing Goffman's approach to other paradigms seems not only to be a negation of the creativity of this writer, but is strongly disliked by Goffman (1981b) when such comparisons have nothing but labelling as their purpose. It is not the function of this paper to place frame analysis in one or another theoretical pigeon-hole. Frame analysis is a sociological approach in its own right. Nevertheless, Goffman accepts different standpoints of symbolic interaction (G.H. Mead), ethnomethodology and phenomenological sociology (A. Schutz) even when he denies others. I intend here to present the differences and similarities between Goffman's frame analysis on the one hand, and Blumer's symbolic interaction, Schutz's phenomenological sociology, and Garfinkel's ethnomethodology on the other hand in function of three questions. (1) What are the presuppositions in relation to reality, knowledge, man and society used in the four paradigms? (2) What is the object of sociology? (3) What are the methodological principles? Moreover, I want to show that in spite of different accents, the frame-analysis approach can already be found in the earlier work of Goffman.

Something must be said about why these four micro-sociological paradigms have been selected. First, Goffman, although sometimes leaning toward the ideas of Schutz, Mead and Garfinkel, presents his work as different from theirs. Instead of using Mead's work in this paper, I will use Blumer's (1969a) seminal book, because of its major influence on symbolic interactionism.[1] Second, they try to give an analysis of the 'ongoing activity' as it appears 'here and now' and are interested in the interpretation of reality. Third, although three of them do not limit their interest to the study of micro-structures, all start by studying face-to-face relations. Fourth, there is a relationship between Goffman's frame as 'the organization of experience', 'the definition of the situation' as used in symbolic interactionism, the phenomenological 'meaning contexts' and ethnomethodological 'indexicality' and 'reflexivity'. Fifth, frame analysis is considered to be a formal sociology (Jameson, 1976), a symbolic interactionist approach (Littlejohn, 1977; Glaser, 1976), ethnomethodological and semiotic (Jameson, 1976) and structuralist (Gonos, 1977). Here, frame analysis will be considered as a special approach and cannot be forced into one of these categories.

Frame analysis in the other works of Goffman
Let us first examine the extent to which the frame analysis approach is present in Goffman's other works. Although he denotes a great deal of attention to a sociopsychological problem formulation, the structures within which the actors move and via which they approach reality form a substantial portion of his earlier work. Where does one find evidence for this thesis?

Already in *The Presentation of Self in Everyday Life* (1959), Goffman wonders what techniques actors use to give others a specific impression of themselves or of a situation. Instead of 'techniques', one could just as well use the term 'frame' here ('framework of appearances', Goffman, 1959: 242). These frameworks are outlined in detail in this book and concur with those of *Frame Analysis*. However, Goffman still talks in this first book about the dramaturgic presentation of an activity. Used in this approach (Goffman, 1959: 8, 17, 107, 112, 70, 175, 176, 141) are terms such as 'concealment, discovery', 'performance', 'front region', 'backstage', 'fabricators', 'staging talk', 'team collusion' and 'secrets'.

The anthology, *Interaction Ritual* (1967), four articles of which had originally appeared before 1959, also deals with similar problems. Goffman bases himself here on the study of the social 'gathering', a collection of people who meet each other superficially at the same place and shortly thereafter leave that place. At the moment, the members of this gathering try to disclose their appearance in a particular way, the facial expression being an important instrument. Goffman (1967: 77) studies how one can hide or betray one's facial expression, what ritual is used, and what attitude is adopted or how we behave in order to lead or mislead the other. The offering of a chair to a visitor, for example, is an expression of deference. Its meaning can be changed, however, should one do it brusquely ('demeanour') (Goffman, 1967: 81).

Further, he studies within what frames 'embarrassment' occurs among the actors and what forms of alienation of a situation can be distinguished (Goffman, 1967: 97ff., 117ff.). In the longest article, 'Where the Action Is', finally, a keen analysis is given of the 'action' that can be found in the world of gambling, card playing and sports. This is a particular form of action: the actor takes risks which flow from the situation but which actually can be avoided. Goffman studies here the structures within which the 'action' takes place.

Encounters (1961a) gives the structure in which table games take form ('Fun in Games'), and how individuals can distance themselves from the roles they have to play ('Role distance'). Here, too, the theme of the first book recurs, namely, what individuals want to manifest of themselves to the other. Much attention is devoted to the frames which make this possible and which will refer to his description in *Frame Analysis*.

This problem can also be found in *Asylums* (1961b) and *Stigma* (1963a): what frames are used there to evaluate the behaviour of patients in a psychiatric hospital and of people who are stigmatized? Goffman (1961b: 283, 331) describes how the structure within which the psychiatric patient and the stigmatized individual act provides the frames in order to see the social reality in a well-determined manner.

In *Behavior in Public Places* (1963b), the face-to-face behaviour of people in the daily circumstances of the gathering is again central. This behaviour must be seen within the situation where the gathering takes place. This means that the actor takes account of the spatial environment into which he or she steps in order to become part of a gathering (Goffman, 1963b: 18). The typical characteristics of these situations impose differing norms on the actors: for example, how one has to manifest one's familiarity or unfamiliarity with someone and where the limits of this behaviour lie (Goffman, 1963b: 112ff.). A number of frames of *Frame Analysis* are also found here already, such as 'talking to oneself', 'delusionary states', 'open regions', 'concealment' and 'boundary collusion' (Goffman, 1963b: 72, 75, 132, 176, 181).

Strategic Interaction (1969) consists of two important essays. The first is entitled 'Expression Games', and Goffman here searches for the conditions under which an individual receives, gives or hides information. For in the encounter with the other, there is always doubt about what the other really means; it is a kind of game situation in which one tries to find out what the other really wants to express. The standpoint is formed by the simple moves of the other that one tries to understand (Goffman, 1969: 11), for they are applied by the other to present the reality in a particular manner. Frames as concealment and fabrication form essential components of these expression games (Goffman, 1969: 28, 58, 80). The same can be said about the second essay, which bears the same title as the book: 'Strategic Interaction'. Here, too, 'keying' (Goffman, 1969:

115, 116, 140), 'frame analysis', 'concealment' and the like are mentioned. These frames are used by Goffman to apply a game theory analysis to the study of strategic interaction. In a strategic interaction, two parties meet each other in a well-structured situation. Each party tries to find out what the other party thinks about him or her. In this way, one tries to foresee what movement the other party will make in order to adapt one's own movements. Goffman studies further what frames are used to make possible and to hinder this strategic interaction.

Finally, frame analysis is not absent from *Relations in Public* (1971). The object of the research is the face-to-face behaviour in daily life: Goffman wants to give a picture of the ground rules and the behavioural patterns of public life. Via the study of these ground rules, he again arrives at the frames which help the actors to read the reality. The manner in which an individual appears in the world and the territory of the self become comprehensible only through the frames used. Thus, for example, one uses signs to define one's territory (Goffman, 1971: 41), but one's territory can also be removed when one fouls it oneself or when others succeed in penetrating it (Goffman, 1971: 52, 57). Brief encounters between people consist of a 'supportive' and 'remedial interchange'. This exchange is a kind of ritual that confirms the relations between the actors or reroutes on a good path those that threaten to become conflictual. Ritual also plays an important role in the signs that are used to clarify our bond with others. All these elements allow the reality to be read as normal or abnormal. The entire series of frames from *Frame Analysis* is already provided in *Relations in Public* (1971: 113, 140, 211, 269, 284, 314, etc.).

In *Gender Advertisements* (1976) and *Forms of Talk* (1981a), Goffman very definitely applies the frame analysis approach. These two works were, in fact, published after *Frame Analysis*. The first work concerns the manner in which people manifest their sexual identity to others and how this is used in the world of advertising. Goffman does this by means of a long series of advertising photographs, and explains what frames we use to interpret them (Goffman, 1976: 10–23). The second work deals with linguistic usage and consists of articles that were written between 1974 and 1980. The frame analysis approach is here applied to the very simple forms of discussion, response cries, and also to ways of speaking, lectures and radio talk. Part of this problem has already been discussed in *Frame Analysis* (1974: 496–559).

In conclusion, one may state that the frame analysis problem formulation is a constant motif throughout all of Goffman's work. Of course, it is not so significant in his earlier work as in *Frame*

Analysis and in his later work. Nevertheless, in one way or another, Goffman is always looking for the frames that we use in order to answer the question, 'what is it that is going on here?' The result is an unmasking of a socially concealed world. But, in addition, a world becomes visible that is established in its smallest details. This will now be examined further.

The world picture

Research cannot be understood apart from the world picture of the researcher (Strasser, 1973; Radnitzky, 1970). This world picture is crucial and gives the researcher a particular image of man and society and the relation between both. The researcher will choose a particular research programme in function of this view. So the social world can be considered as a material reality in which different impersonal powers react upon the material components. There are also sociologists who consider the social world as peopled by individuals creating meaning and reacting upon each other. Both exemplar points of view are applied in sociology and are considered useful for the understanding of social reality in function of the world picture practised by the sociologists. World pictures are thus presuppositions about physical reality, man and society (Radnitzky, 1970: xxviii). Although these hypothesis are of a metaphysical order, they have a major influence on the research and methods of sociologists.

What are the world pictures of frame analysis, symbolic interactionism, phenomenological sociology and ethnomethodology?

Reality

Goffman (1974: 10) uses a rather ambiguous concept of reality. This is clear in his definition of the term 'strip':

> The term 'strip' will be used to refer to any arbitrary slice or cut from the stream of ongoing activity, including here sequences of happenings, real or fictive, as seen from the perspective of those subjectively involved in sustaining an interest in them.

Three points must be considered. In the first place, Goffman speaks of 'real or fictive sequences of happening', but both can be real. 'Actions framed entirely in terms of a primary framework are said to be real or actual, to be really or actually or literally occurring.' (Goffman, 1974: 47.) But even when these actions are keyed, i.e. transposed into another frame, it does not mean that these actions are not real. Indeed, the keying actually occurs. What is considered as real depends on the perspective, either primary or transformed, from which actions are considered by the actor.

Reality always appears to the actor from a particular perspective. This perspective is given by the frames we use, which frames are seen as particular organizations of experience. In a certain sense, we can put that reality into a construction by the actors, taking into account framing, keying and fabrication (i.e. the creation of a 'false belief about what it is that is going on'). But Goffman stresses that it would be ridiculous to say that reality is totally created by the actors: reality is also pre-given. It is not sufficient to define something as a parking place if there is no place at all.

This position is not a break with Goffman's position in his earlier books. Although he gives a very important place to the idea of the 'definition of the situation', an idealistic stance towards reality, he is aware of the fact that reality is outside the individual's mind. In view of the description of encounters, this idea becomes clear (Goffman, 1961a: 27–8). Encounters characteristically produce direct interaction between the participants of the encounters. This does not imply that these participants create the total reality. Indeed, interactions take place in a particular historical sequence, which means that there is already a meaning given to this reality. Moreover, there are unintended acts that are part of the encounter without constituting the main parts of the encounter, e.g. coughing and sniffling. However unimportant they seem to be, they are part of reality, which is out there.

Third, this perspective on activity is formulated by the individuals who are interested in what is happening. Reality is thus also something defined by the actor, which forms the bulk of Goffman's book, *Frame Analysis*. Actually, this book is not about the core concerns of sociology, i.e. social organization and social structure, but about the 'organization of experience — something that an individual actor can take into this mind' (Goffman, 1974: 13). Every individual faces the problem of 'what is it that is going on?' To answer this question people apply frameworks. Applying these frameworks can make experience vulnerable. Indeed, it is possible that an actor can misframe events.

Reality is thus an outer happening independent of the individual actor, but it also gets its meaning from the involved individuals, although they are using pre-given frameworks, keyings, etc., to look at it.

While Goffman takes reality as it is given to him, Alfred Schutz starts from the experience that we are put into the world and that we are intentionally directed towards the world. We are aware of the world around us. We fear for, hope and we long for something. This way we meet our world and realize that it is a pre-given, organized and intersubjective reality. But as a thinking subject we are aware of the act of thinking and consider the 'purified sphere of conscious life'. Therefore, Schutz applies phenomenological reduction to the objects of thinking, i.e., he puts the existence of the outer world between brackets. He abstracts from the possibility that the world could be otherwise than as it appears to us. Schutz is not interested in the objects as such, but in the objects as they appear to him (Schutz, 1967: 99–117), so he does not deny the existence of the world. His interest is rather in the meaning of the world.

Schutz adapts a point of view totally different from Goffman's in these matters. If Goffman's (1981b: 69) admission that he himself is moving towards positivism can be considered to be the correct formulation of what he wants to say, then he does not bracket the existence of reality. Schutz, on the contrary, sees reality as it appears to him.

According to Schutz (1967: 208–29, 3–34), as scientists we have to go back to the pre-scientific reality i.e., the reality that seems self-evident to people remaining within the natural attitude. For Schutz this is the reality of the everyday life-world, i.e., 'that province of reality which the wide-awake and normal adult simply takes for granted in the attitude of common sense' (Schutz and Luckmann, 1974: 3).

As wide-awake adults we experience this world as pre-given, intersubjective, and not created by ourselves, except for a small part. This life-world is not considered to be composed of merely material objects, but also of 'meaning strata which transform natural things into cultural objects'.

This everyday life-world is nevertheless more than the sensibly perceivable world, which was designated by William James as the paramount reality. This life-world also embraces my fantasies and dreams, so it is more than the physical world. Reality is thus constituted by the meaning of our experience rather than by the ontological structures of objects. We have different finite provinces of meaning: that of the everyday life-world, of the world of dreams, of the world of science, etc., which worlds are not necessarily consistent. Each of these provinces is part of a specific style of lived experience, i.e., a cognitive style. In the same day, we can change from one province of meaning to the other. But for Schutz, the everday life-world or 'the world of working' is the paramount reality from which we start to come to scientific knowledge. In this world, purposes-at-hand determine the relevancy of the reality under consideration: it is in this way that we build up a particular province of meaning. According to Schutz we approach reality by looking at it from different 'frames'.

Like Schutz, Garfinkel (1967: 35) stresses reality as a social reality. In his view, people treat 'the natural facts of life' as 'a real world and as a product of activities in a real world'. This starting point for the analysis of social reality is the analysis of the attitude of daily life as described by Schutz. Thus he agrees with Schutz's presupposition that for the actor 'the objects of the world are what they appear to be' (Garfinkel, 1963: 210–14). But this social reality is not just out there. Indeed, the characteristics of the real society are to a certain extent produced by the persons. Meaning is furnished by creative actors (Garfinkel, 1963: 214–15; 1967: 122, 53–6). For the ethnomethodologist this is a paradox, but it does not raise special problems. He should be indifferent towards the problem of choosing between reality as out there or in people's mind. Indeed, Leiter (1980: 20–1) contends that ethnomethodology brackets the existence of the outerworld, as Schutz does.

Contrary to Schutz and Garfinkel, Blumer's (1969a: 21–3) position does not rely on the intentionality of our thinking. For him, the exterior world of gestures and acts is reality. We see people indicating things and we understand the meaning of those gestures. Perception is a necessary condition of finding meaning in the world, and this perception is not just a product of a single actor but is an interplay between the individual and social environment.

Blumer takes an empirical standpoint: reality exists only in the empirical world. For this reason, he rejects traditional idealism and realism and cannot accept that reality exists just in human pictures or conceptions of it. The empirical world can talk back; it is not just something living in our minds. Nor does this obdurate quality of reality produce an extreme realism. This is impossible because the reality — and for Blumer this is social reality — cannot be fixed or immutable and so it is not to be studied as would the advanced physical sciences.

In conclusion, it can be said that Goffman defends a positivistic position: reality is there for him as researcher. And he accepts that every actor acts as if there were a correspondence between his perception and the organization of what is perceived (Goffman, 1974: 26). Instead of using the label 'positivism', as Goffman does, it is perhaps better to speak of naïve realism. Blumer (1969a: 68–9) on the other hand, although speaking of an obdurate reality, states that objects are real in the sense that people have given meaning to them. Schutz does not deny reality but puts it between brackets. This means that because of phenomenological reduction, actors look for the images they have in their minds. But there too, Schutz produces a special *epoché*: a bracketing of the natural attitude. Actors bracket the fact that the real world is different from the way it appears to them (Schutz, 1967: 229; Schutz and Luckmann, 1974: 27). Garfinkel's standpoint can be considered to be the same as that of Schutz. Although the four paradigms propose a different position in relation to reality, none of them holds that reality is totally created by people: it is pre-given.

If reality is seen from different standpoints, the ways to be followed to attain knowledge are different as well. What different options are taken?

Since Goffman (1974:10) sees his task as describing the 'frameworks of understanding available in our society for making sense out of events' and 'the special vulnerabilities to which those frames of reference are subject', he is convinced that, as a researcher, he can unveil the concealed reality. Let us take 'fabrication' (Goffman, 1974: 83–113). One of the parties involved in a fabrication is brought to a false belief about what is going on. The fabricating party knows that it is a fabrication. What is hidden for the deceived party is not only perceivable for the fabricators but also for the researcher. But is it not possible that the total act of the two parties is a benign fabrication for the researcher? This may be, but ultimately the sociologist will see it. Goffman seems to defend the classic positivistic stance: 'What I see, I see.' A researcher considers himself the ultimate judge, able to catch social reality. Just as Goffman supposes that there is a correspondence between the perception of an individual and the organization of what is perceived, he holds that a researcher can perceive reality the way it is.

Blumer, on the other hand, puts himself somewhere between an extreme idealism and a realism that has its roots in physical science. Thus, experience is the ultimate criterion of knowledge because of the obdurate character of reality. A sociologist must perceive social and material reality freed from all theoretical presupposition, and his starting point must be perception of outer reality. Even if this perception is a social act, which means that it is a concatenation of defining processes made by different actors, Blumer holds that the actor as well as the researcher has come to the knowledge of the same reality.

The option taken by Schutz to attain knowledge differs from those of Goffman and Blumer. Schutz brackets the possibility of experiencing the world. His starting point is the everyday life-world of the situated person, who meets that world as organized and intersubjective. In this everyday life-world, we act and meet the other in face-to-face relations. That is the place where I meet my fellow-men ('*Mitmensch*'). But in many situations, I meet only a 'world of contemporaries' ('*Mitwelt*'). The only way to grasp this '*Mitwelt*' is to use typifications of interactions and motives that are built up by using 'in-order-to' and 'because' motives, which are reciprocal between the actor and the partner.

Like a partner, a scientific observer does not experience the other as an actor does in his everyday life-world: he is a disinterested observer (Schutz, 1967: 245 – 59). As an observer, he does not live in a we-relation and cannot immediately grasp this life-world. To bridge this gap, the observer builds types, puppets, that are compatible with the experience of the everyday life-world. He builds ideal types that have meaning adequacy and causal adequacy (Schutz, 1932: 260–61). To accomplish this, Schutz applies the postulate of subjective interpretation, the postulate of consistency and compatibility of all propositions, the postulate that all scientific thought has to be based on tested observation, the postulate of clarity and distinctness of all terms, the postulate of adequacy, and several others.

Garfinkel on the other hand takes most of his inspiration from Schutz's work, so he disagrees with Goffman and Blumer as well in relation to the question of how to attain knowledge of social reality. The experience of daily life of the actor is the main starting point for Garfinkel as for Schutz. The actor behaves in the world as if he grasps it immediately and as 'known in common with others'. To attain this common sense knowledge, the actor uses several presuppositions (Garfinkel, 1963: 210–15), i.e. the reality of the world as it appears to be, the practical interest of the actor, the time perspective of daily life, the et cetera assumption, the continuity of appearances, the commonly entertained scheme of communication, the reciprocity of perspectives and the form of sociality. And Garfinkel continues by defining eleven determinations to see an event as placed in a common-sense environment. Nevertheless, actors have not to be conscious of these determinants. Indeed, the more an event is institutionalized the more the actor takes the act for granted.

According to Garfinkel (1963: 76–103) this common-sense knowledge is also a substantial part of sociological research. He contends that the sociologist doing research relies on and cannot decide about meaning or facts other than by using common-sense knowledge of social structures. On the other hand, scientific knowledge does not suffice for action in everyday life, because scientific theorizing develops according to other principles (Garfinkel, 1963: 283).

Conception of man and society
Another part of the world picture dealt with by sociologists and other social scientists is the conception they have about man and

society. Depending on the vision they have of man as, for example, a bunch of nerves or as meaning-creating actor or of society as a unity in its own right or a collection of individuals, different methodological approaches are developed in sociology.

Man is considered by Goffman to be a personal ongoing identity, consisting of flesh, blood, etc. (i.e. animal nature). Thus, man is a human actor, who stores information in his skull. But this does not mean that he is just a black box (Goffman, 1974: 524, 513–14). Placed into time development, he is the self-same object that has a memory and a biography (Goffman, 1974: 128). As a person, he fulfils many functions or capacities, i.e. roles. Indeed, Goffman differentiates between the person (individual, player) and the role (capacity, function). Although a person's acts are partly a product of the self — and we can find something of the self behind the roles — this does not mean that a person has no freedom. The individual can choose between the total range of actions that are available in fulfilling his role. Moreover, the claims of the role can be forgotten by the individual actor, e.g., when a person leaves a conversation to answer the telephone, or when one is sniffling, coughing, etc., which is not really a part of one's role in a conversation (Goffman, 1974: 273). In this sense, there is never complete freedom nor complete constraint between the individual and his role. The individual acting upon and in the world becomes part of the ongoing world and cannot be studied independently of that social world. A reduction of social reality to its component parts is, therefore, unacceptable.

Society, although consisting of intelligent actors able to act upon the world, must be seen as situated in a natural order. There are natural constraints within which an actor has to behave in society, e.g., we need a voice to speak and a body to make gestures. Goffman's assumption is 'that, although natural events occur without intelligent intervention, intelligent doing cannot be accomplished effectively without entrance into the natural order' (Goffman, 1974: 23). Consequently, the actor needs two kinds of understanding: (1) the understanding of the natural world by which he is encompassed; and (2) the understanding of the special worlds. For this understanding, actors use primary frameworks, both natural and social. This does not simply mean that individuals are merely passive users of the given frameworks. They also can act upon the world. But they act within a world that is framed, keyed or fabricated. 'Framed' means that there happens to be an 'organization of experience' that is given to us. By keying or fabricating, the original framework is transposed or transformed. For example, when two people play checkers, they have to follow the rules of the game that are pre-given. The same happens when these frameworks are keyed or fabricated. For example, contests are a kind of keying of social reality. Wrestling seems to be fighting, but the rules of the sport of wrestling put limits on the aggressive acts. Although keying and fabrication mean a change of the meaning of particular frameworks as seen by the participants, they are given structure to the keying or fabricating actors. Here, Goffman describes emerging realities that differ from the individual construction of reality. These structures are independent of the participants, but, nevertheless, it must be stressed that the participants are aware of the alteration of meaning.

From Goffman's earlier work, it can be confirmed that he considers man and society as real. Since *The Presentation of Self in Everyday Life* (1959), he has adopted both sociological nominalism and sociological realism. The analysis of man, although using different concepts, consolidate this opinion. He speaks about 'human' and 'socialized' selves (Goffman, 1959: 56), about 'fabrica- tor' and 'character' (Goffman, 1959: 251–54; 1967: 31), each being an active and passive part of the individual.

This individual must be studied as part of society, meeting in social encounters, social gatherings, social situations and social occasions (Goffman, 1967: 44, 144; 1961a: 9; 1963b: 248). All these factors are strong socialization instruments. They are so important that Goffman (1963b: 248) concludes at the end of *Behavior in Public Places* that: 'More than to any family or club, more than to any class or sex, more than to any nation, the individual belongs to gatherings, and he had best show that he is a good member in good standing.'

For this reason, the interpretation by Helle (1977: 165) of Goffman's work as an 'anaskopic' approach cannot be accepted, although it can perhaps be defended for the earlier work of Goffman, in which the definition of the situation takes an important place. It certainly is no longer the standpoint of Goffman when he analyses the organization of social reality. Sociological realism and sociological nominalism are methodologically translated into an 'anaskopic' and 'kataskopic' approach.

Discussing the methodological consequences of the conception of reality, I stressed above that, in phenomenological sociology, the main experience we have as actors is the intentionality of the individual actor. We do not ask for evidence about the fact that we are placed in an organized, intersubjective everyday life-world. We have knowledge-at-hand of this life-world. My fellow-men are immediately given in my work and communication in the world. Through our communication, we not only become conscious of the other, but also of our own characteristics. To reach others in face-to-face relations, a stock of knowledge is given, and, to the extent we are remote from others, we use a stock of knowledge equipped with idealizations, i.e., types of what the others want to do. These are expressed in linguistic typifications and recipes for behaviour that are given to us by our predecessors. The others, like the actor, are purpose-directed individuals who can act upon the world.

As an individual I am aware of the social dimension of my life-world, i.e., a society that transcends myself. This is the basis of an 'objective' order, an order that is given to me. To this objective order belongs my subjective 'meaning-context' as well as 'my subjectively experienced adumbrations and modes of apprehension' (Schutz and Luckmann, 1974: 18).

It is in this social world that a personal self is developed. This happens when a child gets a personal self. Since a child is situated in a social life-world, he comes to an 'intersubjective mirroring'. He meets a world-structure that is pre-given and not invented by the child and that appears to him as institutionalized and encompassed in a meaning-context. This meaning-context is objectivized in speech and institutions, which are the instruments by which a child can become a fellow-man. There is an historical and social structure that is met by this child 'here and now' (Schutz and Luckmann, 1974: 295, 244). Institutions (e.g. language, meaning-context) are an important part of the social world and provide knowledge about social reality that transcends the possibilities of individual experience.

None the less, society is composed of individuals who experience society as a pre-given structure. Society must be conceived as a priori to the individual. Like Goffman, the individual recognizes the emergent character of the world structure. Nevertheless, Schutz does not agree that it is methodologically possible to know social reality without taking into account individual intentionality.

Garfinkel speaks about man and society in almost the same way Schutz does. A person is a motivational type, equipped with a body, which is used to designate meaning to the environment and also to draw meaning from others (Garfinkel, 1956: 420–21; 1967: 104–85). As a human actor with a biography he is intentionally directed to the world. He uses 'seen but unnoticed background expectancies' as a scheme of interpretation of the social world that is given to him as a social system (Garfinkel, 1963, 1967). The individual has an intersubjective orientation toward this social world which is an organized reality, a system of rule-governed activities. These social structures of everyday activities become observable through the study of common-sense knowledge and common-sense activities (Garfinkel, 1967: 35–75). Doing this kind of research, Garfinkel, like Schutz, opts for an approach from the individual. Most of the experiments presented in his main work describe how persons handle common-sense knowledge. Even if this common-sense knowledge is known by the researcher through the individuals, it is not considered to be merely a product of the individual but an emergent reality. Structure is also part of Garfinkel's (1963: 188) analysis to the extent that it is a perceived normal environment, which is a condition for understanding accounts and at the same time it is defined by the attitude of daily life.

Man, according to Blumer, is a human organism having a self. And this self is not a structure but a process. By this point of view Blumer (1969a: 62–4, 78–89) follows Mead's conception of man, and he also agrees with Mead's social behaviouristic approach to man. An individual can make gestures, external acts, that acquire a meaning in the interaction with him or herself and the other individuals. The first thing a self does is designate objects and acts; he gives them a meaning and judges if these objects and acts are suitable for his subsequent actions. Having made the judgement, he decides how to act. Because the individual can indicate something to himself, he has the possibility of interpreting the characteristics of the situation in which he acts. The individual becomes a very active unity, and not just a bunch of reactions. Consequently, it makes no sense for Blumer to look for environmental pressures, stimuli, motives, etc., that precede the act as an explanation for the act. What is important is to know that the individual constructs reality in a process of symbolic interaction and that the individual forms interpretations and acts in relation to others.

This interacting self is the kernel of all ongoing activity. An individual meeting another individual in social interaction is the most fundamental form of human association. Human groups consist of interacting human beings. As a matter of fact, these interacting human beings are not interacting 'roles', but interacting 'people'. Society is thus nothing but a collection of interacting individuals.

In spite of the stress on the individual as the composing factor of society, Blumer does not deny the existence of a social structure in human society. There are social roles, positions, rank order, bureaucratic organizations, social codes, norms etc. Their function is to help the interpretation and definition of the situations that are at the base of 'joint actions'. If people do not take into account these structures, then the ongoing activity has no meaning at all. But even these social structures have no life apart from the definition given by the individuals, even in 'joint actions'.

Society can be characterized as follows: (1) it is an 'ongoing process of action — not ... a posited structure of relations'; (2) actions must be seen as joint interactions, not as separate actions of the participants; (3) actions have a career or history; (4) the common definition of the joint action by the participants keeps this career fixed; (5) but this does not mean that this career has no uncertainties and possibilities.

Blumer clearly presents a nominalistic interpretation of society. Although he recognizes the existence of a social structure, his emphasis is on the paramount meaning of the individual. Take, for example, 'joint interactions' such as a marriage ceremony or a family dinner. It is not considered to be possible to achieve joint interaction without the interpretation given by the individuals of a way they fit together.

The four paradigms stress the process character of man and society. None the less, they assign different places to man and society in the social reality and, as will be shown later, this will have different consequences for their methodological principles. Although none of them denies the existence of social structures, Goffman's frame analysis delivers the most structuralist approach of the three. Structure and society are more than the mere sum of the individuals. Schutz and Garfinkel also recognize this standpoint, but methodologically they turn back to the individual, as does Blumer.

The subject matter of sociology

Sociologists confine the subject matter of research within their frames of the conceptions about reality, man and society. In general, it is shown that the interest of the four has been in the ongoing social reality and the meaningful character of this reality. Thus, it could be expected that the definition of sociology would present, to a certain extent, the same characteristics. Goffman (1974: 564) states that: 'The first object of social analysis ought ... to be ordinary actual behaviour — its structure and its organization.' Schutz (1976: 248) puts it this way: 'The primary task of this science [interpretive sociology] is to describe the processes of meaning establishment and meaning interpretation as these are carried out by individuals living in the social world.'

It must be stressed that Schutz (1967: 226) considers the 'world of working' as the paramount reality. Action is thus part of it. Garfinkel (1967: 11), although speaking about ethnomethodology, makes a similar point: ethnomethodology is 'the investigation of the rational properties of indexical expressions and other practical actions as contingent ongoing accomplishment of organized artful practices of everyday life'. Blumer (1969a: 55) moreover, gives a similar description: 'In a valid sense social action is the primary subject matter of social science. Hence, an accurate picture and understanding of social action is of crucial importance.'

Taking into account what has been said about the visions of reality, man and society, it is normal that the three paradigms would try to grasp daily social action. But the option of Goffman is, nevertheless, different: for him, the main task of sociology is to study the social structure and social organization of actual behaviour. None the less, frame analysis is not about social organization, but rather about the structure of experience. Even if Goffman (1974: 13) puts society first, he is concerned about the 'individual's current involvement'. But frame analysis also has something to say about the structure of social action. With regard to three or four performing individuals, frame analysis can show (1) 'the tracks or channels of activity', (2) 'the laminations' and (3) 'the participation status' (Goffman, 1974: 564–5). So the focus is on social structure (Goffman, 1974: 247).

Emphasizing the organization of ordinary actual behaviour as the subject matter of sociology is not new for Goffman. Even when in his earlier work he gives much attention to social psychology, there is always an important part devoted to the organizational approach of social action (e.g. Goffman, 1967: 2; 1961a, b; 1963b: 156, 193, 231; 1971: x, 63, 138, 362; 1981a: 84). For this reason, a formal sociological approach in the footsteps of Simmel is not unusual (Goffman, 1959: 15; 1967: 16, 63, 65).

However, in *Frame Analysis*, Goffman's main concern is not the structure of social life, but the structure of experience. The problem which he wants to solve is what happens when an individual wonders what is going on. To solve this problem, our perception is focused by the different frames, keys and fabrications. The actor thus interprets the world using pre-given frames such as postulates, rules, lores of understanding and approaches (Goffman, 1974: 21). This can be seen as the basis for a sociology of knowledge.

From this point of view there is a parallel between Goffman's paradigms and the three others. The study of knowledge is also a central point in Schutz's, Garfinkel's and Blumer's work. The former two are interested in the processes of meaning establishment and interpretation, while the latter is involved in objects, social action and joint interaction as defined by the actors.

The main part of Schutz's work (1932, 1967, 1964, 1975, 1974) is devoted to the phenomenological analysis of the life-world with much attention being given to the knowledge of the life-world and society. It is to be noted that this is not the same as an empirical sociology of knowledge (Schutz and Luckmann, 1974: 317–18), but 'the formal types of the social distribution of knowledge can even have a certain heuristic value for the empirical sociology of knowledge'. As pointed out above, the life-world stock of knowledge, the social stock of knowledge and scientific knowledge meet each other through the postulate of adequacy (Schutz, 1967: 44). Schutz considers this as a guarantee for the consistency of the constructs of the sociologist with common-sense knowledge.[2]

Garfinkel's ethnomethodology can also be typified as a sociology of common-sense knowledge. Although he takes Schutz's opinion as a starting point, he changes the methods of research by using experiments. In this way, he shows that sociologists as well as lay people use common-sense knowledge to explain social reality (Garfinkel, 1967: 31, 66–103). He points out that scientific rationalities cannot replace common-sense knowledge; they can even hinder social interaction (Garfinkel, 1967: 277–83). Ethnomethodology can help in this way to expose the common-sense reasoning in sociological research.

Blumer (1969a: 55–6), finally, although he is interested in social action as constructed by the participants, looks for processes of knowledge:

> In this situation, he [the actor] notes, interprets and assesses things with which he has to deal in order to act. The collectivity is in the same position as the individual in having to cope with a situation, in having to interpret and analyse the situation, and in having to construct a line of action. Basically put, it means that in order to treat and analyse social action one has to observe the process by which it is constructed.

One last comment is related to the general label 'micro-sociological paradigms'. Only Garfinkel's work is confined to the study of face-to-face relations or small groups, which is the core subject of micro-sociology. Goffman speaks about such things as riots, colleges, passengers and structures; Schutz about social collectives and artifacts; and Blumer about social structures and joint action. Why are these four paradigms then considered to be micro-sociological? A common characteristic of the four is that in each the analysis of social action starts with the interpreting individuals acting in relation to each other in small units. Because of this starting point, these approaches can be considered micro-sociological.

Methodological principles
Speaking about reality and the subject matter, I argued that the four paradigms are keenly interested in daily knowledge. In all of them, individuals are considered to be meaning-endowed entities. As a consequence, it could be expected that they would apply an interpretive sociology to a certain extent, i.e., they would look for

the aims, motives, or plans of the actors as the means of understanding social action.

It is accepted by the four paradigms that acting individuals have life plans, expectations, wishes, etc. Explaining social reality consequently supposes an interpretive approach. This is a necessary but not a sufficient condition. While Schutz (1932: 247–85), Garfinkel (1967) and Blumer (1969a: 60, 40, 58) reduce the methods of sociology to an understanding of the acting individuals within a social setting, Goffman (1974: 10–11) does not consider this approach as sufficient: 'I assume that definitions of a situation are built up in accordance with principles of organization which govern events — at least social ones — and our subjective involvement in them.'

Frames, keys and fabrications organize our experience in a particular way. They are given to the actors, who do not even have to be aware of the primary frameworks they use. Although they may use them improperly, they can apply them effectively. Primary frameworks are, indeed, the central part of the culture of the group. In this respect, frameworks enable the actor to understand his world (Goffman, 1974: 21-7). Goffman stresses a situational '*verstehen*'.

Indeed, in his earlier work the idea of 'definition of the situation' takes a central position. Nevertheless, already in *The Presentation of Self in Everyday Life* (1959: 254–5) he denies that social reality is just a construction by individuals. Even if an individual wants to present an untrue picture of himself, he is using *real* techniques. Consequently, it would be wrong to confine the explanation of social reality to the individual definition of the situation. For that reason, contrary to the classical pragmatic standpoint, Goffman stresses that 'the meaning of an object, no doubt, is generated through its use, as pragmatists say, but ordinarily not by particular users' (Goffman, 1974: 39), a remarkably different standpoint from those of Schutz and Blumer.

What are the consequences of these points of view for methodological research principles?

Scientific reasoning
Philosophy of science has designed the different patterns of reasoning that are followed or have to be followed in scientific research. Most researchers follow these patterns, although the importance of imagination in finding new ways is often stressed. The four paradigms, although not abandoning all the generally recognized scientific principles, give proof of and demand an important place for imagination. Schutz proposes that creativity build up ideal types, while Blumer asks for a creative approach to

overcome the limited possibilities of traditional research patterns. Garfinkel uses very original experiments in which he asks the experimenters to handle or think in deviation from the background expectancies. Goffman's work is an overwhelmingly creative presentation of frames, keys and fabrications drawing on the most unusual sources of research, like comic strips, novels, cartoons, biographies and the cinema. His originality does not lie in the fact that these sources are used, but in the way he uses them.

The paradigms are different, too, as far as the general pattern of scientific reasoning is concerned.

In general Goffman works very impressionistically. He follows no strict pattern to collect facts; he does not worry about the representativity of the facts; he neglects serious quantitative argumentation to make general statements. The overall pattern is inductive, but he gathers facts rather to illustrate than to prove a generalization. There is no systematic falsification or verification; it is more free-wheeling. The standpoint of Goffman (1981b: 65) — 'I would have thought it moves me farther and farther (even further and further) in positivism' — cannot be considered to be an option for the systematic reasoning of the positivistic researcher.

Frame Analysis consists of a long list of frames used by people experiencing social reality. The explanation pattern used most often is explanation-by-concept (Hempel, 1965: 453–7). In the strict sense, this is not considered an explanation, but rather a description of the different characteristics of a phenomenon. These are seen as the constituent elements of a phenomenon and, in this sense, a kind of condition. For example, let us consider keying. A key is,

> the set of conventions by which a given activity, one already meaningful in terms of some primary frameworks, is transformed into something patterned on this activity but seen by the participants to be something quite else. The process of transcription can be called keying. (Goffman, 1974: 43–4)

This definition is preceded by a description of the fighting of animals, which can be done playfully. A much longer description is then given to what keying is. It is a list of conjunctions of symptoms, that need to be present to have a keying. One of these characteristics is: 'Participants in the activity are meant to know and to openly acknowledge that a systematic alteration is involved, one that will radically reconstitute what it is for them that is going on.' (Goffman, 1974: 45) It does not seem to me that these participants are considered to be the causes of the keying. This is only a description of how people are supposed to look at reality when they are keying.

The rest of the chapter, 'Keys and Keying', is spent on the definitions of the different keys and on illustrating them by very disparate examples. Even when this list seems to provide an amazing amount of facts to support a particular key, it must not be forgotten that Goffman (1974: 15) does not consider them as proof or evidence, but merely as simple illustrations.

Goffman also uses other explanation patterns, one of them being based on the dispositions of the acting individuals when they construct fabrications (1974: 87ff.). For example, 'playful deceit', 'benign fabrication', is possible because the victim accepts in good sport to be deceived for a short time.

Nevertheless, the interest of frame analysis is mostly in the questions of 'how' and 'what' and less in the question of 'why'. This is not a very unusual practice for the author, as John Lofland (1980: 31–7) has shown in analysing the earlier work of Goffman.

The standpoint of phenomenological sociology is different. This sociological paradigm wants to observe and understand the life-world. It explicitly chooses a subjective interpretation. This means that the explanation must take account of the actor, not as seen by the researcher, but by the actor himself (postulate of subjective interpretation). As I mentioned above, the sociologist, being an objective observer, has to build ideal types. By these ideal types, the act of the actor can be understood by the researcher. It can also be understood by the actor and his fellows since the act occurs in their life-world (postulate of adequacy). An ideal type must be constructed like the typifications used in the everyday life-world. Moreover, an ideal type, as Weber has put it, must be both causal and meaning-adequate. So it is not sufficient that the motives have some meaning for the realization of the typical act, there must also be some evidence that a meaning-adequate type has some chance of occurring, as experience shows (Schutz, 1932: 247–85). Empirical observation is consequently the basis for verification.

Garfinkel (1967: 77–9) also stresses observation, but uses interpretation or the documentary methods (Mannheim) and experiments. This documentary method takes an 'actual appearance as "the document of", as "pointing to", as "standing on behalf of" a presupposed underlying pattern'. This actual appearance is interpreted within the common-sense knowledge of social structures. Indeed, social facts, which the researcher gets within accounts or ethnographies, are indexical and reflexive. These two characteristics are conditions for interpretation. Garfinkel goes even further. He uses the documentary method to find how understanding happens in daily events. Therefore he uses experiments. Most of the experiments start with a stable system and Garfinkel (1963; 1967: 36–8) tries then to create trouble by asking experimenters to act deviantly. The aim is to show how persons interpret the new deviant situation in order to learn what they consider to be the normal structure. Garfinkel is firmly convinced that these are not proper experiments, but a kind of documentary method to aid his imagination. They are seen more as a source of illustration than as a proof for a thesis. Causality is not the main concern of Garfinkel; he is more interested in how meaning is given to social reality.

On the other hand, symbolic interactionism explicitly takes an inductive stance. The classic patterns of research, the traditional testing of hypotheses, and the confinement to operational procedures are rejected because of their stereotyped structures. A researcher has to return to the empirical social world, i.e., 'the actual group life of human beings' (Blumer, 1969a: 35). Hence the researcher must bridge the distance between his life-world and that of the studied group. Therefore, it would be best for the researcher to become a participant of the group. Doing research means that two steps are taken. In the first place, there is 'exploration', which means that the researcher adapts questions and methods to the interpretation made by the life-group. In the second place, there is 'inspection': the task of scrutinizing the relationship between analytical elements (i.e. general or categorical items) and empirical reality. This method, as formulated by Blumer (1969a: 21–47), forms an inductive sociology using facts to build up theoretical propositions. For Blumer (1969a: 30), this includes confirmation as well as falsification.

I have contended that the paradigms take different methodological stances according to their ontological options, and I suggested that scientific reasoning would follow these differences.

Goffman's frame analysis has a peculiar position in relation to this problem. If we agree that he is moving closer to positivism (Goffman, 1981b: 65), it could be expected he would pay more attention to inductive thinking. And, in a certain sense, he does, but the main thrust of his argument is an enumeration of concepts and illustrations that can be used to recognize structures.

Theory

Theory is a very ambiguous concept in methodology. It can be considered as a universal proposition explaining facts, or as a law, an hypothesis or something in between. The function of theory is also variously defined. This makes it difficult to give an assessment of whether frame analysis, symbolic interactionism, ethnomethodology or phenomenological sociology have attained theory status. Here I would ask only: what is theory according to the three paradigms?

If more attention in *Frame Analysis* is paid to explanations-by-concept, it might be expected that little would be said of laws and theories. None the less, Goffman (1974: 14) wants 'to construct general statements', which was not his aim in *Relations in Public* (1971: xiv). Here he does not want to produce absolute or statistical generalizations. He prefers to speak about practices occurring 'routinely', 'often' or 'on occasion'. Moreover, he is aware that his analysis is confined to Western society, and more particularly to Anglo-American society, in which he pays more attention to middle-class behaviour (Goffman, 1961b: 182; 1963b: 5; 1971: xiv, 40, 75, 382; 1974: 521–2) than to any other category. He does not deny class differences (Goffman, 1961a: 50; 1963b: 206), but it is not his primary intention to contribute to class analysis (Goffman, 1974: 14).

Relying on a vast number of illustrations and his creative analytical power, he makes many general statements in *Frame Analysis*. For example:

> When the individual in our Western society recognizes a particular event, he tends, whatever else he does, to imply in this response (and in effect employ) one or more frameworks or schemata of interpretation of a kind that can be called primary ...
> When no keying is involved, when, that is, only primary perspectives apply, response in frame terms is not likely unless doubt needs combating, as in the reply: 'No, they're not merely playing; it's a real fight' ...
> The more vulnerable the dominant participant to deviant subordinate response, the more selection apparently there is in regard to subordinates ...
> When more generalizations have accumulated concerning face-to-face interaction, there will be greater resources to draw upon for intentionally unhinging the frame of ordinary events. (Goffman, 1974: 21, 46, 429, 495.)

Statements of this kind are numerous, also in the earlier work (Lofland, 1980: 33–4), but they are rarely the product of a systematic collection of corroborating facts.

As a totality, however, frame analysis seems to make the general statement that, as a rule, individuals use a mixture of classified frames. Even though the list of frames is not exhaustive, we all use them when answering the question of what it is that is going on.

According to phenomenological sociology, theory is one of the main concerns of a sociologist. Theory means, 'the explicit formulation of determinate relations between a set of variables in terms of which a fairly extensive class of empirically ascertainable regularities can be explained'(Schutz, 1967: 52).

The universality and the predictive value of these theories is rather restricted. But even though these generalizations have their limitations, they do have a certain nomothetic value. Ideal types are, indeed, constructed in perfect anonymity and, in this way, tell how this typical actor acts in general.

Because the scientifically ideal types must be built in conformity with an everyday and social stock of knowledge, Schutz (1967: 59) considers it necessary to detect the general principles by which an actor grasps his everyday life-world. For this reason, all the general statements made in relation to the knowledge of the life-world and society are of importance for constructing a sociological theory (Schutz and Luckmann, 1974).

Symbolic interactionism is as outspoken as phenomenological sociology. Blumer (1969a: 140) sees the purpose of theory as the development of analytical schemes of the empirical world. But theory has too long been considered to be a result of empirical research with no notice being given to the way empirical facts are approached in enquiry. It must be seen as a result of a dialectical process: 'Theory, inquiry and empirical fact are interwoven in a texture of operations with theory guiding inquiry, inquiry seeking and isolating facts, and facts affecting theory.' (Blumer, 1969a: 141.)

For this reason the empirical reality must be stressed and concepts must be reconsidered in close relation with reality: 'sensitizing' concepts have to be used.

Garfinkel approaches classical sociological theory as critically as does Blumer. He borrows from Schutz for his analysis, but expands the methods. He refuses to accept that common-sense knowledge and activities are just assumed, but makes it an issue of inquiry. He shows that a sociological researcher or theorist assumes common-sense knowledge and presuppositions to explain social phenomena, to interpret answers of questionnaires, biographies, folders, and so on.

Concepts

Frame analysis, phenomenological sociology and symbolic interaction speak about concepts as the sacred instruments for research. The nature of these concepts differs in all three paradigms, and so their functions differ.

Like Goffman's earlier work, *Frame Analysis* is a brilliant construct of concepts concerning the structure of experience, but it is more a taxonomy than a theory. As typifications of what is going on in daily life, these concepts are closely related to everyday language, and most of his definitions are illustrated by large numbers of examples.

For many concepts he relies on the definitions given by other authors, without always taking into account their methodological options. For example, 'social selves' of W. James (Goffman, 1959: 48), 'rules of irrelevance' of H. Garfinkel, 'frame' of G. Bateson, 'sociability' of G. Simmel, 'bureaucracy' of M. Weber and T. Parsons, 'role-set' of Merton, 'role-sectors' of N. Gross and others, 'profane' and 'sacred' of Durkheim (Goffman, 1961a: 19, 21, 22, 87, 152), 'eye-to-eye looks' of Simmel (Goffman, 1963b: 93), 'interchange' of E.D. Chapple, 'ideal sphere' and 'adventure' of Simmel (Goffman, 1967: 19, 62, 162), 'strategic interaction' of T.C. Schelling (Goffman, 1969: 100), 'interaction synchrony' of W.S. Condon, 'prestation' of M. Maus, 'round' and 'exchange' of H. Sacks (Goffman, 1971: 52, 62, 119).

Rarely does he make a comparative analysis of the concepts before proposing a new construct, like he does in the chapter 'Role Distance', in his book, *Encounters* (1961a). These concepts have the form of Weberian ideal types. Some of these stress the motivational aspect. This is the case for make-believe, experiments, fabrications and benign fabrications, to cite only a few (Goffman, 1974: 48, 73, 83, 87). Other concepts concern how something is seen by the actors, e.g., keying, performance, cosmological interest, fortuitousness and demonstration (Goffman, 1974: 43–4, 124, 30, 33, 66). As a totality, they delineate the different perspectives from which social reality is met by actors in the world and describe a pre-given structure of the experience of daily life.

Often these concepts are part of typologies, as can be seen when frames, keys and fabrications were presented. Goffman does not consider these typologies as an exhaustive description of the phenomena, but as a result of 'a caricature of systematic sampling'. Moreover, these types seem to be postulates and not assertions to be proven or tested (Lofland, 1980: 30).

The conceptualization in phenomenological sociology develops directly along the line of Weberian ideal types. I have had occasion to mention this above with regard to scientific reasoning and theory. While the homunculi (= ideal types) must be built adequate to everyday knowledge and to the social stock of knowledge, the significance of pre-scientific knowledge for sociology has to be stressed. Schutz and Luckmann (1974: 306–31) give a good example of this in relation to the study of professionalization. The types, i.e. the layman, the well-informed and the expert, form an interesting starting point for further research.

Few sociologists have so forcefully drawn attention to the mistakes made in the construction and application of concepts as Blumer (1969a: 153–82). In his opinion, traditional empirical sociology uses concepts erroneously. Scientific concepts need a particular degree of abstraction, but they must be meticulously scrutinized in close relation to social life. For Blumer (1969a: 147–8), scientific concepts are 'sensitizing' and not 'definitive', only providing general orientations for the researcher. In this respect, they make possible new orientations and new experiences in social research.

Like Blumer, Garfinkel stresses that concepts, sentences, utterances, etc., must be considered in close connection with the setting in which they are used. The meaning of concepts is consequently not fixed, but depends on the context in which they are employed. Each account must be interpreted taking into account the indexicality of the expressions. In addition he employs ideal types as does Schutz (Garfinkel, 1967: 106, 263). But here again, their meaning is determined by the context in which they are placed. Concepts are thus not just research instruments but are to be scrutinized.

Methods
In view of the different methodological standpoints of the four paradigms, it could be expected that their research methods would differ. Although, in principle, most of the usual research techniques are considered to be useful, there is much criticism of the conventional survey and experimental methods. None of the four sociologists uses the conventional methods in the traditional way.

If Goffman's option for positivism is taken seriously, *Frame Analysis* involves a very unorthodox approach. He ignores systematic gathering of data to verify hypotheses and build theories. Moreover, the facts used in *Frame Analysis* differ considerably from traditional sociological data. Field-work, as such, is not used, although some of Goffman's examples come from participant observation. Instead, Goffman (1974: 15; 1971: xiv; 1976: 24) works with illustrations found in popular books, newspapers, novels, the cinema, comics and theatres etc., and he admits that it is 'a caricature of systematic sampling'. For this reason, it does not matter whether his stories are reliable or not. This point of view is acceptable if the aim is to give a limited description of the structure of experience. If not, the selection of the examples would limit the capacity of frame analysis to find all the possible structures.

Goffman sees himself as an 'ethnographer of small entities'. Being a student of Lloyd Warner and E.C. Hughes, he was trained to do this kind of work. But the major part of his work, and certainly *Frame Analysis*, is not a product of direct observation. He performed field work only three times: a study of a small community on the Shetland Islands (*Communication Conduct in an*

Island Community, 1953), a study of a mental health hospital (*Asylums*, 1961b) and an unpublished study about behaviour in casinos. Like *Frame Analysis*, most of his work relies on illustrations, gathered from personal experience, and the haphazardly collected strips of reality presented in true or fictitious stories of novels, films, research reports etc. The selection of this material happened 'over the years on a hit-or-miss basis using principles of selection mysterious to me' (Goffman, 1974: 15). Sometimes he does have a pattern to collect facts, like the ethology in *Relations in Public* (1971) or game theory in *Strategic Interaction* (1969).

The use of ideal types in phenomenological sociology demands a study of the everyday life-world as it appears to the actor, and the main method in Schutz's work is phenomenological analysis of the life-world of the actor. Good examples of this are found in his papers 'The Homecomer' and 'The Stranger' (Schutz, 1964: 91–119). The attempt to imagine what life in the everyday life-world is like seems to be the main research technique, and it must be augmented by empirical observation.

Garfinkel has a similar position, i.e. ethnography and accounts are the main methods of data collection in ethnomethodology. These phenomena are approached interpretatively as seen by the members of society. To facilitate this approach, Garfinkel uses experiments, but in a way totally different from that of the main tradition. In these experiments, the experimenters are mostly students who are not chosen in function of a representative picture of the problem. Very often they are not trained for the experiment and are given no clear rules to write the accounts. The experimenters also use interviewing, but their objectives are different from the conventional interview techniques. Even when Garfinkel counts the distribution of the phenomena, they can be considered only as illustrations for a particular interpretation of social reality; he is not concerned about the representativity of his material. Like Goffman, Garfinkel uses also ethnography, but, because of his typical ethnomethodological standpoint, the points of interest are completely different.

The ongoing social life, according to the symbolic interactionist, cannot be grasped by classic scientific procedures, which destroy the possibility of getting valid information about the empirical world. The researcher has to come as close as possible to the object. This can be done by becoming an observant participant who explores and inspects. For exploration all kinds of techniques are allowed, such as direct observation, interviews, listening to conversations, life histories, letters and diaries and group discussion. The particular method to be used cannot be determined in advance but has to be adapted in the course of the project.

Conclusions

The purpose of this chapter is not to evaluate the four paradigms. To do this properly the explanatory power of each approach to particular problems would have to be evaluated. But the works of the four authors are too divergent to do this. Whether the frames analysed in *Frame Analysis* give an adequate picture of the structures of experience can be answered only empirically. But this was not the aim of this chapter.

In spite of the specificity of the paradigms, it is obvious that 'the basic frameworks of understanding available in our society for making sense out of events' (Goffman, 1974: 10) are embryonically recognizable in Schutz's social stock of knowledge and Garfinkel's common-sense knowledge of social structures. The epistemological base is, of course, different, but the study of structural phenomena is clearly part of phenomenological sociology and ethnomethodology.

I have suggested that differences in the world pictures would reveal different methodological options. Frame analysis appears as a positivistically inspired reaction against the solipsism of other micro-sociological paradigms. Reality does not live just in the minds of the knowing individuals. Reality is a given and can be recognized as such. Although phenomenological sociology, ethnomethodology and symbolic interactionism try hard to escape the label of solipsism, the knowing subject is undeniably the central source of knowledge for these paradigms.

From an ontological perspective, Goffman stresses the emergent character of society and the ongoing identity of man. Society and the individual are also assigned an important place in the sociology of Schutz and Garfinkel, although they bracket the existence of the world, while Blumer reduces social life to the joint interaction of individuals. Thus, the structural approach is of central concern for both frame analysis and phenomenological sociology, as well as for ethnomethodology.

In spite of these differences the programmes of the four paradigms are similar: they all want to study 'ongoing social action'; they all start from face-to-face interactions, but they do not confine the study to small groups, with the exception of Garfinkel; and they develop a base for a sociology of everyday knowledge.

From the methodological standpoint, there are big differences between frame analysis, phenomenological sociology, ethnomethodology and symbolic interactionism. Frame analysis can be characterized as an approach that is more interested in answering the questions of 'how' and 'what', rather than 'why'. Theory is reduced to generalizations that are formulated on the basis of a selection of illustrations. For the description of the different frames, a vast list of concepts is created, in which very often the personal motivation of the actor is considered. The fact-gathering is haphazard, which is justified by the structural interest.

Taking into account the ontological perspectives, it is shown that a subjective interpretation from the standpoint of the actor is the concern of the three other paradigms. All three stress observation, but are highly critical of the conventional survey and experimental methods, although the arguments are different. There is no concern for representative observation; collected facts are rather illustrations. Using this kind of experience, Schutz and Garfinkel show the meaning of common-sense knowledge for scientific reasoning, Blumer is more interested in interacting individuals. Concepts are used differently. Schutz and Garfinkel apply ideal types, Blumer 'sensitive' concepts, and Garfinkel pays much attention to the meaning of concepts in relation to the social setting.

Whatever the epistemological standpoint of the critic may be, it cannot be denied that frame analysis delivers a brilliant description of the structure of our experience. This structural approach was already present in Goffman's earlier works, although less pronounced. None of the three other paradigms has produced anything similar, although there is a basis for this structural approach in Schutz's analysis of the social stock of knowledge and Garfinkel's work. This approach is important because it puts structural analysis back into the study of small groups, and creates interest for frames, structures and organizations, rather than for interaction.

Notes

*This article is an expansion of the paper presented under the same title at the symposium 'Revisions and relations among modern micro-sociological paradigms' of the Tenth World Congress of Sociology, Mexico, August 1982. I am grateful for the critical remarks of Joan Aldous, Karel Dobbelaere, Horst J. Helle, Tamotsu Shitbutani and Dominique Vancraeynest.

1. We do not consider here the symbolic interactionism of Manford Kuhn, which takes different stances on various points.

2. The postulate of adequacy is actually a *deus ex machina*. Indeed, how is it possible, that a sociologist who approaches society as a 'world of mere contemporaries' and never as a world of 'fellow-men' can ever get a picture of his fellow-men? For Schutz, the solution is to be found in the ideal types.

References

Blumer, Herbert (1969a) *Symbolic Interactionism. Perspective and Method*. Englewood Cliffs, NJ: Prentice-Hall.
Blumer, Herbert (1969b) 'Collective Behavior', pp. 65–121 in A.McClung Lee (ed·), *Principles of Sociology*. New York: Barnes and Noble.
Blumer, Herbert (1977) 'Comment on Lewis's "The Classic American Pragmatists as Forerunners to Symbolic Interactionism"', *The Sociological Quarterly*, 18(2): 285–9.

Blumer, Herbert (1980) 'Mead and Blumer: the Convergent Methodological Perspectives of Social Behaviorism and Symbolic Interactionism', *American Sociological Review*, 45(3): 409–19.

Davis, Murray S. (1975) 'Review Symposium of Frame Analysis', *Contemporary Sociology*, 4(6): 599–603.

Denzin, Norman K. and Charles M. Keller (1981) 'Frame Analysis Reconsidered', *Contemporary Sociology*, 10(1): 52–60.

Ditton, Jason (ed.) (1980) *The View from Goffman*, London: Macmillan.

Ditton, Jason and W.W. Sharrock (1976) 'Review Symposium of Frame Analysis', *Sociology*, 10: 329–34.

Frank III, Arthur W. (1979) 'Reality Construction in Interaction', *Annual Review of Sociology*, 5: 167–91.

Garfinkel, Harold (1956) 'Conditions of Successful Degradation Ceremonies', *American Journal of Sociology*, 61(4): 420–4.

Garfinkel, Harold (1963) 'A Conception of, and Experiments with "Trust" as a Condition of Stable Concerted Actions', pp. 187–238 in O.J. Harvey (ed.). *Motivation and Social Interaction. Cognitive Determinants.* New York: Ronald Press.

Garfinkel, Harold (1967) *Studies in Ethnomethodology.* Englewood Cliffs, NJ: Prentice-Hall.

Garfinkel, Harold and H. Sacks (1970) 'On Formal Structures of Practical Actions', pp. 337–66 in J. McKinney and E.A. Tiryakian (eds), *Theoretical Sociology. Perspectives and Developments.* New York: Appleton Century Crofts.

Garfinkel, Harold (1975) 'The Origins of the Term "Ethnomethodology"' pp. 15–18 in R. Turner (ed.), *Ethnomethodology.* Harmondsworth: Penguin Books.

Glaser, Daniel (1976) 'Review of Frame Analysis', *Sociology and Social Research*, 61(2): 246–7.

Goffman, Erving (1959) *The Presentation of Self in Everyday Life.* Garden City, NY: Doubleday.

Goffman, Erving (1961a) *Encounters. Two Studies in the Sociology of Interaction.* Indianapolis: Bobbs-Merrill.

Goffman, Erving (1961b) *Asylums. Essays on the Social Situation of Mental Patients and Other Inmates.* Harmondsworth: Penguin Books.

Goffman, Erving (1963a) *Stigma. Notes on the Management of Spoiled Identity.* Harmondsworth: Penguin Books.

Goffman, Erving (1963b) *Behavior in Public Places. Notes on the Social Organization of Gatherings.* New York: Free Press.

Goffman, Erving (1967) *Interaction Ritual. Essays on Face-to-Face Behavior.* Garden City, NY: Doubleday.

Goffman, Erving (1969) *Strategic Interaction.* Philadelphia: University of Pennsylvania Press.

Goffman, Erving (1971) *Relations in Public. Microstudies of the Public Order.* New York: Harper and Row.

Goffman, Erving (1974) *Frame Analysis. An Essay on the Organization of Experience.* Harmondsworth: Penguin Books.

Goffman, Erving (1976) *Gender Advertisements.* New York: Harper and Row.

Goffman, Erving (1981a) *Forms of Talk.* Oxford: Basil Blackwell.

Goffman, Erving (1981b) 'A Reply to Denzin and Keller', *Contemporary Sociology*, 10(1): 60–8.

Goffman, Erving (1983) 'The Interaction Order', *American Sociological Review* 48(1): 1–18.

Gonos, George (1977) '"Situation" versus "Frame": The "Interactionist" and the "Structuralist" Analyses of Everyday Life', *American Sociological Review*, 42: 854–67.

Helle, Horst Jürgen (1977) *Verstehende Soziologie und Theorie der Symbolische Interaktion*. Stuttgart: B.G. Teubner.

Hempel, Carl G. (1965) *Aspects of Scientific Explanation*. New York and London: Free Press and Collier Macmillan.

Jameson, Frederic (1976) 'On Goffman's Frame Analysis', *Theory and Society*, 3: 114–33.

Leiter, K. (1980) *A Primer on Ethnomethodology*. New York and Oxford: Oxford University Press.

Lewis, J. David (1976) 'The Classic American Pragmatists as Forerunners to Symbolic Interactionism', *The Sociological Quarterly*, 17(3): 347–59.

Littlejohn, Stephen W. (1977) 'Frame Analysis and Communication', *Communication Research*, 4(4): 485–91.

Lofland, John (1980) 'Early Goffman: Style, Structure, Substance, Soul', pp. 24–51 in J. Ditton (ed.), *The View from Goffman*, London: Macmillan.

Manning, Peter K. (1977) 'Review of Frame Analysis', *American Journal of Sociology*, 82(6): 1361–4.

McPhail, Clark and Cynthia Rexroat (1979) 'Mead vs. Blumer: the Divergent Methodological Perspectives of Social Behaviorism and Symbolic Interactionism', *American Sociological Review*, 44(3): 449–67.

McPhail, Clark and Cynthia Rexroat (1980) 'Ex Cathedra Blumer or ex Libris Mead?', *American Sociological Review*, 45(3): 420–30.

Natanson, Maurice (ed.) (1969) *Essays in Phenomenology*. The Hague: Martinus Nijhoff.

Radnitzky, Gerard (1970) *Contemporary Schools of Metascience*. Göteborg: Akademiförlaget.

Schutz, Alfred (1932, 1960) *Der Sinnhafte Aufbau der Sozialen Welt. Eine Einleitung in die Verstehende Soziologie*. Wien: Springer Verlag.

Schutz, Alfred (1964) *Collected Papers II. Studies in Social Theory*. The Hague: Martinus Nijhoff.

Schutz, Alfred (1967) *Collected Papers I. The Problem of Social Reality* (first published in 1962). The Hague: Martinus Nijhoff.

Schutz, Alfred (1970) *Reflections on the Problem of Relevance*. New Haven and London: Yale University Press.

Schutz, Alfred (1976) *The Phenomenology of the Social World*. London: Heinemann Educational Books.

Schutz, Alfred (1975) *Collected Papers III. Studies in Phenomenological Philosophy*. The Hague: Martinus Nijhoff.

Schutz, Alfred and Thomas Luckmann (1974) *The Structures of the Life-World*. London : Heinemann.

Strasser, S. (1973) *Fenomenologie en Empirische Menskunde. Bijdrage tot een Nieuw Ideaal van Wetenschappelijkheid*. Deventer: Van Loghum Slaterus.

Swanson, Guy (1975) 'Review of Frame Analysis', *The Annals of the American Academy of Political and Social Science*, 17: 218–20.

Vancraeynest, Dominique (1982) *De Sociologie van Erving Goffman. Positie en Inhoud Toegelicht*. Licentiaatsverhandeling, Leuven, Katholieke Universiteit.

6

Out of ethnomethodology

Arthur W. Frank

It is eighteen years since the publication of Garfinkel's *Studies in Ethnomethodology*. One understanding of this passage of time is that ethnomethodology (written hereafter as EM) has developed from being an unruly child (duly chastized by such elders as James Coleman and Lewis Coser) to being a middle-aged bore, about whom Sherri Cavan asked, in the title of a session at the 1983 Pacific Sociological Association meetings, 'Where have all the ethno-methodologists gone?'

The issue is not, to put it properly, something called EM, but rather the activity of a group of practitioners who identify their practice as EM. In response to Cavan's question, I know colleagues who have, to various extents, identified themselves as ethnometho-dologists who are getting out of EM in terms of self-identification, but at the same time they are doing work which takes its auspice from ideas formulated in the activity of EM. My title is designed to suggest both the need for a movement of sociological thought out of (away from) EM, and also the persistence in future sociological work of ideas in some sense out of (derivative from) EM.

EM at eighteen, to use that metaphor a little longer, is most appropriately understood as in an adolescent separation crisis: going 'out of' (or, in EM terms, 'doing "out of"') is a complicated process. The complication, in the case of EM practitioners as in that of many adolescents, revolves round the conflict between the feeling that it is time to move on and, opposed to this, a sense of debt to what is being left and a need to acknowledge that debt. To reflect on and thus facilitate the going 'out of' process, this paper begins with an acknowledgement of what EM has been and then uses EM to introduce a yet more unruly infant, the 'deconstruction' of Jacques Derrida. A deconstructionist critique of EM suggests both why it is time to get out, as well as why future work will always be, in some sense, ethnomethodological.

Acknowledging ethnomethodology

At this point in the paper, some readers might expect me to define, or at least circumscribe, EM and to do this by listing certain of its central concepts and providing glosses of these, with appropriate citations. Of course the notion of glossing is itself an EM concept, so a gloss of glossing would have to be included, and writing this is an example of reflexivity, even though I am not going to provide the set of glosses. More interesting than the actual provision of such glosses is why any such provision would fail. I take it that no matter how articulate I might be, no set of glosses could ever be satisfactory to ethnomethodologists as a re-presentation of their concepts. Why no glosses could be satisfactory is far from simple. In a review of a recent textbook on EM, Maynard writes about the author's attempt to explicate 'accounts', 'reflexivity' and 'indexicality'. 'These concepts have been defined and illustrated in as many ways as there are secondary sources on ethnomethodology, but I suspect they remain inaccessible to the untutored reader.' (Maynard, 1982: 716.)

What is Maynard doing with this sentence? An ethnomethodologist would first recognize the formulation of a contrast set: the opposition of the tutored and the untutored. Who is to be included in each of the respective sets is indexical; that is, knowing what it means to be among the tutored or untutored requires particular background knowledge. The nature of this background knowledge is such that what, or exactly how, the knower knows can never be fully stated. The tutored presumably include Maynard himself, possibly the book's author (who is accused of being 'abstruse' but not of being untutored), and probably others, but the criteria for admission are not, and cannot be, fully specified. By whom, for example, does one have to be tutored in order to become a proper tutor? And even if we had a list of all those who were proper tutors, there would still be the questions of what counts as tutoring, how long must one be tutored, and so forth. Can one become tutored by taking a seminar, or is it necessary to be a teaching assistant, a dissertation advisee, or even a journal article collaborator?

That these questions could not be answered is the essence of indexicality. Maynard could, as a practical matter, identify any particular case as being or not being tutored, but he could not provide exhaustive theoretical criteria which would be sufficient to allow anyone else (i.e., someone untutored) to make such an identification. Maynard's knowledge allows him to do certain things, for example, to classify candidates for the tutored, but it is insufficient to allow him to claim that he is acting on principle. And that — to know, in the sense of being able to do, more than one knows in the sense of being able to provide principles for — is not only the nature of what is produced by tutoring, but the nature of most of what we call our knowledge.

An alternative statement of EM's lesson of indexicality is that it is futile on two levels to expect specificity of extensional reference (e.g., to expect to be able to specify all who might be included in the tutored and untutored). It seems commonsensical to expect that when we use terms, we should be able to specify that to which those terms refer. Such an expectation is futile, first, because it seems to be the nature of language to be, in EM's phrase, irremediably indexical (see Garfinkel and Sacks, 1970). Second, the expectation is futile because it is, in everyday life, a non-issue. To do the work most sentences do in interaction, specificity of extensional reference is not necessary. People can 'make sense' — they can use the sentence — without exact extensional specificity.

The real peculiarity of indexicality, which EM has elucidated, is not that understanding sentences requires particular background knowledge; we should expect that. What is peculiar is this paradox: even those speakers who invoke the indexical item can never provide a fully satisfactory statement of what the required background knowledge is (e.g., what makes for a proper tutor), but this deficiency does not seem to matter to those who use that item in a sentence. Despite the lack of required background knowledge, the sentence makes sense anyway. What, if no one apparently knows what is being talked about, can 'making sense' mean? 'Making sense' means the sentence is usable: it can be used to do some interactive work in some particular context, e.g., in a book review.

Given the (irremediably) indexical nature of 'the tutored', it is particularly interesting how Maynard manages, in the same sentence, to place himself among them. He could have placed himself in many ways, i.e., citing some of his articles and his degrees, providing personal testimonials such as typically occur in prefaces and dust jacket comments (and indirectly in acknowledgement footnotes), but none of these tactics is particularly convenient in the journal format in which Maynard is writing, so he places himself reflexively. His sentence refers to its own implicit condition of intelligibility: for the sentence to make sense, whoever wrote it must be among the tutored.

Making the sentence perform this reflexive task is no simple matter. Maynard could not simply have written 'they [the concepts as explained] remain inaccessible to the untutored reader', because that sentence could have been written by such an untutored reader, reflecting on his own lack of comprehension (i.e., complaining about the book's inadequacy in tutoring him). Instead, Maynard writes: 'I suspect they remain inaccessible to the untutored reader'. The verb 'suspect' is thus a double performative. First, to say 'I suspect' is to do the action of suspecting. Second, the verb performs the reflexive task of telling those who read it in the particular sentence that since the writer, Maynard, is qualified to suspect something about the untutored, he is not himself among the untutored, since he is unable to write from his own experience. Thus the verb first places Maynard among the suspicious, and then it places him among the tutored.

Lest it be forgotten, the Maynard quotation was introduced as my way of accounting for not doing something I might normally have been expected to do, that is, provide glosses of the basic EM concepts such as indexicality, reflexivity and accounts. An 'account' here does not mean simply an excuse or justification, but suggests that action is never sufficiently self-explanatory as it is performed, so one must build into one's action reflexive statements about what one is doing, lest others lose their places. It helps that the structures of most actions, e.g., conversations, provide conventional places or 'slots' for doing particular sorts of things. In so far as I was correct that most readers would have expected, at some particular place in this paper, glosses of some EM concepts, that expectation on their part reflects the presence of a slot in academic papers. The conventional structure of a paper about some 'theory group' helps the reader keep his or her place in the paper by providing an expectation that certain matters, such as 'reviewing the concepts', will be attended to, and where they will be attended to. The explication of slots has been a major accomplishment of those ethnomethodologists involved in analysing conversation. Since there was a slot which I did not fill in the conventional way, how does Maynard provide me with an account?

The first clause of Maynard's sentence ('These concepts have been defined and illustrated in as many ways as there are secondary sources on ethnomethodology') tells us that the failure of the book to bring its untutored readers among the tutored is not the result of some fault of this particular author, since all authors have failed, and I in my turn could hardly have expected to do any better. Instead of blaming individual authors, Maynard is suggesting that the problem lies in something about the nature of explanations in textbooks. To understand what, we need to return to the contrast set. The complications of who is to be included among 'the tutored' have been discussed. The composition of 'the untutored' is easier: we know that each of its members is, at minimum, a reader. What the sentence states is that even if someone reads all the secondary sources on EM, that reader would remain untutored. Can one then become tutored by reading the primary sources? Apparently not, since Maynard concludes by recommending that the book is useful 'given the difficulty of some primary sources'. Albeit this difficulty is qualified ('some'), but the implication is that the primary sources are difficult without the secondary sources; unfortunately, these are also inadequate. How then can someone untutored become tutored?

Another sentence provides the answer. 'The writing is dense and at times cryptic,' Maynard writes, 'so that an instructor's own understanding and involvement in presenting the material is a necessity.' (Maynard, 1982: 716.) Again a contrast set is proposed, this time between written text and instructor 'involvement', and this contrast provides for the inference that what counts as 'involvement' is engagement in face-to-face talk with students. At first, each — the writing and the involvement — appears supplementary to the other; on reflection it appears that the involvement is the *sine qua non* of the writing, since writing is inadequate by itself. Becoming properly tutored, then, cannot be simply a matter of reading, but requires the personal involvement of a tutor.

As a gloss of Maynard's notion of an instructor's 'involvement', I propose Wittgenstein's statement, 'if a person has not yet got the concepts, I shall teach him to use the words by means of examples and by practice' (Wittgenstein, 1958: 83e). Wittgenstein compares words to tools and chess pieces; to know them is to know how to use them in the context of particular activities and games. Language is learned in the course of participating in activities; language is part and parcel of these activities, and its use comes about — and can only come about — as an aspect of the doing of activity. The cases in which we can learn language as Augustine believed it was learned, by association of some phonetic sound with some object in the world, are the restricted, not the general cases. Thus, EM concepts can be learned only in the course of the activity of EM, and their usage makes sense only in the context of that activity.

What is curious is not this idea that EM concepts can only be learned by participation in EM activity, since this would be true for any theory group. In attending to it, EM only displays a greater sensitivity to the nature of learning language and to the mutually constitutive relation of language and activity. What is curious is the idea that certain difficulties of learning through texts are surmounted when learning takes place in person; that is, the idea that the text is supplementary to the speech situation. What is at issue here is not a matter of pedagogy but one of epistemology, and the epistemological issue which is raised suggests an essential limitation in the present formulation of EM.

There is an implication in Maynard's quotation that when an instructor who has 'understanding' becomes involved — when, in other words, a face-to-face speech relationship is established to which the relation of untutored reader to written text (secondary or primary) is supplementary — then some privileged (tutored) understanding of EM is possible. The opposition of the contrast set implies that some do 'know', and that others can learn: a 'real' understanding can be 'had' through tutoring, as opposed to the confused understanding which is attained through reading.

This opposition of understanding through reading versus understanding through speech both formulates and presupposes what we can call the 'problem of the textbook', which in turn becomes the more general 'problem of the text' since primary sources are equally deficient for learning. The insight on which this 'problem of the text' rests is fundamental to EM: the irremediably indexical and reflexive nature of language, full as it is of glosses, accounts and so forth. To read a text outside the activity of which that text is (only) a part is necessarily to misunderstand what is written; the untutored reader can never become tutored by the text alone. But the text does not simply share in a general state of linguistic indexicality; instead some language, that in texts, seems to be more indexical than other language, speech. Thus with regard to its own 'problem of the text', it is possible to propose a remedy, i.e., the personal involvement, the tutoring, of the instructor. Apparently EM speech, then, can remedy what is irremedial both in EM texts and in the speech of everyday life.

Maynard suggests that an untutored student face-to-face with an understanding instructor is somehow in a better position to become tutored than the same student as reader facing a text. Face-to-face speech, at least with an ethnomethodologist, is thus treated as being able to clarify at least some of the uncertainties of reading texts. These uncertainties of indexicality, of knowing how a concept is used in the language game of those who do use it, are quite real, and EM's contribution has been to explicate them. What the privilege of speech over text seems to forget is that these uncertainties are no less real in face-to-face contact than in reading a text. The game is played no better and no worse in speech than in writing; there is no privilege of one over the other. What is the privilege which Maynard attributes to the personal instructional situation? It seems to be that the instructor has a personal presence in speech which is lacking in writing, and this presence is a sort of remedy to the usual indexicality of language.

Why should this positing of a presence in speech be such an issue, such a failure of EM? Because: in positing, initially, that language use is irremediably indexical — that indexicality is its very nature — EM followed Goffman (1959) in demonstrating what had been taken to be the scandal of language to be its essence. The 'scandal' of Goffman's argument had been the necessity of interpretation. In interaction, the self only senses and interprets signs of the other; the 'presence' of the other is no longer 'in' that other him or herself, but 'in' the signs which mediate between other and interpreting self. The interpretation of these signs had been understood as a mere supplement to the originary presence of the other, and a corrupt supplement, risking as it does the very possibility of 'distortion'. Goffman's work demanded the premise that because the presence of the other is always mediated by signs, the interpretation of these signs is the very possibility of that presence. Each is not removed from the other by the necessity of interpreting that other's presence; rather the other is constituted as a presence in a multiplicity of interpretive acts.

What EM contributed with ideas such as indexicality was the recognition that interpretation is always incomplete. The presence of the other is not only made possible by, and even is nothing but, its surrounding aura of interpretations, but this surrounding aura is one of interpretive uncertainty. It is this insight of the irremediable uncertainty of interpretation which is undercut when one kind of interactive situation, e.g., personal instruction, is held to be privileged over another (the text), in the sense of not requiring the same interpretive activity.

The privilege of the instructor's speech over the written text is, as will be shown below, a consistent reflection of the epistemology of EM, the consequences of which are most evident in the practices of those ethnomethodologists engaged in analysis of conversation. Maynard's sentence is not the inconsequential phrase of a particular writer, nor is it a function of its context, a review of a book rather than a review of classroom instruction. Even if it were conceivable that classroom speech had somehow been under review, the opposite sentence — that the instructor's speech is dense and at times cryptic, so the presentation of the material in a text is a necessity — would have been as inconsistent with the rest of EM, and the rest of sociology, as the sentence as written is consistent. That one sentence and not the other is possible suggests an incompleteness in the epistemic break of EM from preceding sociology and the need for new theoretical resources in order to complete this break.

Deconstructing ethnomethodology
One objection to what has been written above might be that it is hardly proper in a 'sociological' paper to be pinning such involved arguments on such slim data. How can I claim that one sentence, extracted by an unexplained procedure of sampling from a text of minor importance (a book review of a textbook), can be 'repre-

sentative' of EM? How can I justify making claims about EM based on inferences about one sentence, and particularly that one sentence?

My decision to quote from the Maynard review — certainly an ephemeral text even to the corpus of Maynard's work, much less to EM — was both eccentric and concentric: eccentric (ex, kentros) in the sense of 'not having the same centre' (Webster's *Third International Dictionary*), and concentric (con, centrum), 'having a common centre'. That is, I chose the quotations from a stance both out of and in EM. The choice was concentric in so far as basing an analysis on a single text chosen according to no particular logic of sampling is a typically ethnomethodological thing to do; see, as an example, Sacks (1974). In following this procedure my choice could be called reflexively concentric. My choice is also concentric in so far as I artfully selected a datum which would provide for the analysis I wanted to do, and my acknowledgement of this artful selection is also a typical move in the EM game. My choice is eccentric in so far as EM has not taken its own texts as objects of analysis. Other sociological work has been analysed on the premise that sociology is simply another form of social activity and analysable like any other, but this premise has not generally been extended to the corpus of EM itself.

This question of the possibility of a simultaneously concentric and eccentric stance, of a simultaneous interiority and exteriority, seems to be an essential reflection on the possibility of EM itself. To demonstrate this idea it is convenient to specify one variety of EM work. Although any work would do, my choice is made from a concentric stance: the short answer to Cavan's question is that the ethnomethodologists (if not everyone, at least most) have gone to analysing conversation and so conversation analysis (written hereafter as CA) is the most appropriate variety of current EM about which to write. The *locus classicus* of current CA probably remains Sacks, Schegloff and Jefferson's 'A Simplist Systematics for the Organization of Turn Taking in Conversation' (1978), and that paper is the most approximate referent for what is said about CA below.

In doing CA the ethnomethodologist is not a participant observer, present at the talk and having some status among the speakers. Instead, he or she listens to a tape-recording of the talk (recorded no matter how, possibly for non-social-scientific purposes) and then makes a transcription. The analysis is based on a study of the transcription, with possible reference back to the tape. Since in much of the work little or no reference is made to the situation in which the conversation took place, and little may in fact be known about it, the ethnomethodologist is exterior to his or her materials for analysis. But in the method of analysis, the ethnomethodologist grants him or herself a significant interiority: he invokes his competence as a member of the same speech community as the speakers in order to claim to know enough of what they are doing in the speech to enable him to get on with the analytic problem of how these doings are accomplished, i.e., what conventional resources are required. The analytic stance is thus simultaneously exterior and interior.

Being simultaneously exterior and interior is no easy business, to wit: what if I were to provide a quotation to support my assertion, above, that conversation analysts depend on their knowledge as competent members of a speech community shared with those they study? I could, for example, quote Turner: 'It is by virtue of my status as a competent member that I can recurrently locate in my transcripts instances of "the same" activity' (Turner, 1974: 204–5). What would such a quotation count as? Would I confirm my own interiority by displaying that I can quote from the corpus of material (EM) about which I am writing, or would it suggest my exteriority by contrasting the weight of my opinions to those of Turner, whose quotation is presented as necessary to buttress my own statement, which is perhaps not fully defensible if left to stand on its own?

I have thus created a position which is neither interior nor exterior, and this position is an analogue to that of the ethnomethodologist *vis-à-vis* society. The ethnomethodologist as a member of society is competent to know some things (e.g., to make decisions regarding 'sameness'), but his member's competence is somehow incomplete, because other issues require analysis. Judging 'sameness' is apparently a matter of competence being sufficient by itself, but other matters, such as those which Turner (1974: 205) calls 'how utterances come off as recognizable unit activities', require analysis which is outside the play of normal competence. Thus, the ethnomethodologist simultaneously maintains an attitude of interiority (competence) and exteriority (analysis) *vis-à-vis* society.

One way to describe being simultaneously interior and exterior, both eccentric and concentric, is that it is to be decentred. With regard to the theme of decentring I am required, by academic convention, to inscribe into my text a citation, '(Derrida, 1976; see also Silverman, 1978)'. As a reflexive display of what decentring is, let me consider what such a citation does. In citing Derrida, I mark my arguments as concentric to his and eccentric to EM, in the corpus of which Derrida is not normally cited. But in so far as this is a paper 'about' EM, do I not also suggest that one (Derrida, EM) is about to be brought into the orbit of the other (but who into which?)? Most citations are concentric: by the act of citation, the author centres himself within some group of others whom he cites, the commonality of whom is both the topic and resource, the project and the possibility, of his writing. Citing Derrida in a paper ostensibly about EM is eccentric, and by its eccentricity becomes an act in which the author is decentred: is he an ethnomethodologist or a post-structuralist, and what relation between the two is suggested? An opposition is established, and the expectation created that one term of this opposition will come to govern the other, e.g., Derrida will be assimilated to EM, or vice versa. The point of decentring is to frustrate this expectation, maintaining instead that the utility and even the intelligibility of either term depends on the continuing opposition of the other.

Or, decentring could be described as the effect of placing the citation in quotation marks, by which it is simultaneously a citation and a prototype for a citation. I am now treating it as a prototype, but since this treatment is suggested by the texts cited, it is simultaneously a real citation and an example of a citation. Decentring is the refusal to establish a hierarchy, as, for example, a hierarchy is established within the citation between Derrida and Silverman. By writing 'see also', I relegate the text of Silverman's to a status somehow (though exactly how is indexical) supplementary to Derrida's. Without the 'see also', the relation of Silverman and Derrida would be recursive: each would have to be read simultaneously in terms of the other, the reader being decentred between both; with the inscription 'see also', this recursivity becomes a hierarchy, and both Silverman and the reader are placed in concentric relation to Derrida.

This decentring is precisely the situation of the ethnomethodologist who is both interior and exterior to some conversation, and it is the situation of the speech which is both lived in conversation and analysed in a transcript, and it is the situation I claimed for myself in choosing the Maynard quotation. To place oneself within such an opposition, rather than taking a stance at one or the other of its poles, is to perform an act of decentring. What such an act tries to accomplish is an escape from a traditional logic of place, by which something is somewhere and therefore not elsewhere. Within this logic, I am either an ethnomethodologist or not, and the ethnomethodologist must act as either a member of society or an analyst of society.

What underlies the situations defined by such a logic of place is a logic of supplementarity, and at the centre of my critique of CA is its formulation of the supplementarity of the transcription. Analysts of conversation use the transcription as a supplement to the tape-recording, which is in turn considered supplementary to the live conversation. Ethnomethodologists would prefer to play a tape rather than to present just a written transcript (which always stands to be corrected by the tape), and member-speakers in situ are understood to 'know' what their speech acts are doing, the problem of analysis being to recover this knowledge at a reflective level.

What is important about supplements is that they inscribe a hierarchy in which the form judged to be supplementary is subordinated: in this case, the live conversation enjoys a privilege over the tape, which in turn is privileged over the transcription. Thus, analysts, looking at the transcription, who dispute matters of competence seek resolution by listening to the tape, and disputes over how the tape is to be heard (i.e., what is a competent hearing) could, at least in principle, be resolvable by reference to how members in the situation acted. Jokes have been particularly good topics for conversational analysis, since members laugh at the end of what they hear as joking, thus providing behaviour in the situation which warrants the analysts' own competent understanding that 'joking' was the activity being practised.

Oppositions thus suggest a logic of supplementarity, and supplementarity suggests hierarchy, e.g., the text evaluated as supplementary to personal instruction is subordinated to it. This paper is designed to generate a hierarchy of sorts, but the sort desired is a sort of counter-hierarchy. The need for such a counter-hierarchy, and the serious problem for EM, is that usual notions of hierarchy are mis-taken; by taking matters one way rather than another, something has been missed. Of course if matters had been taken the other way, something else would have been missed too, so the problem is not to reverse the hierarchy, but to comprehend what it might mean to be decentred within it.

What, then, does it mean for something (me, the ethnomethodologist, the conversation) to be decentred? At the end of the first section I wrote that, 'The presence of the other is not only made possible by, and even is nothing but, its surrounding aura of interpretations ...' This statement can now be glossed. In the necessity of interpretation, the speaker/writer is decentred by being externalized in the sign and then internalized in the other's interpretation of this sign. The signs presented in speech or text decentre the presence of the speaker/writer by becoming themselves the objects of the interpretation of some other. Speech and text are not supplements to a presence which exists in unmediated form 'elsewhere', but rather they are the constitutive form of any possible presence, which can only be always already decentred.

One of the principle contributions of Derrida has been to assert the nature of presence to be always already decentred in the multiplicity of interpretive acts of its auditors. The early EM of indexicality, reflexivity and glossing had already grasped this idea with the insight that the interpretation of the sign is always uncertain. In later EM, however, the centrality of irremediable uncertainty got lost: speech, i.e., the speech of Maynard's instructor, is afforded a kind of privilege, and this privilege mirrors that afforded to the speaking subject by analysts of conversation. Derrida's work seems necessary to understand this loss.

Returning to the transcription, what it ought to be understood as is not a supplement to speech, but a decentring of speech. The essence of this decentring is that no one position of speech is privileged, neither conversation in situ, nor on tape, nor in writing. Instead, the possibility of being of each of these is understood as dependent on the others. The relation of speech, tape and transcript exemplifies what Derrida calls 'differ-ance', which is perhaps most simply described (to the untutored) as a double pun (see Derrida, 1973: 129ff.; 1981: 27ff.). In one movement of this pun Derrida combines the verbs 'to differ' and 'to defer', the latter principally in the sense of 'to put off'. Thus, the tape and the transcript differ from each other, and the transcription represents a deferring, in time, of the tape which precedes it, just as the tape itself defers the presence of a conversation which took place at an (again) earlier time.

The pun is further intensified in the case of CA by the process of 'deference' through which the understanding of the tape and the production of the transcription alternatively defer to the other. The tape is afforded the privileged status, with the transcription always in some sense derivative and supplementary, but the recording does not simply generate the written word, because in the act of transcription what is written also reorganizes the sense of what is heard. What is curious is that the original speech is maintained to be outside of any relation of constitutive reciprocity with tape or transcript; such a relation could be posited, much as Sontag (1977) posits the reciprocal relation between lived experience and the experience of, and in, photographs.

In the second movement of his pun Derrida changes the spelling of 'difference' to 'differance', the latter spelling being marked in English by writing it as 'differ-ance'. The significance of this move is that the change of 'e' to 'a' is visible in the written text but not (in French) in the spoken word. Derrida's early work emphasizes the consequence to Western thought of the opposition of speech to writing, and the privilege traditionally afforded to speech within this opposition. His objective is not to reverse the traditional hierarchy, but rather to function in his own writing as a corrective to its excess.

Such undoing of traditional, oppositional hierarchies is the beginning of what Derrida calls 'deconstruction'.

Why, then, did I choose the quotation from Maynard? Because it is a supplementary text, and in affording it some privilege I undid the hierarchy which suppresses such texts. The eccentricity of the selection is thus itself an elemental act of deconstruction. More important, the hierarchy which the quotation formulates, tutored and untutored, depends on affording a privilege to the spoken word (the instructor's involvement) over the intelligibility of the written text. This hierarchy is not incidental in Maynard's review, but rather it recapitulates the presupposition of the practice of conversation analysis. In this practice, the original insights of EM, which involved the decentring of presence through the necessity of interpretation, have become lost. The deconstructive project, which is out of ethnomethodology, is to decentre the text of talk, and in doing so to decentre the notion of sociology itself.

Decentring sociology
In its relegation of the text (either textbook, primary source or transcription) to a position of supplementarity, EM has, to its peril, followed sociology in general. In sociology, the written texts are understood as derivative descriptions of the world, or as supplementary to a reality which has its existence elsewhere; these supplements may be more or less useful, but they are supplements none the less. The texts, the writings of sociology, are treated as nothing more than traces — provisional, ephemeral approximations of the presence of a world which is always outside the text. The texts mediate our understanding of this world, but this mediation is a lapse, a falling from the grace of immediate vision. For a sociologist to take the writing or reading of texts too seriously is to perpetrate a decadence which is one of the typical scandals of sociology (known as 'navel gazing'). The essence of this scandal is claiming for the text a presence of its own, which is not supplementary but complementary to the presupposed presence of 'the real world'.

Taking the writing and reading of the text seriously threatens a certain conception of sociology by called attention to the mediation of sociological knowledge by its written form. Knowledge in sociology, like any knowledge, is mediated by numerous layerings of interpretation; those least attended to are the textual. The ideas of 'reliability' and 'validity' seek to neutralize the intrusion of interpretive activity; by rhetorically constructing 'the data' as the unmediated presence of the world, the possibility of direct knowledge is sustained. Taking the text seriously, and understanding the possibility of 'the data' as dependent on certain rhetorical conventions of social scientific writing, undercuts the possibility of direct experience of the world.

Ethnomethodologists have with few exceptions (e.g., Garfinkel, 1967: 285–8; Wieder, 1974) never been particularly attentive to the production of their own texts. Ethnomethodologists write defences, apologies, critiques of 'other' sociologies, but when has EM provided a critique of its own practices? Not only in CA but also in recent sociology of science work (see Garfinkel et al., 1981) the direction seems to be towards self-effacement rather than self-reflection. The EM of '"Good" organizational reasons for "bad" clinical records' (Garfinkel, 1967) might have asked why all the textbooks seem inadequate, i.e., '"good" epistemological reasons for "bad" textbook definitions'. I miss such an interest in present work. Possibly it would be unrealistic to expect such an interest. The nature of life and texts may be such that critique must always await the next generation.

What is necessary as a completion to the task of EM is to decentre sociology between text and world. In order to undo the hierarchy which has existed heretofore, I propose to treat the text — the writing of sociology — not as supplementary to society, individuals etc., but as foundational. Eventually, text and world must be understood as mutually constitutive in this sense: the problems of reading and writing texts, problems of working through layers of interpretive possibilities and never being able to justify on principle the choice of one interpretation (reading) over another, are the problems of everyday social life. Interaction is the problem of interpreting some presence of the other when presented with the text of that other's conversation and action, and the essence of that text is to be indexical, reflexive and so forth. One social actor cannot 'know' another; he can only suggest interpretive possibilities, glosses, out of which that other is constituted.

The creation of an epistemological milieu in which neither text nor world enjoys a privilege over the other can begin with Derrida's suggestion (1981: 41–2) that to undo a traditionally maintained hierarchy, it is necessary to effect a temporary reversal of its terms. If it is necessary, in order to decentre sociology, to undo the hierarchy of the presence of the world over the text, that undoing begins by locating sociological practice as having its existence in texts, and so I have attempted to locate the present argument in the text of EM and the counter-text of this paper itself.

A final example: what was done in 1967, what was the 'practical accomplishment', in the naming of 'ethnomethodology'? A difference was created, the difference of EM and not-EM. In the formulation of that difference, each term became meaningful in so far as it diferred from the other, and thus an understanding of either presupposed not just an act of deferring the other, but also the possibility of understanding either required some deference to the understanding of the other. The possibility of sustaining a relation of differ-ance was, however, apparently unthinkable on both 'sides'; what counted was to gain privilege in what was conceivable only as a hierarchy. Depending on one's stance, what ethnomethodologists variously call 'conventional sociology' (i.e., non-EM) was merely prefatory to EM, or as critics such as Colemen and Coser asserted, EM was, at most, a perverse supplement to sociology.

The inevitability of this controversy originates in an act of naming. Recall another such act: Odysseus escapes the cyclops Polythemos as long as he refuses to name himself; when he finally shouts back his name, the curse of Poseidon falls upon him. Until he names himself, Odysseus is no-body; he is decentred, and being decentred gives him certain invulnerability. In naming himself, he centres himself and thus becomes (again) an object in that sequence of hierarchical struggles which war has been and his homecoming will be. In this chapter I have inscribed the name of 'deconstruction' into the terms of theoretical controversy in sociology. I propose deconstruction as a corrective to EM, but more specifically as a displacement of its name. A relation of displacement, Freud has taught us, is a decentring relation in which both terms retain their force. Thus any hierarchy based on displacement is a counter-hierarchy, because the relation of its terms is never based on subordination, but can only be one of differ-ance.

Deconstruction is not an '-ology', a study of; rather it continues to assert its connection to its verb form, 'to deconstruct'. To do deconstruction, as it has been done in philosophy and literary criticism and as I am now proposing to do it in sociology, is to create texts which inscribe themselves in other texts. Thus Derrida's work is a self-inscription in such texts as those of Nietzsche, Heidegger, Husserl, the Romantic poets, Lévi-Strauss, Freud, Foucault and Lacan. My introducing deconstruction into sociological discourse by its inscription into a collection of texts, e.g., EM, is not only a concentric choice but an inevitable one — deconstruction can always only be inscribed in other texts. There is no new hierarchy because there is no deconstruction in itself, only a series of deconstructive inscriptions.

Deconstruction is pure differ-ance; it can only exercise its process (or process its exercises) in other texts. The 'being' of deconstruction requires being in the other text, within which its difference from that text is expressable, and in this expression of difference the other text is deferred. But this deferring is itself a kind of privilege:

deconstruction does its work by the attention of reading which its inscriptions afford those texts. Thus the principle of deconstruction is to privilege those texts, or aspects of texts, which have been suppressed by traditional hierarchies, and so to undo the epistemological ordering inscribed by those hierarchies. Being neither coextensive with those 'other' texts nor independent of them, deconstruction is always already decentred. What the preceding exercise in deconstruction inscribes is: out of ethnomethodology.

References

Derrida, Jacques (1973) *Speech and Phenomena.* Translated by David B. Allison. Evanston: Northwestern University Press.

Derrida, Jacques (1976) *Of Grammatology.* Translated by Gayatri Spivak. Baltimore: Johns Hopkins University Press.

Derrida, Jacques (1981) *Positions.* Translated by Alan Bass. Chicago: University of Chicago Press.

Fish, Stanley E. (1982) 'With the Compliments of the Author: Reflections on Austin and Derrida', *Critical Inquiry*, 8(4): 693–721.

Garfinkel, Harold (1967) *Studies in Ethnomethodology.* Englewood Cliffs, NJ: Prentice-Hall

Garfinkel, Harold and Harvey Sacks (1970) 'On Formal Structures of Practical Actions', pp. 337–66 in John C. McKinney and Edward Tiryakian (eds), *Theoretical Sociology: Perspectives and Development.* New York: Appleton Century Crofts.

Garfinkel, Harold, Michael Lynch and Eric Livingston (1981) 'The Work of a Discovering Science Construed with Materials from the Optically Discovered Pulsar', *Philosophy of Social Science*, 11: 131–58.

Goffman, Erving (1959) *The Presentation of Self in Everyday Life.* Garden City: Doubleday.

Maynard, Douglas W. (1982) 'Review of Warren Handel, Ethnomethodology: How People Make Sense', *Contemporary Sociology*, 11(6): 715–6.

Sacks, Harvey (1974) 'On the Analysability of Stories by Children', pp. 216–32 in Roy Turner (ed.), *Ethnomethodology.* Harmondsworth: Penguin Books.

Sacks, Harvey, Emanuel A. Schegloff and Gail Jefferson (1978) 'A Simplist Systematics for the Organization of Turn Taking in Conversation', pp. 7–55 in Jim Schenkein (ed.), *Studies in the Organization of Conversational Interaction.* New York: Academic Press.

Silverman, Hugh (1978) 'Self-Decentering: Derrida Incorporated', *Research in Phenomenology*, 8: 45–65.

Sontag, Susan (1977) *On Photography.* New York: Delta Dell.

Turner, Roy (1974) 'Words, Utterances and Activities', pp. 197–215 in Roy Turner (ed.), *Ethnomethodology.* Harmondsworth, Penguin Books.

Weider, D. Lawrence (1974) *Language and Social Reality.* The Hague: Mouton.

Wittgenstein, Ludwig (1958) *Philosophical Investigations.* Translated by G.E.M. Anscombe (3rd ed.) New York: Macmillan.

7
Talk and identity: some convergences in micro-sociology*

Paul Atkinson

This chapter deals with two approaches to sociological work which are often included under the rubric of 'micro-sociology', although that designation in itself is not one I should wish to endorse. I wish to remark on some relationships between 'ethnography' and 'conversational analysis', illustrating my argument primarily with recent British studies on organizational settings. In such a brief paper I am forced to oversimplify: I acknowledge from the outset that the two areas discussed are not homogeneous, and that debates about their relative status are by no means clear-cut. My review of the empirical literature is necessarily partial.

I shall argue for a principled and systematic rapprochement between ethnography and conversational analysis, despite the fact that many commentators portray them as mutually exclusive categories and others find no relevance in one or the other. Furthermore, I shall suggest that my argument in fact makes a virtue out of necessity: in the context of particular empirical studies, such rapprochement has taken place *de facto*. Finally I shall suggest that such developments represent a retrieval of conversational analysis rather than a dilution or corruption. I do not intend to propose that the two approaches are 'really the same', nor to attempt some grand synthesis. In the first instance my aim is much more modest: I shall argue that differences between the two are by no means as radical as is sometimes suggested, and that principled, selective trade-offs are possible and desirable. In the course of this paper I shall confirm my remarks on 'ethnography' to empirical investigations which, broadly speaking, derive from 'interactionist' perspectives. I recognize that this in no sense exhausts the usage of the term, and that 'ethnography' as such is not tied directly to any one theoretical tradition, while having family resemblances with several.

A number of proponents of ethnomethodology have explicitly announced the incompatibility of conversational analysis and ethnographic approaches. Atkinson and Drew (1979), in introducing their work on the organization of courtroom proceedings, make the distinction quite sharply. In attempting to justify their own approach, which is essentially conversation-analytic, they argue that the ethnographer is necessarily confronted by insurmountable problems, not least in the problematic status of his descriptions. As Atkinson and Drew (1979: 25) put it:

> The selection and design of the descriptions appearing in the final report can thus be seen to be only the latest practical solution to a long line of descriptive problems which will have been arising and being resolved continually during the course of the research ... A general implication of all this is that there is a very considerable distance between the empirical data ... and those who read, hear and assess the reports on the data.

Here Atkinson and Drew draw on the classic forms of ethnomethodological critique, in particular the notion of analysts' reliance on members' knowledge:

> For the ethnographer, then, the problem of coming to terms with the ethnomethodological constraint against the unexplicated reliance on members' competences in doing research is particularly acute. Thus, however reflexive he tries to be about the way his research was directed by taken for granted commonsense knowledge, and achieved through the use of everyday methods of practical reasoning, he will never be able to explicate them satisfactorily for his readers. For one thing, a pre-condition for being able to do such a thing would be that ethnomethodology's topic (members' competences) had already been extensively explored and documented to a point where a detailed explication of how members' methods worked to produce ethnographic reports could be provided. (Atkinson and Drew, 1979: 25)

Here, and in similar arguments from other authors, is articulated the distinction — fundamental to the ethnomethodological programme — between 'topics' and 'resources'. It is this issue which is held to mark the epistemological divide between the ethnographic and the conversation-analytic. This is a point to which I shall return, when I shall argue that the topic/resource distinction has been rendered in terms which are too rigid and absolute.

To a considerable extent, the tension between ethnography and conversational analysis is detectable *within* ethnomethodology, as well as between it and constructive sociology. Button (1977), for instance, argues for such a distinction within the ethnomethodological tradition. He identifies two tendencies: 'fine-grained sequential analysis' and analyses having 'an ethnographic character'. Button's distinction would include, as instances of the latter, Zimmerman (1969), Wieder (1974) and Sacks (1972). In practice, particular ethnomethodological studies draw on elements of both tendencies: for instance, Schegloff (1968) on insertion sequences, and on formulating place (1972). The coexistence and intermingling of these two strands with ethnomethodology may suggest that the sort of distinction Atkinson and Drew insist on is exaggerated.

In recent years the distinction has been blurred by a growing number of researchers engaged in the production of what can be termed 'ethnomethodologically informed ethnography', in which elements of sequential analysis are drawn on. In this context I would instance published work on features of educational settings (e.g. Hammersley, 1974, 1976, 1977, 1981) and on medical settings (e.g. Dingwall, 1980; Hughes, 1982). None the less, it would appear to be the case that many ethnographers, for instance those working in the interactionist tradition, have not paid systematic attention to conversational analyses: selective uses of ethnomethodological notions have been on an *ad hoc* basis.

The apparent failure of interactionist sociology to borrow or to develop a systematic approach to language use in natural settings is in itself remarkable, given the centrality of communicative acts to the epistemology of the tradition — 'understated' though its theoretical formulations may be (Rock, 1979). Indeed, the very reliance upon an understated, oral tradition has not been conducive to conceptual clarity. Knowledge has largely been warranted by the investigation's transactions in and with the social world, without explicit analysis of the form and content of such transactions.

Advocacy of rapprochement does not deny that there are important differences between much ethnography and much conversational analysis. Hammersley (1981) has captured one major dimension of difference, in terms of the distinction between 'action' and 'competence' models:

> In the competence approach, particular instances or recurring patterns of human activity are treated as competent displays of culture memberships, and the discovery of the rules or procedures by which that activity was, or could have been, produced is taken as the exclusive goal.

Under this rubric Hammersley collects the ethnography of speaking, speech act analysis, conversational analysis and discourse analysis. In contrast,

> Action theory ... while similarly anti-behaviourist, treats patterns of activity as the product of interaction between groups with different concerns and interests, who define situations in distinctive ways and develops strategies for furthering those interests, often by means of negotiation and bargaining with one another. In relation to any particular action, the action theorist asks what intentions and motives

underlie it and how these relate to the actor's perspective or definition of the situation.

Here Hammersley locates interactionist ethnography, transactional anthropology and social phenomenology.

Now, as I have already indicated, there are aspects of 'action' approaches which have been notably underdeveloped — not least interactionism's paradoxical failure adequately to theorize language. Similarly, many aspects of 'action' methodology — including ethnography — remain poorly developed. However, I am not persuaded that this is an argument for celebrating a conversation-analytic 'competence' approach at the expense of the other. Like Hammersley, I remain sceptical of the insistence on the priority of 'social order' as the problematic for a competence-based sociology. Such formulations run the risk of recapitulating the errors of a normative-functionalist analytic framework. Such dangers are compounded when the proponents of conversational analysis avoid the explicit formulation of any theoretical or methodological stance: 'Because it lays great stress on the identification of issues and actions which are of significance to participants, and because it has no theories about interaction that it is concerned to test, the procedure of analysis is primarily inductive.' (Wootton, 1981.)

Rather than denigrate or abandon ethnography, then, my aim is to recognize its problems and its shortcomings, and to examine possibilities for its development. Now, it seems to me that there are two senses in which the ethnographer is to benefit from his or her colleagues who practise conversational analysis. The first concerns the conduct of ethnographic fieldwork, and the second concerns issues of analytic, substantive significance. In the last analysis these two are identical. The logic of interactionist ethnography is predicated on the homology between the social action as observed, and participant observation as social action: that is, the identity of the social actor as known object and as knowing subject. This is, after all, central to Mead's theory of knowledge as well as implicit in the empirical investigations of interactionist researchers (Rock, 1979). I shall, however, consider them separately for the purposes of argument.

In the classical conception of ethnography, knowledge is rooted and warranted in the transactions through which the researcher explores so-called 'social worlds'. There is no difference in principle between the ethnographer's activities as researcher and 'lay' everyday social action. The difference lies in the 'attitude' of the former. The ethnographer should aim to place him or herself in the position of Schutz's 'stranger', who is the prototype and metaphor of the phenomenological enquirer (Schutz, 1964). While commentators on ethnography often appeal to a commitment to 'naturalism', that should not be interpreted as a commitment to the researcher dwelling in the 'natural attitude'. Quite the reverse, the ethnographic commitment to reflexiveness (which is rooted in interactionist anthropology) resists the natural attitude. Indeed, the possibility of 'discovery' lies largely in the space created by such resistance.

Critics like Atkinson and Drew are, therefore, right to remark that the ethnographer depends on members' competence — in the most general sense — but wrong to imply that particular interpretive methods or procedures are invoked in an entirely uncritical fashion. This does not blind us to the fact, however, that interactionists and ethnographers may be less than perfectly equipped to do so. And while perfection is unattainable, we can nevertheless attempt to be more systematic or more principled in establishing the underpinnings of ethnographic enquiry.

Many aspects of ethnographic method rest at the level of an oral tradition of advice, maxims and personal experience. While the 'competence' (in both senses) of the ethnographer is developed through apprenticeship and experience, it is poorly understood and articulated. Now, *pace* some ethnomethodologists, some reliance on tacit knowledge is characteristic of probably all scholarly and scientific activity (cf. Polanyi, 1974; Ravetz, 1973). It would be a mistake were one to strive for an exhaustive, inductively derived foundation.

On the other hand, the formal insights of conversational analysts, together with those of discourse analysts, speech act theorists, linguistic anthropologists and the like, can help to inform the reflexive competence. As Williams (1981) has recently suggested in a discussion of research methods training:

> there have been a number of contributions to the direct analysis of naturally occurring talk that are of particular relevance to the conduct of field research, both at the level of fieldworker conduct and the level of data creation. Three types of work seem especially exciting and noteworthy: 'the ethnography of speaking', 'dialogue analysis' and 'conversation analysis'. Each of these contributions have developed slightly different ways of working, but each is closely related to the traditional interests of sociological fieldwork. While they differ in the extent of the imperialism of their claims to offer relevant advice to fieldworkers, exposure to all of them only serves to increase the resources available to those who wish to conduct ethnographic research.

As Williams suggests, the search for formal foundations does not look to conversational analysis alone, but it clearly represents a major contribution to such an undertaking.

In a similar vein, the conversation analytic tendency suggests convergence at a substantive level. I shall now go on to outline a number of themes which illustrate this latter contention.

I begin with the commonplace observation that natural language use is a matter of interest for the conversational analyst and the ethnographer alike. The 'traditional', interactionist ethnographer should be concerned with the exploration of the formal properties of talk in given social settings. Language is — in terms of interactionist theory — constitutive of everyday action.

The potential relevance of an awareness of the formal properties of natural talk may be illustrated by reference to ethnographers' abiding concern with the social production, transformation and display of 'selves' and 'identities'. As Rock (1979) underlines, the self lies at the heart of interactionist thought: 'Symbolic interactionism thus conceives the self to be the lens through which the social world is refracted. It is the medium which realizes the logic of social forms.' Hence many empirical studies in this tradition focus on the social formation and reproduction of actors' 'selves', their 'moral careers' and the like.

Furthermore, the interactionist actor is essentially a speaking subject. The self is identified as a locus or space within a conversational system: the dialogue of self and other, and the dialogue of the reflexive subject-object. In interactionist anthropology, then, the maintenance, transformation and reproduction is (or ought to be) fundamentally a matter of speech or discursive practices.

But these latter issues have tended to escape interactionist ethnographers. They may acknowledge Mead as a 'founder' or inspiration, but the spirit of Mead is poorly reflected in the work of his would-be followers. Moreover, the treatments of language that do appear have particular limitations. By and large language practices are dealt with primarily in terms of 'naming' or 'labelling', with corresponding lack of attention to the formal properties of language use, or to the analysis of language as social action.

It is abundantly clear, however, that close attention to the organization of talk can directly inform an ethnographic interest in the social production and display of 'selves' or 'identities'. In this task, the analytic machinery of conversational analysis furnishes a powerful resource. (I shall return to my quite deliberate use of 'resource' in this context towards the end of this chapter.)

I want to exemplify this by reference to the notion of 'recipient design'. As Sacks et al. (1974) suggest:

> RECIPIENT DESIGN [is] perhaps the most general principle which particularizes conversational interactions. [It refers] to a multitude of

respects in which talk by a party in a conversation is constructed or designed in ways which display an orientation and sensitivity to the particular other(s) who are the co-participants.

In other words, it is asserted to be a universal feature of talk that an utterance produced by any party is designed to 'take account of' the audience to whom it is addressed. A particular sketch of talk is therefore recipiently designed in so far as it can be heard as oriented to an identifiable feature or features among the many which may be used to 'identify' members.

Seen from this point of view, then, 'identities' and 'identifications' will be regarded by the ethnographer as matters of language practice. But such activity will be treated in terms which transcend mere naming of 'labelling'. The recipient design of conversational talk provides one way in which identity-relevant work may get done through the social organization of talk itself.

This can, perhaps, be illustrated with the following extract from a transcribed tape-recording of a higher education seminar. In doing so I shall not attempt to reproduce a faithful and detailed conversational-analytic account as such: that is not my purpose here.

At a gross level of characterization, one may describe this particular sequence of seminar talk as beginning with a 'disagreement' between a student (S) and a tutor (T), over the criminality of minor traffic offences (lines 9–27). While there are other parties to the talk, who witness, and to some extent participate, I shall address my remarks particularly to this dispute between student and tutor. The 'trajectory' of this dispute shifts as the discussion develops and as the parties develop their respective 'positions'. The dispute (grossly put) 'boils down to' the potentially criminal status of the student (S8 — lines 48–53).

In the light of the later direction taken by the discussion, the point at which the student first speaks, and the fact that each of his successive turns in the talk are disagreements, appears to be far from coincidental. With this in mind, let us now turn to a more detailed consideration of the data extract, with regard to the interactional consequences — and identity-relevant work — of the organization of the talk.

We begin with the tutor's formulation of her example of those crimes which are not immoral (lines 1–8). While an empirically adequate specification of the phenomenon, the particular formulation proposed has interactional consequences. By designing her utterances as she does ('a lot of people would see … minor … traffic offences … as immoral') the tutor clearly avoids the issue of whether she herself sees those crimes as immoral. Thus she

DATA EXTRACT

1	T:	...You can also have behaviour the other
2		way around which is criminal but not immoral,
3		a lot of people would see: un-traffic offences
4		Y'know the minor ones in particular, not perhaps
5		dangerous driving th- as not particularly
6		immoral offences = but they are criminal
7		offences, you'd be- you're subject to fine: by
8		the courts. (S) If you um y'know ⎸(if you)
9	S_8:	⎹Aren't you
10		Stressing it a bit by calling a traffic offence a
11		crime?
12	T:	Well ⎸in the technical sense it is – ⎸it is a crime
13		⎹Is it not an offence ⎹it is a crime is it?
14		
15	S_3:	It's punishable by law isn't that the // definition?
16		It's punishable by law
17	T:	Right
18	S_8:	Well that is not what one normally thinks
19		of a: criminal a criminal is somebody who's-
20		uh well somebody who's been to prison
21		very often, but not an ordinary citizen who:
22		um- (S) commits a parking offence to regard
23		him as a criminal you wouldn't in the
24		normal accepted sense of the term, regard
25		a person like that as a criminal. Would
26		you?
27	S_5:	(Well the person isn't asking that)
28	S_8:	(Would you?)=
29	T	Yes this is indeed raising that-that//very
30		question.
31	S_3:	mm:
32	T:	I m'n technically=
33	S_8:	Well that is what I want to get clear. Do we
34		regard as criminals every person who commits
35		an offence, whatever is the nature of the offence=
36		Whether its a small offence or a big offence?.
37	T_1:	What (do the- the) rest of you think?
38	S_7:	=Its according to your point of view. Whatever
39		you think uh you've gathered from the various
40		accounts (maybe reading these) and you've
41		got your own sort of opinion= We've all
42		got different opinions an' what we think is
43		particularly relative at that particular time
44		maybe even in our life span.
45	T:	But at the same time we c'd there's
46		probably a majority view. I think (George) y- y-

```
47            in a sense you're saying│there's certainly offences are
48    S₈:                             │Yes well I've committed tw-
49            two offences in recent months (of which) I was
50            very annoyed, parking offences, and//I was fined
51            six pounds for each (an' they're=) under a)//
52            fixed penalty. But I don't regard myself as
53            a criminal do you?=
54    T:      mm: mm
55    T:      Right, yes.
56    T:      =No=
```

simultaneously avoids the interactional consequences, whatever they may be, of 'stating an opinion' (cf. Sacks, 1976).

While the tutor's turn is apparently designed to convey an 'objective', 'matter-of-fact' categorization of traffic offences, it also appears to be treated as a statement of 'opinion' by the student (S8) who challenges what he hears as the tutor's view (lines 9–11): 'Aren't you stressing it a bit by calling a traffic offence a crime?' (This particular turn can also be said to 'pre-sequence' agreement/ disagreement — see Schegloff, 1968.) Stating an opinion or aligning oneself with a particular position or point of view can have consequences, and this may be attended to in an utterance's design. This accounts for example, for such displays of 'distancing', 'tact' or 'mitigation' as: 'in my humble opinion ...'; and what Stubbs (1973) identifies as 'Personal-Point-of-View Prefaces': 'personally I think we really ...'; 'my real opinion is ...'; 'I certainly don't ...' (cf. Burton, 1980: 146ff.).

Throughout the remainder of the sequence various utterances are designed with their status as possible 'opinions', and hence designed with respect to their potential interactional significance. Each of the tutor's successive turns, except for one (line 56) to be dealt with later, are constructed with a view to establishing the non-opinionated character of the first turn. The use of phrases such as 'in the technical sense' (line 12), 'it is a crime' (line 12), I m'n technically' (line 32) and 'a majority view' (line 46) are all indicative of this orientation. Similarly, with regard to the student's turns, the following items exhibit the same concern: 'is it not an offence' (line 13); 'what one normally thinks' (line 18); 'a criminal is somebody who's ... been to prison' (lines 19–20); 'but not an ordinary citizen who...' (line 21); 'you wouldn't in the normal accepted sense ...' (lines 23–5); 'do we regard as criminals ...' (lines 32–3).

It would appear, throughout these various utterances, that while the two parties are formulating matters of opinion and matters of fact, they are concerned to display their personal independence or distance from the issues they address. This can be related directly to the fact that many of the turns in the sequence are simultaneously constructed as disagreements or agreements. In themselves, agreements and disagreements are interactionally implicative and 'identity-relevant'. (See Pomerantz, 1975 and 1978, for a consideration of the organization of disagreement sequences.)

As the argument develops, it is apparent that the participants' respective positions come closer together. At the end of the sequence (lines 45–56), the tutor's turn admits of the possibility of a 'majority view', or opinion, which may or may not be her own. This admission occasions the introduction by the student (lines 48–53) of identity-relevant material ('well I've committed two offences ...'). Simultaneously, within the same turn, the student produces an opinion ('I don't regard myself as a criminal') and what might be termed an 'opinion elicitator' with the use of the 'tag question' ('... do you?'). At this point the tutor also voices an opinion (line 56), in agreement with the student's prior turn. Thus, as invited to do so, the tutor reciprocates the production of an opinion with an equivalent.

In this review of the sequence of talk, then, we have seen how the formal arrangement of turns as components of agreement/ disagreement sequences can be related to the student's identity revelation in lines 48–53. This student's prior turns, in which the tutor's formulations are challenged, are thus explicable in terms of the avoidance of the categorization as 'criminal'. Were this student to volunteer his personal 'experience' prior to the 'argument' then he might lay himself open to the implicit acceptance of the categorization 'criminal'.

The particular interactional issue in this sequence, therefore, revolves round the contested nature of 'criminality'. The process of identity negotiation entailed here involves protecting a participant's identity from a 'real' challenge, by establishing that the challenge is 'merely' a matter of 'opinion'. Throughout this sequence, then, we find matters of relevance to 'identity' being delicately managed through the sequential organization of the talk itself.

Here we find precisely displayed the sort of analytic concerns of interactionist sociology, and typically addressed in ethnographic research. In pursuing such investigations of the 'fine-grained' organization of natural language use, we may thus take seriously the commitment to view language as constitutive of social selves and social order, rather than paying lip-service to it.

In making this observation we do not claim that no other authors have drawn on such analysis of natural language. French and

Maclure (1979), Hammersley (1977), Payne and Hustler (1980) are among those who have displayed such interests.

The issue of 'recipient design', for example, has implicitly informed the investigation of the construction of teachers' questions and pupils' answers. Hammersley (1977), for example, shows how teachers' questions are constructed with a view to the pupils' perceived resources-at-hand: likewise, he comments on how pupils may draw on their understanding of such recipient design in searching for the appropriate 'right' answer (cf. also Mehan, 1974; Maclure and French, 1980). For a parallel treatment of 'recipient design' in a medical context, see Heath (1982). Heath comments on general practitioners' use of medical records to identify patients and topics with a view to appropriate recipient design in the organization of consultation talk.

Several discussions of the 'strategies' of teacher-questioning have remarked that they could be thought of as 'pseudo-questions', in that the question is not a genuine request for information (cf. e.g. Stubbs, 1975). On the other hand, the fact that such questions display 'recipient design', they share in a feature common to all such exchanges. Whether or not the questioner knows the answer, he must construct a request or elicitation on the basis of the assumed identity, knowledge, competence and so on of the party to whom it is addressed. Such recipient design thus has major consequences for interactional work between the parties, with regard to identities and information-states.

It is by virtue of recipient design that a teacher may construct a turn very precisely in order to monitor pupils' attention, discipline them for inattention, 'show them up' and so on. Hence the teacher may formulate a question which should be answerable by any member of the class and address it directly to a pupil who is suspected of inattention, and whose shortcomings may be exposed by a failure to answer correctly. As Hammersley (1977) puts it: 'On such occasions the teacher is attempting to maximize the attention of the class by demonstrating the potential built into directly selective questions for the embarrassment of pupils who have not been "following" the lesson.' 'Recipient design' thus emerges as a fundamental issue in the formal organization of talk, which provides a powerful analytic resource in dealing with issues of the social production and distribution of 'identities' in given settings. A similar point may be made with reference to the notion of 'repair'.

The organization of 'repair' is a pervasive feature of naturally occurring talk (Schegloff, Jefferson and Sacks, 1977). Initiated either by another, or by the speaker himself, 'repair' points to trouble or potential trouble in a conversation: troubles and misunderstandings are located and formulated in the sequential organization of turns at talking. (Compare also Heritage and Watson, 1979, on conversational 'formulations'.)

Here again, therefore, we find an issue in the formal sequential organization of conversation which also impinges directly on broadly ethnographic concerns of 'identity'. These interactional phenomena are profoundly 'moral' in their implications. (Compare the 'preference' for self-initiated repair, and the use of uncertainty or mitigation markers in other-initiations.) The organization of 'repair' provides analytic focus on the differential distribution of cultural resources, the management of 'information' and the like.

This is admirably exemplified by Hughes (1982). Writing on the organization of doctor–patient consultations, Hughes draws attention to the relative frequency of other-initiated repair (doctor-initiated) in the context of such settings. These are often linked with doctors' topic-formulations. As Hughes himself summarizes some of these issues:

> Repair initiations ... may have a highly leading format in relation to subsequent answers. Clarificatory exchanges sometimes developed into a series of speaker turns where the doctor offered candidate formulations of further relevant dimensions of described symptoms for the patient's confirmation or disconfirmation.

Confirmations and disconfirmations are directly linked to membershipping within the consultation, where,

> any implicit challenge to membership implied by a disconfirmation of a doctor's formulation has the added dimension of constituting a challenge to an expert's membership by a layman, and the production of a disconfirmation itself poses technical difficulties that do not apply to confirmations. Whereas confirmations merely require an indication of agreement or absence of response and do not entail a recapitulation of preceding topical talk, a disconfirmation needs grounding and requires the provision of an alternative formulation.

Hughes thus provides us with a most pertinent example of the particular significance of some general conversational features. Indeed, his own paper is grounded in a recent dispute about the description of doctor–patient encounters. Sharrock (1979) had taken to task a number of other commentators (e.g. Bloor, 1976; and West, 1976) for their attempts to portray the medical consultation as an unequal transaction, in which 'control', is exercised by the medical practitioner. Authors like Bloor and West had argued for a micro-analytic, ethnographic portrayal of 'professional dominance' and 'control' through the practitioner's organization of talk in the consultation. Sharrock takes such commentators to task, in that they depict the doctor–patient relationship as one of 'struggle' and 'conflict'. The remarkable thing, Sharrock suggests, is that doctor–patient talk is orderly — that doctors 'get their way' with so little overt, demonstrable 'conflict'. Sharrock's critique suggests that the local management of interaction is largely irrelevant in comparison with general normative expectations of both parties.

Now, although Sharrock's criticisms of Bloor and West are pertinent, there is no need to extend his argument to suggest that there is no point of contact between a formal or 'fine-grained' analysis of consultations, and ethnographic concerns. On the contrary, the investigation of 'repair' and conversational formulations provides a precise penetration of the asymmetry of such encounters: there need be no recourse to vague unexplicated notions of 'dominance' and 'control'.

Indeed, these latter remarks on asymmetry serve to remind us that the kinds of analysis referred to and advocated above rest on the analysis of turn-taking in spoken interaction. Increasing numbers of studies are being produced in which 'speech-exchange systems' are revealed where rights to speak are differentially distributed. These include what Dingwall (1980) refers to as 'orchestrated encounters':

> An orchestrated encounter is characterized by the cession of the right to organize speech-exchange to one of the parties for the duration of the encounter. Examples of such organization include that that party may act as an authorized starter and closer and as an arbiter of the distribution of the right to hold the floor and to introduce new topics.

Dingwall's own analysis is based on tutorials observed in a study of health visitor training. Similar perspectives on educational settings as 'orchestrated encounters' are provided by Mehan (1978), McHoul (1978) and Atkinson (1981), among others. A similar, though by no means identical, issue is raised via the notion of 'pre-allocation' (cf. Atkinson, 1977; Atkinson and Drew, 1979).

There has been a tendency on the part of conversational analysis to treat 'pre-allocation' and 'orchestration' in purely formal terms. That is — in terms redolent of Simmel's formal treatment of the dyad and the triad — such matters are treated as reflections of the management of turn-taking in multi-party settings. But as Dingwell remarks,

> this concentration on pure numbers is an instance where speech-exchange analysts have been misled by their insistence on decontextualized data. What is, I suggest, more critical is the degree of difficulty in sustaining orientation to joint action, where numbers are only one of

many obstacles. Even two-party encounters may be orchestrated or pre-allocated. Examples of the former might include interviews and professional-client consultations where one party is trying to sustain a particular thematic orientation and to keep the other addressing that theme, rather than introducing themes of his own.

Central to such interactional organization is the differential distribution, not merely of rights at turn-taking, but also of cultural resources. In rendering such encounters explicable, then, we are forced to take such resources into account. And, by the same token, such formal foundations are available to ethnographers. Indeed, the two enterprises of ethnography and conversational analysis are demonstrably much closer together than authors like Atkinson and Drew (cited at the beginning of this chapter) would suggest.

Some further remarks can be appended briefly here. It will be apparent that in advocating the use of formal speech-exchange approaches, I am questioning the preservation of the topic/resource distinction as insisted upon by some ethnomethodologists. The identification of 'topics' is fundamental, but the distinction should not be treated as a once-for-all, absolute affair. There is no a priori reason why interactional matters which have been topicalized should not be drawn on as analytic resources subsequently or simultaneously. It is important that the interactional foundations should be explicated, and describable in principle: it is not necessary that all other descriptions or analytic levels be suspended *sine die*.

Furthermore, it seems to me that a rapprochement between ethnography and conversational analysis does much to retrieve the latter from the dangers of an empty formalism. Some versions of contemporary conversational analysis seem to me to have distorted the original ethnomethodological inspiration. Whereas the latter drew attention to the 'seen but unnoticed' in an essentially phenomenological sense, the former rests on an essentially behaviourist concentration on 'the fleeting': tacit knowledge is replaced by the timing of pauses in chains of spoken behaviour. (This is by no means true of all analyses, but is discernible in those who portray themselves as 'purists' in the field.) The ethnographer ignores at his peril the interactional foundations and interpretive procedures he draws on. But the conversational analyst treads on equally thin ice if he becomes seduced by the ideal-type of the decontextualized, 'mundane' talk of the two-party encounter in which rights and resources are equally available.

As the late Erving Goffman (1981: 25ff) remarked, we must take account of both the 'ritual' and 'system' constraints of talk.

Note

* This chapter is partly based on work with David Shone: the data extract derives from his MSc (Econ.) dissertation *The Social Organization of Seminar Talk*, Cardiff: University of Wales, 1981.

References

Atkinson, J. Maxwell (1977) 'Sequencing and the Accomplishment of Shared Attentiveness to Court Proceedings', pp. 257–86 in G. Psathas (ed.), *Everyday Language*. New York: Wiley.

Atkinson, J. Maxwell and Paul Drew (1979) *Order in Court*. London: Macmillan.

Atkinson, Paul (1981) 'Inspecting Classroom Talk', pp. 98–113 in C. Adelman (ed.), *Uttering, Muttering: Collecting, Using and Reporting Talk for Social and Educational Research*. London: Grant Macintyre.

Bloor, Michael (1976) 'Professional Autonomy and Client Exclusion: A Study in ENT Clinics', pp. 52–68 in M. Wadsworth and D. Robinson (eds), *Studies in Everyday Medical Life*. London: Martin Robertson.

Burton, Deirdre (1980) *Dialogue and Discourse*. London: Routledge and Kegan Paul.

Button, Graham (1977) 'Remarks on Conversation Analysis', *Analytic Sociology*, 1: D09.

Dingwall, Robert (1980) 'Orchestrated Encounters: An Essay in the Comparative Analysis of Speech-Exchange Systems', *Sociology of Health and Illness*, 2 (2): 151–73.

French, P. and MacLure, M. (1979) 'Getting the Right Answer and Getting the Answer Right', *Research in Education*, 22: 1–23.

Goffman, Erving (1981) *Forms of Talk*. Oxford: Basil Blackwell.

Hammersley, Martyn (1974) 'The Organization of Pupil Participation', *Sociological Review*, 22 (3): 355–68.

Hammersley, Martyn (1976) 'The Mobilisation of Pupil Participation', pp. 104–15 in M. Hammersley and P. Woods (eds), *The Process of Schooling*. London: Routledge and Kegan Paul.

Hammersley, Martyn (1977) 'School Learning: The Cultural Resources Required to Answer a Teacher's Question', pp. 57–86 in P. Woods and M. Hammersley (eds), *School Experience*. London: Croom Helm.

Hammersley, Martyn (1981) 'Putting Competence into Action: Some Sociological Notes on a Model of Classroom Interaction', pp. 47–58 in P. French and M. MacLure (eds), *Adult-Child Conversation*. London: Croom Helm.

Heath, Christian (1982) 'Preserving the Consultation', *Sociology of Health and Illness*, 4 (1): 56–74.

Heritage J.C. and D.R. Watson (1979) 'Formulations as Conversational Objects', pp. 123–62 in G. Psathas (ed.) *Everyday Language*. New York: Wiley.

Hughes, David (1982) 'Control in the Consultation: Organising Talk in a Situation Where Co-Participants Have Differential Competence', *Sociology*, 16 (3): 359–76.

MacLure, M. and French, P. (1980) 'Routes to Right Answers', pp. 74–93 in P. Woods (ed.) *Pupil Strategies*. London: Croom Helm.

McHoul, A. (1978) 'The Organisation of Turns at Formal Talk in the Classroom', *Language in Society*, 7: 183–213.

Mehan, H. (1974) 'Accomplishing Classroom Lessons', in A.V. Cicourel et al. *Language Use and School Performance*. London: Academic Press.

Mehan, H. (1978) 'Structuring School Structure', *Harvard Educational Review*, 48 (1): 32–64.

Payne, G. and D. Hustler (1980) 'Teaching the Class: The Practical Management of a Cohort', *British Journal of Sociology of Education*, 1 (1): 49–66.

Polanyi, M. (1974) *Personal Knowledge*. Chicago: University of Chicago Press.

Pomerantz, Anita (1975) 'Second Assessments: A Study of Some Features of Agreements/Disagreements'. Unpublished PhD Dissertation, University of California at Irvine.

Pomerantz, Anita (1978) 'Compliment Responses: Notes on the Co-operation of Multiple Constraints', in J. Schenkein (ed.), *Studies in the Organization of Conversational Interaction*. New York: Academic Press.

Ravetz, J.R. (1973) *Scientific Knowledge and its Social Problems*. Harmondsworth: Penguin Books.

Rock, Paul (1979) *The Making of Symbolic Interactionism*. London: Macmillan.

Sacks, H. (1972) 'An Initial Investigation of the Usability of Conversational Data for Doing Sociology', pp. 31–76 in D. Sudnow (ed.), *Studies in Social Interaction*. New York: Free Press.

Sacks, H. (1974) 'An Analysis of the Course of a Joke's Telling in Conversation', pp. 337–53 in R. Brauman and J. Sherzer (eds), *Explorations in the Ethnography of Speaking*. Cambridge: Cambridge University Press.

Sacks, H. (1976) 'On Getting the Floor', *Pragmatics Microfiche*, 1.8, D11–ES.

Sacks, H., E.A. Schegloff and G. Jefferson (1974) 'A Simplest Systematics for the Organization of Turn-Taking for Conversation', *Language*, 50: 696–735.

Schegloff, E.A. (1968) 'Sequencing the Conversational Openings', *American Anthropologist*, 70 (4): 1075–95.

Schegloff, E.A. (1972) 'Notes on Conversational Practice', in D. Sudnow (ed.), *Studies in Social Interaction*. New York: Free Press.

Schegloff, E.A., G. Jefferson and H. Sacks (1977) 'The Preference for Self-Correction in the Organisation of Repair in Conversation', *Language*, 53: 361–82.

Schutz, Alfred (1964) 'The Stranger: An Essay in Social Psychology', *Collected Papers Vol. II* (ed. A. Brodersen). The Hague: Martinus Nijhoff.

Sharrock, W. (1979) 'Portraying the Professional Relationship', pp. 125–46 in D. Anderson (ed.), *Health Education in Practice*. London: Croom Helm.

Stubbs, M. (1973) 'Some Structural Complexities of Talk in Meetings', Working Papers in Discourse Analysis No. 5, mimeo, University of Birmingham.

Stubbs, M. (1975) 'Teaching and Talking', pp. 233–46 in G. Chanan and S. Delamont (eds) *Frontiers of Classroom Research*. NFER: Windsor.

West, P. (1976) 'The Physician and the Management of Childhood Epilepsy', pp. 13–31 in M. Wadsworth and D. Robinson (eds), *Studies in Everyday Medical Life*. London: Martin Robertson.

Weider, D.L. (1974) *Language and Social Reality: The Case of Telling the Convict Code*. The Hague: Mouton.

Williams, Robin (1981) 'Learning to do Field Research: Intimacy and Inquiry in Social Life', *Sociology*, 15 (4): 557–64.

Wooton, A.J. (1981) 'Conversation Analysis', pp. 99–110 in P. French and M. MacLure (eds), *Adult-Child Conversation*. London: Croom Helm.

Zimmerman, D.H. (1969) 'Tasks and Troubles: The Practical Bases of Work Activites in a Public Assistance Organization', in D.A. Hansen (ed.), *Explorations in Sociology and Counselling*. Boston: Houghton-Mifflin.

8
Micro-sociological theories of emotion

Steven L. Gordon

Social relationships evoke guilt, love, envy, humour and other emotional experiences among interacting individuals, but these powerful and distinctively human social feelings have rarely been the object of systematic sociological analysis. Micro-sociology has emphasized cognitive and behavioural interaction disproportionately, neglecting emotional patterns and experiences in social life. In recent years, however, a sociology of emotion has developed (Collins, 1975, 1981; Gordon, 1981; Heise, 1979; Heiss, 1981; Hochschild, 1975, 1979; Kemper, 1978, 1981; Scheff, 1979; Shott, 1979). This new field promises to increase our understanding of many forms of social interaction, such as the sociology of culture, family sentiments and conflict, and political coalitions. As different micro-sociological theories define and explore the sociology of emotion, we have an opportunity to compare their assumptions and distinctive emphases. The goals of this chapter are to examine several of the micro-sociological theories of emotion, to identify some of their potential contributions, and to consider fundamental questions raised by each theory about the nature of emotion in social interaction.

Key issues in the sociology of emotion

The theoretical and research literature in the sociology of emotion has examined a diversity of topics, but five issues appear to stand out as important problem areas for the field to pursue.

The first issue is the sociological significance of emotion's biological components. How does emotional physiology influence the expression, recognition, duration and other aspects of emotion at the social level? Let us consider jealousy as an example. Is jealousy part of human biological nature? Does a biological origin facilitate our expression and recognition of jealousy? Do bodily sensations determine the onset and duration of jealousy? Sociologists disagree about the connection between emotion's biological and social levels.

Second, how is emotion differentiated into qualitatively distinct sentiments? This differentiation issue examines how social interaction establishes and maintains distinctions among the variety of emotions that are socially recognized. Under what conditions is jealousy felt, but not envy or hatred, for example? How can we explain the cultural availability of these different kinds of emotional experiences?

The socialization of emotion is a third issue. What facets of emotion are culturally learned, and how does this occur? For example, how are we socialized to know how to recognize jealousy in others and how to react to it? How do we learn to identify jealousy as our own feeling, and what determines when we become jealous and how we show it? The socialization issue also involves differences across cultures and within a society, such as between women and men, in what social factors cause jealousy, how intensely it is felt, and what actions are taken to express it.

Individuals and groups appear to regulate and modify their own expression and experience of emotion. This issue of emotional management asks how persons and collectivities act upon emotion's quality, intensity, visibility, direction and other variables. Returning to our example of jealousy, we ask: what social forces determine when jealousy is openly expressed, when is it muted, and when is it disguised as another emotion? When and why is jealousy sometimes displayed although no corresponding feeling is present? The issue of emotion management focuses on individual and collective attempts to guide the direction of interaction.

Fifth, how does large-scale societal change affect the expression and experience of emotion by individuals? This structural issue links the seemingly private emotional life of persons to economic, political, cultural, demographic, religious and other societal structures and trends. How do the political and economic changes in women's roles modify the sources of jealousy and how it is expressed, for example? How is jealousy altered by the changing values round sexuality and self-indulgence generally, or by the increasing prevalence of singlehood? The structural issue places micro-sociological processes of social emotion in the larger cultural and historical context.

Having identified five main issues for the sociology of emotion, we now turn to an examination of three micro-sociological theories of emotion: behavioural exchange theory, conflict theory and symbolic interactionism. Each of these perspectives is a major type of micro-sociology, and each has generated major new works in the sociology of emotion. The intention is not to summarize or criticize the theories, but rather to explore their implications and develop the questions they suggest. A careful scrutiny of these theories will contribute not only to the sociology of emotion, but will also generate insights into the assumptions and substance of each perspective itself.

Behavioural exchange theory of emotion

This perspective explains emotions as psychological reactions to outcomes of specific social-interactional dimensions. This model of emotion has been outlined briefly in the works of George Homans (1961, 1974) and Peter Blau (1964), and has been greatly developed by Theodore D. Kemper (1978, 1981). Interactional conditions are defined in terms of a very limited set of relational dimensions, such as status, power and the ability to provide rewards. Psychological responses to these social stimuli are assumed to cause people to experience specific emotions. For example, failure to receive a reward expected from another person leads to frustration and anger (Homans, 1974: 38).

According to this theory, social structure causes emotions through fundamental and universal principles of human behaviour, derived from psychology, specifically behaviourist stimulus-response conditioning. The relational stimuli for emotions are defined by the culture, but the stimuli instigate specific emotions only to the degree that they signify the key relational variables such as power, status or ability to provide rewards.

The image of the person in this theory is that of one who is self-interested, motivated to pursue pleasure, status and/or power, and to avoid punishments, costs or loss of power and status. These gains and losses occur in the exchange of these social stimuli. The image of emotion in this theory is of a rational, self-centred evaluative response. The special contribution of this theory may be in explaining the reflexive, self-oriented emotions that are reactions to how a relational outcome — such as status loss or gain of reward — reflects upon self-interest. Emotions like shame, fear, envy, pride and gratitude may be explained by this perspective; but how would the theory account for indignation at injustice done to others, or reverence for a deity, or patriotism towards another abstraction, a nation? The scope of the theory also seems to exclude non-rational, spontaneous emotion in which self-interest is irrelevant, or where other considerations take precedence and rational calculations are unwanted or impossible.

A broad variety of emotions is predicted by Kemper's (1978) theory, however, from combinations of felt excess or deficit in power or status, and from agency — whether self or other is responsible for the excess or deficit. Thus, adequacy of power produces a feeling of security, while excess power due to one's own agency leads to guilt, but if the other is responsible for our excess of power, we feel combined anger and hostility towards the other, resembling megalomania (Kemper, 1978: 54). Not only is the emotional differentiation issue linked to specific relational outcomes, but biological differentiation is also seen as parallel to social differentiation: 'particular social stimulus keys fit particular physiological locks to produce particular emotions' (Kemper, 1981: 338). By assuming the biological fixity of specific emotions, behavioural exchange theory can argue that particular social stimuli activate specific emotions consistently. This is a clear and bold statement, in contrast to other positions which either ignore the biological components of emotion or rely upon vague conceptualizations of emotion.

Correspondence between biological and sociological levels of differentiation is not essential for the validity of a sociology of emotions, however, as we shall argue below. The biological correspondence argument raises further questions as well. If the quality of an emotion is defined by the activation of innate physiological response patterns, how can long-term relationships be explained, in which enduring feelings of love, hatred, loyalty and other sentiments persist well beyond the activation of bodily sensations? Arousal is not constant in social relationships. Does an enduring sentiment cumulate, perhaps, from situational emotional arousal? If so, the ambivalent or mixed feelings in lasting relationships might be explained as resulting from the shifting patterns of status, power, reward, etc., between individuals over time. As social stimuli change, so must emotional responses change. If an overall sentiment about a relationship is an accumulation of *mixed* feelings, however, then the establishment and maintenance of emotional differentiation is not explained. Behavioural exchange theory may be most applicable to account for emotions in a given situation, but may lack the temporal framework to account for emotion in enduring, complex relationships.

The socialization of emotion is not explicitly treated in the behavioural exchange theory of emotion, since emotions are assumed to be innate in the human organism. The central socialization problems are how people learn the culture's specific indices or criteria for the more abstract relational stimuli of status, power and so forth, and also how these interactional outcomes become associated with specific emotional responses. Because these outcomes are assumed to be intrinsically pleasurable or aversive, however, little socialization is required after the abstract outcome (such as loss of status) has been learned as the relational meaning of the more concrete outcomes (such as being insulted or getting a poor grade).

Emotion management is scarcely touched upon as an issue by behavioural exchange theory, which focuses upon immediate, unmanaged emotional reactions. Calculation may precede the emotion, but does not follow its onset. Homans (1961: 380) recognized, however, that inauthentic or spurious expressions of emotion may be maintained by reinforcers such as social approval. The institutionalization of grief occurs, he suggested, when some members of a society find expression of genuine grief to be rewarding, and this pattern gradually becomes normative. Other members of the group then express grief because rewards and punishments sanction their behaviour.

Simulated emotion may produce the same interactional outcomes as genuinely felt emotion. This insight has not been incorporated into behavioural exchange theory, which focuses on the causes of emotions but not on their effects. Blau (1964) noted the importance of impression management in social exchange. He suggested that lovers withhold expressions of affection in order to increase their ultimate value, for example. Behavioural exchange theory largely ignores the management and consequences of emotion, however. If simulated emotion can be socially efficacious, the link between innate emotional reactions and specific relational conditions is irrelevant for any social interactions. Many, perhaps most, emotional reactions may be managed or regulated by strategic and normative considerations. A comprehensive theory of emotion should explain emotion's social consequences as well as emotion's social origins.

The structural issue — how emotions are connected to large-scale institutions and change — is potentially a major contribution of behavioural exchange theory to the sociology of emotion. Proponents of the theory generally assert that the same generalized reinforcers or media of exchange (e.g. money, compliance, approval) operate in large-scale social behaviour much as in small groups (Homans, 1974; Blau, 1964). Social scale produces some differences, such as that exchange may be more indirect in complex organizations (Blau, 1964), but the same general theoretical principles (such as reciprocity) apply within large structures much as for individuals. Similarly, Kemper (1978: 31) contends that the relational variables of power and status function for all types of relationships from romantic love to international relations. Principles of exchange, status and power could potentially explain collective emotions, such as when members of a social group or category feel the same emotion (such as anger) because of similar reactions to a shared relational outcome (such as status loss).

Having examined assumptions, unresolved questions and potential contributions of the behavioural exchange theory of emotion, we now turn our attention to another emerging conceptualization of emotion, the perspective of conflict theory.

Conflict theory of emotion

The conflict theory of emotion has been presented in the works of Lewis Coser (1956, 1967) and Randall Collins (1975, 1981), who assert that the crucial determinant of emotion is membership in competing groups and social classes. Emotion is one of the resources which can be mobilized, directed and exploited in conflicts over power (Coser, 1956), and can be used to create emotional solidarity and loyalties (Collins, 1975). Conflict theory finds a close relationship between the biological and social levels of emotion. This resolution of the biological question may derive from a Hobbesian perspective which sees both emotion and an appetite for power and strife to be inseparable in human nature. The image of emotion in this theory resembles psychodynamic theory's view of emotion as a quantity of energy, but here social forces, not psychic forces, mobilize and channel emotion (Coser, 1956).

The biological structure of emotion is also emphasized by Collins (1975), who observes that humans have automatic emotional reactions to certain human gestures and sounds, such as signals of alarm, affection and recognition. This shared responsiveness to gestures and signals permits emotional contagion to be stimulated and manipulated in solidarity rituals. The human propensity for sharing emotions increases collective arousal in rituals, thereby reifying and validating the meanings of the symbols which people think about while emotionally aroused, Collins argues. The group concentrates its attention, aided by stereotyped gestures and formulae, thereby generating a strong emotion which is magnified by emotional contagion among ritual participants.

Human biological nature provides emotion's energy, but the differentiation and management of emotion is achieved by competing groups, who struggle for control over the 'means of emotional reproduction' — the resources for assembling and staging the ritualistic arousal of emotions in support of one's group (Collins, 1975: 58). These means are distributed unequally, so that some groups or classes are better able to stimulate emotion for solidarity, domination over other groups, and establishment of prestige hierarchies for legitimating the standards of emotional experience.

Conflict theory suggests two important insights into the management of emotion. First, people manage not only their own emotions, but also strive to stimulate, suppress and transform emotions in other people. Second, an intermittent energizing may be essential for the continuity and vitality of an enduring emotion. Arousal or excitement makes an emotion seem to be real and valid once again. This testing for the vitality of a lasting emotion may occur in relationships between individuals, as well as between groups, and also may be accomplished in ways other than through collective rituals. A twinge of jealousy may signify the continuing intensity of romantic love, for example.

Conflict theory contributes to our understanding of the factors which manage emotion in collectivities. Experienced hostility from external groups increases in-group solidarity (Coser, 1956). Emotion is intensified by the presence of a large number of people in an expressive ritual (Collins, 1975). Discharging hostile emotions collectively heightens solidarity, provided that basic group values are not threatened by the hostility (Coser, 1956). Hostility will be violently disruptive if the social structure does not allow safe channels for deprived groups to discharge their emotions (Coser, 1956). Emotion may be deflected or absorbed. An individual's membership in overlapping, segmented groups reduces emotional involvement in any one group. Emotion, conceived in conflict theory as energy, is thus dispersed across multiple, cross-cutting allegiances. These kinds of structural relationships among conflicting groups channel the flow of emotion.

The issue of how individual emotion is connected to structural change is addressed by conflict theory in terms of increasing and decreasing a scale of social interaction. Macro-sociological structures may be aggregates of micro-sociological events, Collins (1981) contends. In every encounter, individuals tacitly match resources, such as emotion, acquired from previous encounters. For example, abilities for successfully negotiating emotional solidarity cumulate across episodes. This form of emotion socialization can be augmented by access to large-scale emotional technologies, such as mass communication or emotion-producing specialists. In a decreasing interactional scale, inter-group conflict in relations of domination and revolution governs individual identifications with contending groups and coalitions. This membership in turn determines the types and intensities of emotions individuals will experience.

In reviewing the conflict theory of emotion, it may be noted that the close connection claimed between biological and social emotion is consistent with psychological studies which find that some facial expressions and bodily gestures of emotion are very similar across cultures (see reviews by Ekman and Oster, 1979, and Eibl-Eibesfeldt, 1980). If innate emotional response patterns are augmented by shared expressive norms within a culture, rapid emotional communication among members of a cohesive community should be possible. An unresolved question is whether members of modern, urban and industrialized societies with heterogeneous subcultures actually share many emotional response patterns. If so, how effectively can these predispositions be exploited when full mass assembly is impossible, and where privatized feelings and public apathy and non-involvement seem to reign instead of shared emotional arousal?

On the differentiation of emotions, conflict theory makes an important contribution in noting that intimate relationships tend to produce intensely ambivalent or mixed emotions (Coser, 1956). Close proximity and interdependence breed both love and hatred, generating a potential for sharp conflict within a close group. The full variety of emotions is not embraced within conflict theory, however, which focuses on emotions relevant to political conflict and solidarity, rather than on the total range of human emotions.

In contrast to behavioural exchange theory, conflict theory envisions emotions as being felt towards individuals or groups as evaluations of relationships, not of interactional outcomes as exchange theory suggests. Thus, loyalty is felt towards one's own group, while hostility is felt towards a competing group. Emotions are felt towards social targets, not merely towards the intervening target represented by the relational outcomes which those groups cause. Does the exploited worker hate his or her deprivation, or instead despise the oppressor? Here, the choice of target may be a matter of political consciousness. When I am insulted, however, my anger is aimed not at the interactional outcome (my degradation), but instead at the person who insulted me. When exchange relations become conflict relations, emotions may be aimed beyond interactional outcomes, directly at the social sources of outcomes.

Conflict theory emphasizes collective interests over the self-interest stressed by behavioural exchange theory. Another difference is that conflict theory considers the effects of emotions, as well as the sources of emotion which are behavioural exchange theory's primary focus. In contrast to exchange theory's rationalistic outlook, conflict theory recognizes that non-rational, 'unrealistic' discharges of emotional tensions occur, as in scapegoating or displacement (Coser, 1956). This spontaneous, impulsive emotion need bear no relationship between its original source and its expression, although its substitute target is determined by social forces. The conflict theory of emotion provides a dynamic, compelling explanation of emotions generated by inter-group turmoil.

Symbolic interactionist theory of emotion

Symbolic interactionism conceptualizes emotions as social objects towards which individuals and groups act (Gordon, 1981; Hochschild, 1975, 1979; Shott, 1979; Turner, 1970). This theory emphasizes the uniquely human capacity for creating, manipulating and modifying symbols to direct one's own behaviour and to influence others' behaviour. Thus, love, hatred, anger and grief are emerging acts under construction and redefinition by the individual and group. An emotion signifies symbolically to others what one's response to a situation may be, and hence what may be the meaning of that situation for them. This theory's image of emotion is that it is the object or focus of interaction.

People interpret, explain, evaluate, challenge, justify and alter emotion's intensity, quality and direction. The individual's stance towards emotion is more active, and less determined by the situation or by group membership than in the other theories. For the symbolic interactionist, an emotion is real if it is real in its social consequences — if people interpret and then react to the emotion as a familiar object that is relevant to their social behaviour.

Emotion's biological and social levels do not coincide closely in symbolic interactionism. People act towards emotions according to the meanings they impute to them, not primarily in terms of emotion's biological substructure. The nature of sorrow, contempt or embarrassment is not essentially biological, but is a social nature defined by the meaning the emotion has acquired in the situation and in the surrounding culture through people's interpretations and actions. A distinction has been drawn between biological emotions and social sentiments (Cooley, 1902; Shibutani, 1961; Turner, 1970; Gordon, 1981). An emotion is fixed in the human organism, is experienced concurrently with bodily arousal, and is composed of an unchanging configuration of bodily sensations and gestures in response to standard, simple stimuli. In contrast, a sentiment originates through cultural definition and social interaction, and continues over time in enduring social relationships. The pattern of expressive gestures and internal sensations for a sentiment is culturally defined and can be altered situationally and on a broader cultural scale, because sentiments are not fixed in human biological nature (Gordon, 1981). Fear and surprise may be emotions, but most of the socially recognized feelings such as pity, envy, guilt, love, pride, jealousy and hatred seem to qualify as sentiments.

The differentiation of emotion into distinct varieties of sentiments is not the result of objective relational variables, according to symbolic interactionism. Social situations are too diverse and mutable to permit any precise correspondence between specific sentiments and situational parameters such as power or status. We experience sentiments and emotions in terms of their relevance to our plans in a situation or relationship. Emotion is differentiated through people's mutual adaption to each other's actual or anticipated behaviour. As the course of interaction changes, differences among sentiments are created and redefined continuously throughout an encounter or relationship. For example, sporadic excitement and a vague melancholy may be identified as the love sentiment, but after anger at frustration of my plans and a surge of jealousy over someone's interference with my romantic plans, I may redefine the sentiment as hatred and, eventually, as nostalgia.

The differentiation of emotion into sentiments occurs through interpretation as well as behavioural adaptation. Common social patterns in a culture become reflected in its vocabulary of sentiments, a set of shared symbols and understandings about varieties of emotional experience. Each term — such as 'enthusiasm' or 'gratitude' — provides a symbolic framework by which we can interpret, anticipate and justify emotional gestures, sensations and a relationship's overall meaning. The cultural vocabulary predisposes people towards certain conceptualizations of, and actions towards, sentiments as different social objects. Some sentiments are given considerable elaboration, with precise discriminations among varieties of feeling. Other sentiments are poorly differentiated, often because they are devalued or are of little practical importance in relationships in that society. People have difficulty reflecting upon undifferentiated emotion for lack of an expressive vocabulary.

Emotional differentiation is also guided by the popular knowledge conveyed by the cultural vocabulary about each sentiment's nature, signs, course and desirability. This folk wisdom tells us whether real guilt can be concealed, or whether romance inevitably changes into apathy, or whether we should admire or pity a jealous person, and whether humour and shame are compatible sentiments or not. Such common-sense beliefs are an interconnected system of meanings which supports the social reality of recognized sentiments, and provides criteria by which people may differentiate them through discussion and debate. Boundaries among sentiments are suggested by the cultural vocabulary of meanings for emotion, which is reconstructed tentatively in social encounters.

Emotional socialization includes learning the cultural vocabulary of sentiments, but also involves the emergence of the social self. The individual learns to indicate to the self the possible meanings of an emotional expression by imaginatively assuming another person's viewpoint. As role-taking ability develops, one learns to identify and guide sentiments according to the meanings they have for other people. A person's characteristics and social position influence the socialization opportunities he or she has to express various sentiments, and be exposed to sentiments from other people (Gerth and Mills, 1953; Hochschild, 1975). For example, a physically attractive individual learns to adjust to expressions of envy and sexual desire from others. The poor and handicapped are more likely to be socialized into adapting to expressions of pity directed at themselves. If envy is generally directed upwards in the class structure, the wealthy and powerful have more opportunities to learn to deflect or attract envy. Differential exposure to sentiments produces variable socialization opportunities for people to adapt to those sentiments as objects of social interaction.

Emotional socialization involves more than learning to interact round sentiments as familiar social objects. The individual also interprets sentiments in terms of the meanings they signify for self-conception (Turner, 1979; Turner and Gordon, 1981). Some sentiments may be interpreted as revealing one's authentic, deeper or 'real' self, such as being able to feel compassion for the less fortunate. Other sentiments may seem to represent a spurious or inauthentic self-image, such as an angry outburst which betokens an uncharacteristic loss of temper. Some individuals who are envied may find that the envy elicits pride in their identity and boosts their self-esteem, while other envied persons may feel uncomfortable or guilty about the implications of envy for their self-conception. Role-taking ability and the development of a stable self-conception cause us to feel sentiments about our sentiments and emotions, as one aspect of emotional socialization. We may feel pride at being able to express love spontaneously, and feel shame over a display of jealousy.

The emotion management question is embraced within the symbolic interactionist concepts of 'expression management' and 'emotion work'. Expression management is a form of self-presentation and impression management, as described in the dramaturgical works of Erving Goffman (1959, 1963, 1967, 1971). We establish an identity in a situation through the appearance we present to others, Goffman argues. By managing the impressions others have of ourselves, we facilitate our goals, attract the responses we feel we deserve, and make our situational identity more congruent with our self-conception. Like emotional socialization, expression management often involves inauthentic sentiments. Self-presentation techniques include avoiding or concealing situationally inappropriate emotional gestures, such as laughter at a

funeral. Expression management also includes simulating a sentiment even when it is not felt genuinely, such as a forced smile upon
meeting an enemy. Expressive styles may distance oneself from an
emotional gesture, such as through a half-hearted or overly
dramatic display of anger or grief, establishing an emotional type of
'role distance' (Goffman, 1963).

Expression management is guided by socially shared, implicit
rules about appropriate and inappropriate display of sentiment and
emotion (Hochschild, 1975, 1979). We demonstrate interactional
competence by taking these conventions into account. Others may
feel they are entitled to our expression of love, admiration or
sympathy, because sentiments are socially understood in terms of
rights and obligations. Emotion rules do not determine expression
and experience, but are a normative framework of expectations that
people take into account. One may follow an expressive rule
apathetically or only in part, or take it into account only in violating
it. For example, one may act gloomy to spoil a social occasion
because one knows that cheeriness is the expected expression.
Expression rules are often used retrospectively to justify emotional
gestures. A failure to apologize to a lover for an unkind expression
may be justified by a rule such as 'love means never having to say
you're sorry'.

Through 'emotion work', we actively manage our experience of a
sentiment by inducing or inhibiting feelings (Hochschild, 1975,
1979). Feeling rules define what we should feel in various situations
and entitlement to gestures or feelings; one believes that a gesture
or feeling is owed to oneself or another (Hochschild, 1979). A smile
or a glare is to be repaid in kind, for example. Emotion work also is
exchanged, as individuals agree to commit themselves more deeply
to a sentiment, or mutually to distance themselves from it, as when
agreeing to set aside previous hostilities. The value of a gesture or
feeling in exchange is established by broader ideologies, promoted
by contending groups, that convey folk knowledge about sentiments
and define the rights and obligations attached to sentiments. This
point is one at which symbolic interactionism and conflict theory
may converge (Collins, 1975; Hochschild, 1975, 1979).

Conclusion
The chapter has reviewed theories of emotion as developed within the
behavioural exchange, conflict and symbolic interactionist paradigms. The future of the sociology of emotion will be closely related
to emerging trends in these and other micro-sociological theories. In
her work on emotion, Arlie Hochschild has suggested important

linkages between emotional experience and the larger social structure, a macro-sociological perspective which symbolic interactionism has often been criticized for neglecting. And, in his conflict theory of emotion, Randall Collins has demonstrated how large-scale structural conflicts may be reproduced in micro-sociological rituals of emotion. Through insights such as these, the analysis of emotion in social interaction promises to spur the development of the micro-sociological theories in new directions.

Many unresolved issues and differences among the theories of emotion remain. One issue is whether a theory of emotion can encompass both situational emotion and long-term relationship sentiments. Like sociology and social psychology generally, the sociology of emotion has focused primarily on situational encounters — whether in natural settings, laboratories or surveys — and has largely neglected the affective dynamics of lasting relationships.

The compatibility of social theories of emotion with the major psychological theories of emotion is another important problem. Behavioural exchange and conflict theories are more compatible with those psychological viewpoints which emphasize innate physiological response patterns and expressive gestures. Symbolic interactionism is more closely aligned with cognitive theories of emotion that examine how undifferentiated arousal is identified by individuals in terms of situationally appropriate labels. This difference is clearly reflected in the sociological theories' divergent images of the nature of emotion, and of the individual's relationship to emotional experience. Thus, the person's stance towards emotion in behavioural exchange theory is passive, reacting to emotion rather than acting towards it. Conflict theory sees emotion as a resource employed by groups, and, to a lesser extent, individuals, but also stresses emotion's biological and irrational components. Symbolic interactionism places the individual in an active stance towards emotion, interpreting and transforming it. This perspective also separates the expressive layer of emotion from the experiential layer, recognizing that the two are partially independent and substitutable as variables producing the same effects.

The differentiation, socialization and management of emotion and sentiments will likely remain as very significant problem areas for all micro-sociological theories. Each of these social processes has sociologically emergent properties which resist reduction to the psychological level of explanation. The degree to which research generated by the micro-sociological theories can account for these fundamental processes and emergent properties will provide a basis for the growth of this new field of micro-sociology, the study of social emotions and sentiments.

References

Blau, Peter M. (1964) *Exchange and Power in Social Life*. New York: John Wiley.

Collins, Randall (1975) *Conflict Sociology*. New York: Academic Press.

Collins, Randall (1981) 'On the Microfoundations of Macrosociology', *American Journal of Sociology*, 86 (5): 984–1014.

Cooley, Charles H. (1902) *Human Nature and the Social Order*. New York: Charles Scribner's Sons.

Coser, Lewis (1956) *The Functions of Social Conflict*. New York: Free Press.

Coser, Lewis (1967) *Continuities in the Study of Social Conflict*. New York: Free Press.

Eibl-Eibesfeldt, Irenäus (1980) 'Strategies of Social Interaction', pp. 57–80 in R. Plutchik and H. Kellerman (eds), *Emotion: Theory, Research and Experience*. New York: Academic Press.

Ekman, Paul and Harriet Oster (1979) 'Facial Expressions of Emotion', *Annual Review of Psychology*, 30: 527–54.

Gerth, Hans and C. Wright Mills (1953) *Character and Social Structure*. New York: Harcourt, Brace and World.

Goffman, Erving (1959) *The Presentation of Self in Everyday Life*. Garden City, NY: Doubleday/Anchor.

Goffman, Erving (1961) *Encounters: Two Studies in the Sociology of Interaction*. Indianapolis: Bobbs-Merrill.

Goffman, Erving (1963) *Behavior in Public Places*. Glencoe, Ill.: Free Press.

Goffman, Erving (1967) *Interaction Ritual*. Garden City, NY: Doubleday/Anchor.

Goffman, Erving (1971) *Relations in Public*. New York: Basic Books.

Gordon, Steven L. (1981) 'The Sociology of Sentiments and Emotion', pp. 562–92 in M. Rosenberg and R.H. Turner (eds), *Social Psychology: Sociological Perspectives*. New York: Basic Books.

Heise, David R. (1979) *Understanding Events: Affect and the Construction of Social Action*. New York: Cambridge University Press.

Heiss, Jerold (1981) *The Social Psychology of Interaction*. Englewood Cliffs, NJ: Prentice-Hall.

Hochschild, Arlie R. (1975) 'The Sociology of Feeling and Emotion', pp. 280–307 in M. Millman and R.M. Kanter (eds), *Another Voice: Feminist Perspective on Social Life and Social Science*. Garden City, NY: Doubleday/Anchor.

Hochschild, Arlie R. (1979) 'Emotion Work, Feeling Rules and Social Structure', *American Journal of Sociology* 85: 551–75.

Hochschild, Arlie R. (1983) *The Managed Heart*. Berkeley and Los Angeles: University of California Press.

Homans, George C. (1961) *Social Behavoir: Its Elementary Forms*. New York: Harcourt.

Homans, George C. (1974) *Social Behavior: Its Elementary Forms* (revised ed.). New York: Harcourt, Brace and World.

Kemper, Theodore D. (1978) *A Social Interactional Theory of Emotions*. New York: John Wiley.

Kemper, Theodore D. (1981) 'Social Constructionist and Positivist Approaches to the Sociology of Emotions', *American Journal of Sociology*, 87(2): 336–62.

Scheff, Thomas J. (1979) *Catharsis in Healing, Ritual and Drama*. Berkeley and Los Angeles: University of California Press.

Shibutani, Tamotsu (1961) *Society and Personality: An Interactionist Approach to Social Psychology*. Englewood Cliffs, NJ: Prentice-Hall.

Shott, Susan (1979) 'Emotion and Social Life: A Symbolic Interactionist Analysis', *American Journal of Sociology*, 84: 1317–34.

Turner, Ralph H. (1970) *Family Interaction*. New York: John Wiley.

Turner, Ralph H. and Steven L. Gordon (1981) 'The Boundaries of the Self: The Relationship of Authenticity to Inauthenticity in the Self-Conception', pp. 39–57 in M.D. Lynch, A.A. Noren-Hebeisen and K.J. Gergen (eds), *Self-Concept: Advances in Theory and Research*. Cambridge, Mass.: Ballinger/Harper and Row.

9

Theoretical and metatheoretical themes in expectation states theory

Joseph Berger
David G. Wagner
Morris Zelditch, Jr

Expectation states theory as a theoretical research programme

'Expectation states theory' is not a 'theory' in the usual textbook sense. A 'theory' is usually defined as a set of general, systematically interrelated concepts and propositions that have empirical import. Berger and Conner's theory of the power-prestige process in small, initially undifferentiated, problem-solving groups is a theory in this sense (see Berger and Conner, 1969). In such groups, inequalities in opportunities to perform, performance outputs (problem-solving attempts) and influence regularly emerge. These inequalities are highly intercorrelated and, once emerged, are highly stable. Such empirical generalizations can be explained by assuming that the resolution of disagreements in problem-solving interaction gives rise to differences in underlying, unobservable expectations for future performance. Each of the inequalities of the observable power-prestige order of the group is a probabilistic function of these underlying performance expectations. Once emerged, expectation states change only if behaviour is incongruent with expectations. But the conditions giving rise to such change are themselves direct functions of the underlying expectation states. Hence, the underlying structure, and the observable inequalities that are a function of it, are stable unless disturbed by some exogenous force. This theory is *an* expectation states theory, but it is not *the* expectation states theory; expectation states theory is not *a* theory, it is a family of interrelated theories. It is a more complex theoretical structure, created by the proliferation of the original performance expectation theory, i.e. by its extension (with appropriate reformulations) to a number of other kinds of phenomena. One of the earliest such proliferants was the theory of status characteristics and expectation states which was concerned with the power-prestige order of initially status-differentiated

groups. In groups already differentiated by external status characteristics (such as age, sex, occupation, education, race and
ethnicity), externally created status differences determine the
power-prestige order of the group whether or not the initial status
differences are relevant to the group's task. To explain this
empirical generalization, the theory of status characteristics used
the same concept of a power-prestige order as Berger and Conner,
the same concept of an underlying expectation state, and the same
assumption that observed inequalities in power and prestige are
probabilistic functions of the underlying expectation state. But it
introduced new concepts (including an abstract conception of what
a status characteristic is) and new assumptions (explaining how
status characteristics are involved in the formation of performance
expectations) to extend the performance expectation theory to this
new domain. There have in fact been a large number of such
proliferants of the original power-prestige theory (see Table 1 for a
brief summary). Taken together, these constitute 'expectation
states theory'.

This more complex theoretical structure is not a 'paradigm' in
Kuhn's sense. As is well known, 'paradigm' is a term with a large
number of meanings, from concrete exemplars (like Durkheim's
Suicide) to the underlying values and non-empirical faiths that
orient and guide the construction of theories in a field (like 'conflict'
or 'functional' or 'exchange' theory). Kuhn tended to cover all
aspects of scientific activity by the one term, treating it as a single,
seamless web. But failing to distinguish materially different levels
and kinds of theoretical activity attributes to all of science the
properties of its orienting strategies. Orienting strategies consist of
concepts, values and directives (i.e., prescriptions) that guide the
investigators of a given discipline in identifying significant problems, formulating workable solutions and assessing them. They are
presupposed by an enquiry: they define what the subject matter of a
discipline is, how to conceptualize it, how to reason about it; what
the goals of enquiry are, what one can assume about what there is
and how we know it; they legislate criteria of assessment and derive
from them methods of observation and inference. But because they
are themselves values and non-empirical faiths, they are relatively
incorrigible, conflicts among strategies are relatively irreconcilable,
and change, when it occurs, is discontinuous and non-cumulative, as
paradigm change is. (A good example is the ideal of value-free
enquiry. If one wishes such enquiry one must nevertheless come to
terms with the fact that value neutrality is itself a value and one not
'provable' by reference to any empirical enquiry.) Expectation
states theory is not a paradigm in the orienting strategy sense: its

domain is more limiting, it is in closer touch with empirical reality, it grows and changes more rapidly.

Lakatos (1970) has suggested that the proper unit for analysis of cumulative growth lies somewhere between particular unit theories and paradigms at a level he calls 'theoretical research programmes'. Expectation state theory is a theoretical research programme in Lakatos's sense. Departing slightly from his usage, such a programme can be defined as a set of interrelated theories, theoretically oriented and applied empirical research, such that the theories share some (not all) concepts, propositions, metatheoretical assumptions and methods of observation and inference (called the 'core' of the programme). The theoretical research of the programme is relevant to the theories in the programme and the applied research is grounded in those theories. Relative to orienting strategies, such programmes consist not only of metatheory but also of research that is oriented to testing, refining, extending and otherwise modifying theories. (By contrast, in Kuhn 'normal science' typically involves filling in gaps; very little modification of theory occurs without large-scale revolutions in thought.) They include not only theoretical research, research with a generalizing orientation, but also applied research, research concerned with identifying instances to which the theories of the programme apply and with testing implications of the theory for interventions that modify the empirical world. Relative to theories, such programmes are much more complex and dynamic structures. The most important thing about them is that they continually change, and through such change grow and expand. Such growth is of two kinds: on the one hand, particular theories are *elaborated* — i.e., reformulated to correspond more closely with empirical research, or extended to generalize their scope, or refined to describe more precisely or rigorously the phenomena within their scope. Elaboration displaces an earlier theory by a later, more comprehensive or more rigorous theory. For example, the first theory of status characteristics, which was concerned with a single characteristic, was later displaced by a more comprehensive theory of multiple status characteristics (Berger and Fisek, 1974). On the other hand, theories also *proliferate* — the same ideas are employed to explain different phenomena. Status characteristics theory was a proliferant of the original power-prestige theory. Again, some of the same concepts, propositions, metatheory and methods were used by Webster and Sobieszek (1974) to address the conditions under which a source of evaluations becomes 'significant' for the formation of performance expectations, the concept of a 'source' differentiating this theory from either the power-prestige or status characteristics theories. Proliferation is the process that gives

TABLE 1

Theory	Phenomenon with which the theory is concerned	Sources
Performance-expectations	Emergence and maintenance of differentiated power-prestige orders in initially undifferentiated problem-solving groups.	Berger, 1958; Berger and Conner, 1969; Berger and Conner, 1974; Fisek, 1974; Conner, 1985.
Evaluations and expectation states	Processes by which evaluations of acts lead to formation of expectation states and in turn expectation states lead to the evaluation of acts.	Berger and Snell, 1961; Conner, 1965; Berger et al., 1969; Moore, 1969; Fararo, 1973.
Authority and expectation states	Effects of changes in expectation states on the stability of structures of decision-making control and their joint effects on compliance.	Berger and Zelditch, 1962; Zelditch, 1972.
Status characteristics and expectation states	Formation of expectation states involving externally created status characteristics and maintenance of power-prestige orders in groups initially differentiated in terms of status.	Berger et al., 1966; Kervin, 1972; Freese and Cohen, 1973; Berger and Fisek, 1974; Berger et al., 1977; Berger et al., 1980; Humphreys and Berger, 1981; Skvoretz, 1981; Cohen, 1982.
Decision-making structures and processes	Effects of structural differences in decision-making control on influence behaviours in groups.	Camilleri and Berger, 1967; Balkwell, 1969; Camilleri et al., 1972; Shelley, 1972; Balkwell, 1976; Camilleri and Conner, 1976; Lindenberg, 1981.
Sources of self-evaluation	Effects of evaluators in roles with rights to evaluate on the formation of expectation states.	Webster, 1969; Sobieszek, 1972; Webster and Sobieszek, 1974.
Contradictions and change in performance expectations	Effects of objective feedback about unit performances on stability and change of performance-expectations.	Foschi, 1968, 1971; Foschi and Foschi, 1976, 1979.

Distributive justice	Emergence and maintenance of reward expectations and the meaning of violations of such expectations.	Berger et al., 1968, 1972b; Jasso, 1978.
Personality characteristics and expectation states	Emergence and maintenance of specific and diffuse characteristics of individual actors.	Johnston, 1977, 1978, 1980, 1985.
Sentiments and performance expectations	Interrelations of affect and sentiment processes with expectation-state processes.	Berger and Webster, 1979; Shelley, 1979; Wattendorf, 1979; Webster, 1980.
Reward expectations	Interrelations of status, task and reward expectations and the inequalities created by these interrelations.	Berger et al., 1985.
Second-order performance expectations	Effects of expectation states held by other interactants on formation of expectation states for self and other.	Moore, 1983, 1985.
Interpersonal social control	Interpersonal social control as a state-organizing process.	Talley and Berger, 1983.
Moral characteristics	Relation of non-performance characteristics to status characteristics and expectation states.	Driskell, 1982; Webster, 1982.
Status cues	Effects of diction, speech rate, posture, dress and other verbal and non-verbal cues on formation of status and task expectations.	Ridgeway et al., 1985; Berger, Ridgeway, Rosenholtz and Webster, forthcoming.
Roles of standards in formation of expectation states	Factors determining probability that evaluations assessed under different standards lead to formation of and change in expectation states.	Foschi and Foddy, 1981.

theoretical research programmes their more complex structure: where elaboration displaces one theory by another, proliferation increases the number of theories that, taken together, make up the programme.

The two kinds of growth, taken together, give rise to a theoretical structure that looks something like a growing tree. Through elaboration the earliest theory continues to grow and change. Later theories proliferate from this growing body of work like so many branches of a tree. The metaphor should not be stretched too far, because there is some difficulty in saying exactly what the trunk of the tree is. The original branch is not really the trunk because looking at the tree as a whole it is, after a time, merely one among many branches. What more nearly resembles a trunk is something more impalpable, the 'core' of common concepts, propositions, metatheory and methods of observation and inference that relate the diverse branches of the tree to each other. It is this core that is both the key to the programme's proliferation and what holds it all together. In the second part of the chapter, therefore, we focus on some of the more important theoretical and metatheoretical themes that make up the core of expectation states theory.

**Theoretical and metatheoretical themes in the core
of the expectation states programme**
The core of a theoretical research programme is made up of three kinds of elements: (1) common terms and assumptions that are involved in its theories, such as the concept of an expectation state; (2) common metatheoretical directives that guide the construction of its theories, such as the abstract, general conception of process or the close relation of theory to both theoretical and applied research that have consistently given shape to the expectation states programme; (3) common methods of observation and inference, such as the use of standardized experimental settings for the programme's theoretical research or the use of open-interaction settings in most of its applied research. For reasons of space we limit ourselves to three of the most important of these elements. (For further discussion see Berger et al., 1974.)

The nature of an expectation state process
Expectation state processes belong to a larger class of processes that can be called 'state organizing' processes. The unit of such a process is the situation (not the group, organization or society) and a state organizing process occurs in a situation only if certain conditions

hold true. Given these conditions, it evolves a stable, underlying structure (shaped by the specific features of the immediate situation) that determines the observable behaviour of the process. When the initial conditions are altered, the process terminates. From this perspective, state organizing processes are latent processes that have a constant potentiality of becoming activated given the appropriate conditions in a social situation. But a particular state organizing process is not something that is always there. When the conditions that lead, say, to a status process in a particular family are not present, the differentiated power-prestige order generated by the process will not be observable and the relations among family members may in fact for a time be undifferentiated.

When the conditions giving rise to a particular process are present and the process in fact comes into existence, it is said to be *activated*. (When these conditions change it is *deactivated*.) Conceptualizing a process as a state organizing process will therefore lead an investigator first of all to the question: '*Under what conditions is the process (whatever it is) activated?*' The answer requires conceptualizing the situational conditions involved in generating the particular process. In the power-prestige and status characteristics theories, for example, these are particular status and task conditions (that differ in some respects between the two theories). (See Berger et al., 1974; Berger et al., 1977.)

If the required conditions activate a state organizing process, it will evolve in such a way that it creates a relatively stable underlying structure (the 'state' of the process) that governs observable interaction. In the case of expectation state processes, the states are self-other relations which stably organize behaviour among interactants. But the structure that organizes behaviour is shaped by the specific features of the immediate situation: while expectation states are stable relational structures, their stability is relative to the specific features of the interactive situation. It is contingent on the presence of the conditions that generate the process, on the nature of the particular process or processes that are activated, and on the social characteristics of the particular others with whom the individual is interacting. The same actor can hold any one of an almost infinite number of expectation states, depending on the situation, and a shift in any of its conditions will alter the actor's state. Conceptualizing a process as a state organizing process will therefore lead an investigator, second of all, to the question: '*How are the elements that constitute such states processed and organized in the operant situation?*' The answer requires formulating theoretical assumptions that describe how behaviour, cultural beliefs and special information inputs are processed by the interactants. In a status characteristics theory, for example, these are assumptions describing how status elements become salient, relevant to the situation and related to each other. In general, the task is to describe how a particular process evolves situationally stable states.

It is the state structure evolved by such a process that underlies the observable behaviour of interactants in a given situation. Conceptualizing a process as a state organizing process will therefore lead an investigator to a third question: *'How is a state, once formed, translated into (state governed) behaviour(s) in the particular situation?'* In the power-prestige theory, for example, this involved assumptions which describe how an interactant's expectation advantage relative to others is related to differences in the probability of giving, receiving or accepting opportunities to perform, differences in the probability of communicating positive or negative evaluations of units of performance, and accepting or resisting influence by another. In general, the task is to formulate, within specific theories, assumptions which relate the state structures involved in the particular process to the observable behaviours of that process.

The nature of expectation states
Expectation states as theoretical constructs. The concept of an 'expectation state', which is involved in all the branches of the programme is central to the idea of an expectation states process. This concept has evolved a good deal since the time it was first introduced (in Berger, 1958) because it has been 'stretched' to fit the needs of various theoretical formulations. In this section we describe features that have been common to the theories in the programme.

Expectation states are not observable states. The most important feature of an expectation state is that it is a theoretical construct (see Berger et al., 1962). The role such constructs play in theories is to enable the theorist to generalize and integrate, through underlying abstract concepts, other concepts that describe otherwise disparate features of a process. This mode of theorizing about expectation states is almost as old as the programme itself and was first rigorously developed in the Berger and Snell model (1961).

While they are not directly measured, expectation states are inferred. Inferences about them are made on the basis of (1) known antecedent conditions, such as behaviours, cultural beliefs and special information inputs, (2) observable consequences (for example, inequalities in behaviour), and (3) theoretical specification of the relations between known antecedent conditions, consequent observables and unobservable expectation states. The testability of a theory employing theoretical constructs rests on theoretical specification of the links between them and antecedent conditions and consequent observables. Three of the most important ideas common to the theories of the programme arise out of the way these theories specify these links. Here we simply summarize these most general theoretical 'themes' which are developed (in varying forms) in specific theoretical formulations.

The first of these is the general idea that *expectation states drive behaviour or that behaviour is a function of expectation states*. This is probably the most common idea in the programme, namely, that differences in underlying states and structures lead to differences in behavioural consequences. In general, the consequences that are theoretically linked to expectation states are the interactant's observable social behaviours, as, for example, his power and prestige behaviours.

Second, under specifiable conditions, expectation states themselves are conceived to be functions of behaviour and/or information inputs. That is, *behaviour, cultural beliefs and special information inputs to the actor drive expectation states, just as expectation states drive behaviour*. This idea, conjoined with the first, argues that there exist conditions that involve a 'basic duality' between behaviour and expectations states, i.e., conditions in which behaviour determines expectation states and expectation states, in turn, determine behaviour. This duality is perhaps most explicitly specified in the power and prestige theories of Fisek (1974) and Berger and Conner (1974), and in the models developed by Conner (1965), Berger et al. (1969), Moore (1969) and Fararo (1973).[1]

Third, if expectation states determine behaviour and behaviour determines expectation states, then it is reasonable to assume that *there exist conditions in which expectation states and their behavioural consequences, once evolved, are maintained*. While again these ideas on the maintenance of expectations and the stability of its behavioural consequences are most explicitly specified in the theories and models in the power and prestige branch, they are also tacitly assumed in most other branches of the programme.

Expectation states, interactants and non-interacting observers. Because expectation states are conceptualized as unobservable states and are not directly measured, the methods by which expectation state theorists identify or assess them differ markedly from more conventional attempts to find them in interviews or self-reports. In fact, we believe that interactants, while engaged in interaction, typically are not aware of nor do they consciously reflect on how expectation states are formed, what states are formed or how these states are translated into behaviour. The processes, for example, by which a mosaic of initially unconnected status elements produce a resultant status order are, in all likelihood, largely outside the individual's awareness.

In the perspective of expectation state theory, the interactant *is* capable of and engages in information-processing activities which can be quite complex. The assumptions of different theories describe these activities. In the status characteristic theories (Berger, Cohen and Zelditch, 1966; Berger, Fisek, Norman and Zelditch, 1977), for example, there are 'activation' and 'salience' assumptions which describe how items of information, such as beliefs about self and other, beliefs associated with status characteristics, and so on, become *inputs* to the status process. Similarly, in the power and prestige theories Fisek's (1974) model, Berger, Conner and McKeown's (1969) model, and Berger and Conner's (1974) theory provide assumptions which describe how a variety of different types of behaviour, such as performance outputs, disagreements, exercised influence and so on, become *inputs* to an expectation formation process. Also in the current version of the status theory (Berger et al., 1977) there are information processing principles that describe how the interactant operates on different types of complex status structures (of almost an infinite variety) in forming aggregated expectation states. In short, we believe that the actor's behaviour, while the actor is in the role of an interactant, is governed by complex information-processing principles, which are described by the assumptions in expectation state theories. At the same time we do not think of these as being consciously guided processes, or processes that the actor monitors, or processes that the actor may even be aware of.

But whatever, in fact, is the nature of and role of 'awareness' in these matters, the important point is that current expectation state theories in general make no assumptions, which are formal parts of these theories, that relate the formation of the interactant's expectation states to his conscious processes. Specifically, they make no assumptions about the relation between the way an actor forms expectation states and engages in behaviour and the way in which he reflects about his expectation states and his behaviours.[2]

In expectation states research a sharp distinction is made between the *interactant*, the actor who is directly engaged in the interacting process, and the non-interacting observer of that interaction, the actor, who is reflecting on what has taken place in it, interpreting and making sense of it.[3] Post-session interview, for example, is conceived by expectation states theorists to put the respondent in the role of a non-interacting observer of his or her own behaviour.

The two roles function in quite different social situations, involving different tasks, different inputs and different processes governing their behaviour. Expectation states, inputs to these states and behavioural functions of these states in current theories, are conceptualized from the standpoint of the interactant and not from the standpoint of the non-interacting observer interpreting his own behaviour after the fact. As a consequence, productions of the actor as a non-interacting observer (such as the post-session interview) cannot, from a theoretical point of view, be used to identify his or her expectation state as interactant.[4] By making such an identification the researcher risks the errors that are involved in making theoretically unwarranted inferences. In addition, the researcher obscures an important theoretical problem in all interactionist theory, namely, that of *relating* the cognitive productions of individuals in their role of non-enteracting self-observers to their behaviours and stated in their role of interactants.

The relation between theory, tests and applications
'Expectation states theory' as a programme is built up out of three kinds of components: first, it consists in abstract, general theories, i.e., theories the terms of which are such ideal generalizations as 'diffuse status characteristics', 'specific status characteristics', 'unitary, collective tasks', 'action opportunities', 'performance outputs', etc. Second, it consists of a body of controlled, experimental tests of these theories, in situations that realize as far as it is technically possible the abstract conditions regarded as necessary to test the theory. Third, it consists of a body of applied research, research designed to discover and identify different specific social characteristics in concrete, particular settings and to intervene to alter their more undesirable effects (for reviews of this applied research, see Berger et al., 1980; Cohen, 1982).

The relations among these components are conditioned by three metatheoretical directives common to all the branches of the programme. The first follows directly from the logic of the relation between theories and their application: theories are general, they refer to abstract elements such as 'diffuse' or 'specific status characteristics' in the status characteristics theory. Applications of the status theory involve particular, concrete elements such as race, sex or ethnicity. To apply a theory such as the status characteristics theory, therefore, requires statements asserting that such concrete entities as race, sex or ethnicity are instances of the abstract elements that theory defines as a status characteristic. This means that to apply status characteristics theory requires evidence that race or sex or ethnicity are differentially valued characteristics, the states of which are associated with specific and general expectations. Such 'instantiating' statements can be true or false: race or sex or ethnicity might be status characteristics in Boston but not in Mexico City; in 1982 but not in 2082. But if an instantiation is false, one does not say that the *theory* is false, one says that the theory does not apply to this instance. From this it follows that instantiational assertions are not statements *in* the theory, they are part of a distinct body of applied knowledge. Hence, applied research is necessary in order to relate the abstract theory to the different concrete realities. It is by virtue of such research that one accounts for status organizing effects for particular cases and in particular situations, and describes how these effects can be modified. In this sense, abstract theory is grounded by applications.

But it is also true that applied research, and actual applications and interventions, contribute in crucial ways to the growth and development of theory. They do this in part by suggesting new problems: both their successes and failures contribute to growth, the former because interventions sometimes succeed in ways the theory does not explain, the latter because applications sometimes fail in ways that cannot be explained by challenging instantiational assertions or questioning the scope conditions of the application/ intervention. Thus, in some ways E.G. Cohen's application of status characteristics theory to biracial interaction is almost a textbook case in which, first, a theory was constructed (Berger et al., 1966), then it was subjected to theoretical tests (Moore, 1968; Berger et al., 1972a), then it was applied to biracial work-groups (Cohen, 1971). Cohen and Roper (1972) subsequently took this theory into account in developing a successful intervention to reduce black/ white differences in observed power-prestige. But it is important to note that they ran ahead of the pace set by the development of the theory and ended by driving the theory forwards. Their method was to introduce contradictory performance information into racially defined situations. This raised questions about multi-characteristic status situations that were outside the scope of the initial status characteristics formulation, posing a 'theoretical problem' that, combined with other pressures (including the purely theoretical one of generalizing the theory), led to the extension of the initial status characteristics theory to more complex multi-characteristic, status situations (see Berger and Fisek, 1974). In general, the issues arising from application and intervention research generate theoretical problems whose situations actually shape the specific forms of theory development in the programme. Thus, the first directive governing the relations among theory, theoretical research and applied research in the expectation states programme is: theory is grounded in applications and applications shape theory.

The second directive follows from the nature of theoretical

research as expectation states theory conceives it. *Theoretical research*, in contrast to applied research, is research with a generalizing strategy. Its purpose is to test, refine and extend a theory; its method is to isolate and abstract theoretically relevant aspects of concrete, natural settings and study them under highly controlled conditions. Hence, it mirrors theoretical processes, not natural settings. In fact, it does not describe any natural setting at all. (This is as true of non-experimental as experimental theoretical research.) The whole strategy with which one approaches such research is quite different in basic orientation than is, for example, applied research. The strategy of generalizing research is governed by the primary objective of providing relevant information about theoretical processes. In this context 'relevant information' is information which can be used to test, refine and extend theoretical formulations. Research settings are chosen because they are instrumental to the theorist's primary objective, i.e., they can be manipulated, they can be controlled, effects within them can be magnified (if necessary), and they can be measured. Applied research, on the other hand, chooses settings because of their social importance, or for other reasons in which the setting itself is of paramount importance. Theoretical research will therefore often use settings and techniques that appear special and contrived and irrelevant from the perspective of applied research, and the question that will often arise is: how do you get from such artificial and concretely very different settings to applications and interventions? The directive that the expectation states programme derives from its 'generalizing' orientation is that it is theoretical research that one uses to test, refine and extend theory; and it is theory that one applies to natural settings.

From the nature of applied research and its differences from theory and theoretical research, one derives the triadic structure of the components of a theoretical research programme that, in lectures and more informal occasions (if not actually in print) we have colloquially referred to as the 'holy triangle'. Differences in the strategy of theoretical and applied research give them somewhat different roles to play in the growth and development of theory, but the traditional conception that a theory is assessed primarily (even exclusively) with reference to criteria of theoretical research or those intrinsic to the objectives of abstract theory (generality, testability, confirmation status, relative superiority over other theories) is incomplete. A theory may be general, testable, well-confirmed, superior to alternative theories but still forgotten because it applies only to very special social situations, or it describes a process that is so sensitive to competing processes or boundary conditions that it is difficult to detect in concrete settings, or the theory offers no usable or effective way of manipulating the process it describes to accomplish desired interventions. All these criteria arise from applications and interventions, not theoretical research. Our third directive accepts the fact that the assessment of theory in a research programme is a more complex problem than is traditionally recognized. It argues that theory assessment rests on multiple *kinds* of criteria including those involved in applications and interventions, as well as those involved in theoretical research and in the objectives of developing abstract theory.

The distinction between micro- and macro-sociology and expectation states theory

The distinction between micro- and macro-sociology takes many different forms in sociology; it is partly a dispute between holism versus methodological individualism; partly a distinction between 'levels' of concrete social structure (family, economic, political and other institutions versus small problem-solving groups); partly a distinction between aggregate and individual-level effects; and other things as well. We do not intend a full-scale analysis of these distinctions here, but two points should be made in this context about expectation states theory, which is often thought to be a 'micro' theory in a way that, in our view, is misleading.

The theories in the expectation states programme deal with general social processes such as evaluation expectation processes, status processes and justice processes. These are not theories about particular social structures and social groupings. The unit of analysis for these theories is the 'situation', a unit of analysis at once broader and narrower than such conventional 'levels' as small group, organization or society. It is broader in that a 'situation' is conceptualized in abstract and general terms which are applicable to any kind of concrete social system. Elements such as a 'task', a 'collective decision', a 'status characteristic', or a 'power and prestige order' might be found in families, work groups, complex organizations or small problem-solving laboratory groups. The situation is narrower in that it does not describe the whole of a concrete social structure. No concrete system is in the same social situation all of the time, nor is the same social process occurring all of the time. The analytic elements that make up the situation and describe a particular social process are present some of the time but absent at other times.

Because of its focus on analytic elements such as 'tasks', collective decisions', and more generally on abstractly defined situations within which a social process occurs, expectation states theories cut across the 'macro-micro' distinction that is so common in sociological theory. This does not mean that size, distance, complexity and other properties of larger-scale social systems make no difference to how expectation state processes work. Even the difference between two and three actors makes a profound difference to an expectation states process (cf. Fisek, 1974). But in expectation states theory 'scale' is treated as an analytic property like 'task', 'collective decision', et al., not as a fundamental difference in 'level' of theory.

On the other hand, expectation states theory is a theory about interpersonal processes. Its elements are (abstract aspects of) individuals and their relations. But this does not make it irrelevant to macro-sociology nor make macro-sociology independent of it. Many (though not all) 'macro' theories are theories about the aggregate effects of underlying social psychological processes, and in this case the results of research at the 'micro' level have important implications for 'macro' theories.

One example in particular of this relation between micro and macro theories involves the status characteristic research on multi-characteristic status situations. In general it has been found that at the individual level actors 'combine' information about multiple status characteristics, even if it is inconsistent, in forming a resultant status order (see Berger et al., 1980). The theoretical and experimental expectation states research which claims that information from multiple status characteristics is combined has major implications for macro-sociological theories of status consistency and inconsistency. Such macro theories as those of Lenski (1966), Zelditch and Anderson (1966), Galtung (1966) and others rest in a fundamental way on micro-level social psychological assumptions describing the behaviour of individuals in inconsistent status situations. Lenski (1966), for example, assumed that in a status inconsistent situation the actor eliminates (or ignores) contradictory status information and maximizes his status position by acting in accord with his positively evaluated status attributes. Thus, for example, if a male labourer is interacting with a female professional, according to this view, the male will define his situation in terms of the sex differences alone and the female in terms of the occupational differences. These status simplifying and status maximizing ideas long have been popular in sociological theorizing. In addition, the status simplifying principle also is involved in the other major status consistency theories (see Zelditch and Anderson, 1966; Kimberly, 1966; Galtung, 1966). In characterizing the individual's behaviour in status situations, all of these macro-theories of status consistency *generalize across the range of social situations* which the individual confronts, and for all situations these theories *aggregate over the behaviour of individuals* involved with status consistencies and inconsistencies.

The current research from status characteristic theory argues that for large classes of task-oriented situations these status simplifying principles do not hold. Thus, aside from other problems these macro-theories have, they also may be inadequate because the social psychological principles they use either are not valid or if they are valid it is for a limited set of (unspecified) social conditions. These arguments have not escaped sociologists studying macro-theories of status consistency. Treiman, for example, looking for Lenski-like inconsistency effects on prejudice (which he does not find) has suggested that there may be the operation, on the aggregate level at least, of what he calls a 'mean value theorem', and Crosbie (1979) has directly challenged these macro-theories on the grounds that their underlying social psychological principles may be invalid. All this does not mean that sociologists should not be constructing macro-theories of status consistency. What it does mean, however, is that in constructing such theories the sociologist should explicitly recognize: (1) that these theories rest on individual level social psychological principles, and (2) that the principles they use in constructing these theories should be consistent with (if not actually based upon) the social psychological status theories (of which the status characteristic theory is only one) which are being developed by sociologists.

Conclusion

What evidence is there that these 'themes' are fruitful? The question is difficult to answer because sociologists do not have a great deal of experience in evaluating the growth and development of a theoretical research programme (see Wagner and Berger, 1985). There are other examples in sociology and social psychology — Davis and Moore's theory of stratification, mathematical models of social mobility, Heider's theory of balance, and equity theory, for example — but we are still sufficiently unfamiliar with ways of conceptualizing them that we have few criteria of assessment. Lakatos's criterion (contrasting the 'excess impact' of progressive versus degenerating programmes) applies better to particular branches than to programmes as a whole — expectation states theory, for example, is a mixture of unevenly developing branches, some of which are arrested (like the 'authority-expectations' branch — see Table 1), others of which have long traditions and continue to grow actively (like the status characteristics branch). But even in the case of branches that have shown notable cumulative development, like the power-prestige, status characteristics or source branches, it is too early to assess properly their staying power. The programme is quite young, and most of the work is being carried on by a quite small body of researchers (mostly the original founders, their students or students of their students). What one can say, at this point, is that (1) some of the programme's branches have emerged as well-established traditions that continue as active and growing lines of work; (2) these have proven to be robust and powerful when applied; (3) some of its 'core' themes, such as the notion of a state organizing process and the conception of the 'holy triangle' (i.e., how abstract theory, theoretical research and applications are related), appear to be applicable to the study of a wide range of social phenomena; and (4), perhaps the most important feature of the programme, it is fertile in developing new and important branches of research activity. Finally, while some aspects of the programme's development may be unusual in sociological research, it is nevertheless fully in accord with the premise that whatever else sociology is (and it is surely many things), it is also a generalizing science, and therefore committed to theoretical growth.

Notes

1. This duality does not imply that the relations between behaviour and expectation states are necessarily symmetrical. In the Markov chain model constructed by Berger et al. (1969), for example, we find that while the behaviour of the interactant at time n is a probabilistic function of his expectation state at time n, his expectation state at time n is a probabilistic function of *both* his behaviour and his expectation state at time $n - 1$.

2. While the actor's self-interpretative and self-reflective statements are not used to measure his or her expectation state for the reasons which we described here, such information does have heuristic value and often is so used by expectation state researchers in developing their theoretical principles about expectation states and processes.

3. One of the original sources of this distinction is the very common observation among expectation state researchers that subjects' post-experimental reports on their behaviour (for example, on how many 'S-responses' they made) may bear very little relation to their actual behaviour as it occurred in the standardized experimental situation. As a consequence, we have long expressed the view, in lectures and discussions, that different principles are required to understand the individual's interpretation of his or her experimental experiences as a reflecting observer in a post-experimental interview, than are required to explain his or her behaviour as an actor in the experimental situation.

4. In fact, it is of considerable importance to distinguish findings that bear on the behaviour of non-interacting observers from those that bear on interactants. In a study of Fisek and Ofshe (1970), for example, they found that there was consensus in sociometric rankings among individuals who were members of a group in which there was behavioural differentiation throughout their task session, while there was no such consensus among individuals who were members of a group in which

differentiation emerged during the session. This is a finding about *non-interactant observers* reporting on their own behaviours. Presumably the more uniform and consistent the behaviour they are reporting on, the greater agreement in their observations. Identifying this properly as a finding about non-interactant observers (as opposed to interactants) helps us better to understand the relations between the social constructions of individuals as observers and their behaviours and states as interactants.

References

Balkwell, J.W. (1969) 'A Structural Theory of Self-Esteem Maintenance', *Sociometry* (December), 32: 458–73.

Balkwell, J.W. (1976) 'Social Decision Making Behavior: An Empirical Test of Two Models', *Sociometry*, 39 (1): 19–30.

Berger, J. (1958) 'Relations Between Performance, Rewards and Action-Opportunities in Small Groups' (unpublished doctoral dissertation). Harvard University.

Berger, J., B.P. Cohen, J.L. Snell and M. Zelditch Jr (1962) *Types of Formalization in Small-Group Research*. (Reproduced by Greenwood Press, Westport, Conn. 1980.)

Berger, J., B.P. Cohen and M. Zelditch Jr (1966) 'Status Characteristics and Expectation States', pp. 29–46 in J. Berger, M. Zelditch Jr. and B. Anderson (eds), *Sociological Theories in Progress*, Vol. 1. Boston: Houghton-Mifflin.

Berger, J., B.P. Cohen and M. Zelditch Jr (1972a) 'Status Characteristics and Social Interaction', *American Sociological Review*, 37: 241–55.

Berger, J. and T.L. Conner (1969) 'Performance Expectations and Behavior in Small Groups', *Acta Sociologica*, 12: 186–97.

Berger, J. and T.L. Conner (1974) 'Performance Expectations and Behavior in Small Groups: A Revised Formulation', pp. 85–109 in J. Berger, T.L. Conner and M.H. Fisek (eds), *Expectation States Theory: A Theoretical Research Program*. Cambridge, Mass.: Winthrop.

Berger, J., T.L. Conner and M.H. Fisek (eds) (1974) *Expectation States Theory: A Theoretical Research Program*. (Reproduced by University Press of America, Lanham, Maryland, 1982.)

Berger, J., T.L. Conner and W.L. McKeown (1969) 'Evaluations and the Formation and Maintenance of Performance Expectations', *Human Relations* (December), 22: 481–502.

Berger, J. and M.H. Fisek (1974) 'A Generalization of the Theory of Status Characteristics and Expectation States', pp. 163–205 in J. Berger, T.L. Conner and M.H. Fisek (eds), *Expectation States Theory: A Theoretical Research Program*. (Reproduced by University Press of America, Lanham, Maryland, 1982.)

Berger, J., M.H. Fisek, R.Z. Norman and D.G. Wagner (1983) 'The Formation of Reward Expectations in Status Situations', pp. 215–6 in J. Berger and M. Zelditch Jr (eds), *Status, Rewards and Influence*. San Francisco: Jossey-Bass.

Berger, J., M.H. Fisek, R.Z. Norman and M. Zelditch Jr (1977) *Status Characteristics and Social Interaction: An Expectation States Approach*. New York: Elsevier Scientific.

Berger, J., C. Ridgeway, S. Rosenholtz and M. Webster Jr 'Cues, Expectations and Behaviors' in E.J. Lawler (ed.) *Advances in Group Processes: Theory and Research*, Vol. 3. Greenwich, Conn.: JAI Press.

Berger, J., S.J. Rosenholtz and M. Zelditch Jr (1980) 'Status Organizing Processes', *Annual Review of Sociology* (August), 6: 479–508.

Berger, J. and J.L. Snell (1961) 'A Stochastic Theory of Self-Other Expectations', *Technical Report No. 1*, Laboratory for Social Research, Stanford University.

Berger, J. and M. Webster, (1979) 'Intergrating Social Processes'. Paper presented at the Annual Meeting of the Southern Sociological Society, Atlanta, Georgia.

Berger, J. and M. Zelditch Jr (1962) 'Authority and Performance Expectations', (unpublished manuscript). Department of Sociology, Stanford University.

Berger, J., M. Zelditch Jr , B. Anderson and B.P. Cohen (1968) 'Structural Aspects of Distributive Justice: A Status Value Formulation', *Technical Report No. 28*, Laboratory for Social Research, Stanford University.

Berger, J., M. Zelditch Jr , B. Anderson and B.P. Cohen (1972b) 'Structural Aspects of Distributive Justice: A Status Value Formulation', pp. 119–46 in J. Berger, M. Zelditch Jr and B. Anderson (eds), *Sociological Theories in Progress*, Vol. 2. Boston: Houghton-Mifflin.

Camilleri, S.F. and J. Berger (1967) 'Decision-making and Social Influence: A Model and An Experimental Test', *Sociometry* (December), 30: 367–78.

Camilleri, S.F., J. Berger and T.L. Conner (1972) 'A Formal Theory of Decision-making', pp. 21–37, in J. Berger, M. Zelditch Jr and B. Anderson (eds), *Sociological Theories in Progress*, Vol. 2. Boston: Houghton-Mifflin.

Camilleri, S.F. and T.L. Conner (1976) 'Decision-making and Social Influence: A Revised Model and Further Experimental Evidence', *Sociometry*, 39 (1): 30–8.

Cohen, E.G. (1971) 'Interracial Interaction Disability: A Problem for Integrated Education.' *Urban Education*, 5: 336–56.

Cohen, E.G. (1982) 'Expectation States and Interaction in School Settings', *Annual Review of Sociology*, 8: 209–35.

Cohen, E.G. and S.S. Roper (1972) 'Modification of Interracial Interaction Disability: An Application of Status Characteristic Theory', *American Sociological Review* (December) 37: 643–55.

Conner, T.L. (1965) 'Continual Disagreement and the Assignment of Self-Other Performance Expectations' (unpublished doctoral dissertation). Department of Sociology, Stanford University.

Conner, T.L. (1985) 'Response Latency, Performance Expectations, and Interaction Patterns', pp. 189–214 in J. Berger and M. Zelditch Jr (eds), *Status, Rewards and Influence*. San Francisco: Jossey-Bass.

Crosbie, P.V. (1979) 'Effects of Status Inconsistency: Negative Evidence from Small Groups', *Social Psychology Quarterly*, 24: 110–25.

Driskell, J.E. Jr (1982) 'Personal Characteristics and Performance Expectations', *Social Psychology Quarterly*, (December), 45 (4).

Fararo, T.J. (1973) 'An Expectation-States Process Model', pp. 229–37 in *Introduction to Mathematical Sociology*. New York: Wiley-Interscience.

Fisek, M.H. (1974) 'A Model for the Evolution of Status Structures in Task-Oriented Discussion Groups', in J. Berger, T.L. Conner and M.H. Fisek (eds), *Expectation States Theory: A Theoretical Research Program*. (Reproduced by University Press of America, Lanham, Maryland, 1982.)

Fisek, M.H. and R. Ofshe (1970) 'The Process of Status Evolution', *Sociometry* (September), 33: 327–45.

Foschi, M. (1968) 'Imbalance Between Expectations and Evaluations'. Paper presented at the Canadian Sociology and Anthropology Association Meetings, Calgary, Canada.

Foschi, M. (1971) 'Contradiction and Change of Performance Expectation', *Canadian Review of Sociology and Anthropology*, 8: 205–22.

Foschi, M. and M. Foddy, (1981) 'Standards, Expectations and the Assignment of Abilities to Self and Other'. Grant Proposal to the Social Sciences and Humanities Research Council of Canada.

Foschi, M. and R. Foschi (1976) 'Evaluations and Expectations: A Bayesian Model', *Journal of Mathematical Sociology*, 4 (2): 279–93.

Foschi, M. and R. Foschi, (1979) 'A Bayesian Model for Performance Expectations: Extension and Simulation', *Social Psychology Quarterly*, 42 (3): 232–41.

Galtung, J. (1966) 'Rank and Social Integration: A Multidimensional Approach', pp. 145–98 in J. Berger, M. Zelditch Jr and B. Anderson (eds), *Sociological Theories in Progress*, Vol. 1. Boston: Houghton-Mifflin, 1966.

Humphreys, P. and J. Berger (1981) 'Theoretical Consequences of the Status Characteristics Formulation', *American Journal of Sociology*, (March): 953–83.

Jasso, G. (1978) 'On the Justice of Earnings: A New Specification of the Justice Evaluation Function', *American Journal of Sociology*, 83 (6): 1398–419.

Johnston, J.R. (1977) 'Investigation of Pseudo-Mutuality, Double Binding and Scapegoating — An Expectation-States Approach'. *Technical Report No. 55*, Laboratory for Social Research, Stanford University.

Johnston, J.R. (1978) 'Stereotyping, Scapegoating and Pseudo-Mutuality — An Expectation-States Approach' (unpublished doctoral dissertation). Department of Sociology, Stanford University.

Johnston, J.R. (1980) 'Resolution of Verbal/Nonverbal Contradictions in Communication'. Paper presented at the Annual Meeting of the Pacific Sociological Association. San Francisco.

Johnston, J.R. (1985) 'Personality Attributes and the Structure of Interpersonal Relations', pp. 317–49 in J. Berger and M. Zelditch Jr (eds), *Status, Rewards and Influence*. San Francisco: Jossey-Bass.

Kervin, J.B. (1972) 'An Information Processing Model for the Formation of Performance Expectations in Small Groups' (unpublished doctoral dissertation). Johns Hopkins University.

Kimberly, J.C. (1966) 'A Theory of Status Equilibration', pp. 213–25 in J. Berger, M. Zelditch Jr and B. Anderson (eds), *Sociological Theories in Progress*, Vol. 1. Boston: Houghton-Mifflin.

Lakatos, I. (1970) 'Falsification and the Methodology of Scientific Research Programmes', in I. Lakatos and A. Musgrave (eds), *Criticism and the Growth of Knowledge*, Cambridge: Cambridge University Press.

Lenski, G. (1966) *Power and Privilege: A Theory of Social Stratification*. New York: McGraw-Hill.

Lindenberg, S. (1981) 'Rational, Repetitive Choice: The Discrimination Model Versus the Camilleri-Berger Model', *Social Psychology Quarterly*, 44 (4): 312–30.

Moore, J.C. Jr. (1968) 'Status and Influence in Small Group Interactions', *Sociometry* (March), 31: 47–63.

Moore, J.C. Jr. (1969) 'Social Status and Social Influence: Process Considerations', *Sociometry*, (June), 32: 145–68.

Moore, J.C. Jr. (1983) 'Role Enactment and Self-Identity: An Expectation States Approach'. Paper presented at the West Coast Small Groups Conference, San Jose, California.

Moore, J.C. Jr. (1985) 'Role Enactment and Self-Identity: An Expectation States Approach', pp. 262–316 in J. Berger and M. Zelditch Jr (eds), *Status, Rewards and Influence*. San Francisco: Jossey-Bass.

Ridgeway, C.L., L. Smith and J. Berger (1985) 'Non-verbal Cues and Status: An Expectation States Approach', *American Journal of Sociology*, March, 90: 955–78.

Shelley, R.K. (1972) 'Interpersonal Influence and Decision-making: Monetary vs. Non-monetary Rewards', (unpublished doctoral dissertation). Department of Sociology, Michigan State University.

Shelley, R.K. (1979) 'Sentiment, Prestige and Influence'. Grant proposal to the National Science Foundation, Department of Sociology, University of Ohio.

Skvoretz, J. (1981) 'Extending Expectation States Theory: Comparative Status Models of Participation in N Person Groups', *Social Forces*, 59 (3): 752–70.

Sobieszek, B. (1972) 'Multiple Sources and the Formation of Performance Expectations', *Pacific Sociological Review*, (January) 15: 103–22.

Talley, J. and J. Berger (1983) 'Social Control as a State Organizing Process'. Mimeograph, Stanford University, 1983.

Wagner, D.G. and J. Berger (1985) 'Do Sociological Theories Grow?' *American Journal of Sociology*, 90: 697–728.

Wattendorf, J.F. (1979) 'Interpersonal Similarity/Dissimilarity Bonds: An Expectation-States Approach' (unpublished doctoral dissertation). Department of Sociology, Stanford University.

Webster, M. Jr. (1969) 'Sources of Evaluations and Expectations for Performances', *Sociometry*, 32: 243–58.

Webster, M. Jr. (1980) 'Integrating Social Processes.' Research proposal funded by National Science Foundation.

Webster, M.A. Jr. (1982) 'Moral Characteristics and Status Generalization'. Research proposal funded by National Science Foundation.

Webster, M.A. Jr. and B.I. Sobieszek, (1974) *Sources of Self-Evaluation: A Formal Theory of Significant Others and Social Influence*. New York: John Wiley.

Zelditch, M. Jr. (1972) 'Authority and Performance Expectations in Bureaucratic Organizations', pp. 484–513 in C.G. McClintock (ed), *Experimental Social Psychology*, New York: Holt, Rinehart and Winston.

Zelditch, M. Jr. and B. Anderson (1966) 'Stability of Organizational Status Situations', pp. 269–94 in J. Berger, M. Zelditch Jr. and B. Anderson (eds), *Sociological Theories in Progress*, Vol. 1. Boston: Houghton-Mifflin.

Notes on contributors

H.J. Helle is Professor of Sociology at the University of Munich and Head of the Institut für Soziologie at Munich. In 1982 he chaired the symposium on Revisions and Relations among Modern Microsociological Paradigms at the Tenth World Congress of Sociology. He is the author of *Soziologie und Symbol* (Duncker and Humblot). His special areas of interest are: social psychology, sociology of the family, sociology of religion and sociological theory.

S.N. Eisenstadt is Professor of Sociology at the Hebrew University of Jerusalem. His publications include *From Generation to Generation, The Political Systems of Empires, Israeli Society* and *Revolution and the Transformation of Societies*.

Ralph H. Turner is Professor of Sociology at the University of California, Los Angeles and, since 1980, has been Editor of the *Annual Review of Sociology*. He has published extensively in the fields of collective behaviour, the social aspects of disaster, theory of social roles and sociological theory and methods.

Hans Joas is the Heisenberg Fellow at the Max Planck Institute for Human Development and Education, and 'Privatdozent' in Sociology at the Freie Universitat, Berlin. In Spring 1985 he was Visiting Professor in the Department of Sociology at the University of Chicago. He has major publications on role theory and on the anthropological foundations of sociology. His study of G.H. Mead appeared in English in 1985 with the title: *G.H. Mead: A Contemporary Reexamination of His Thought* (MIT Press).

G. David Johnson is Assistant Professor of Sociology and Anthropology at the University of South Alabama in Mobile. He has published an article on the history of American Social Psychology in *Symbolic Interaction* and articles on gender inequality in the *Journal of Marriage and the Family* and *Sex Roles*. He is currently writing a monograph where he develops a theory of Western family change from a socio-historical comparison of early modern England, France and the American Colonies.

J. Steven Picou is Professor and Graduate Advisor, Department of Sociology, Texas A&M University, College Station, Texas, USA. His publications include *Career Behavior of Special Groups* (with R.E. Campbell) and *American Sociology: Theoretical and Methodological Structure* (with R.H. Wells). He is currently involved in research on the community impact of technological disasters as well as research in the areas of sociological theory, private-sector organizations and clinical sociology.

Jef Verhoeven is Professor of Sociology at the Katholiek Universiteit Leuven, where he specializes in theoretical sociology and the sociology of education. He has published in both these areas and is currently working on a study of metascientific problems in American symbolic interactionism, in addition to further work in the sociology of education.

Arthur W. Frank is Associate Professor of Sociology at the University of Calgary, Alberta, Canada, where he also teaches in the Programs in Communications and in Women's Studies. His research using conversation analysis has appeared in the *Canadian Review of Sociology and Anthropology*, *Semiotica*, and *Human Studies*, and his earlier writings about ethnomethodology have appeared in the *Annual Review of Sociology* (1979). His current interests concern post-structuralism and the relation of text and lives.

Paul Atkinson is a Senior Lecturer in the Department of Sociology, University College, Cardiff. He is the author of *The Clinical Experience* (Gower Press), *Language, Structure and Reproduction* (Methuen), and joint author with Martyn Hammersley of *Ethnography* (Tavistock), as well as editor of three collections of papers.

Steven L. Gordon is Associate Professor of Sociology at California State University, Los Angeles. His publications have been in the areas of: sociology of emotion, children's emotional development, gender differences in close relationships and theory of the self-concept.

Joseph Berger is Professor of Sociology at Stanford University. From 1977 to 1983 he was chair of the Department of Sociology at Stanford. His earlier works include *Status Characteristics in Social Interaction* (with Fisek, Norman and Zelditch) in 1977; *Expectation States Theory: A Theoretical Research Program* (with Conner and Fisek) in 1974; two volumes of *Sociological Theories in Progress* (with B. Anderson and Zelditch) in 1966 and 1972; and *Types of Formatization in Small Groups Research* (with Cohen, Snell and Zelditch) in 1962, a new printing of which appeared in 1980 from the Greenwood Press.

David G. Wagner is Associate Professor of Sociology at Stanford University. He received his BS from Michigan State University (1971) and PhD from Stanford (1978). He has taught at the University of Toronto (1976–1978) and the University of Iowa (1978–1984). His recent work includes *The Growth of Sociological Theories* (1984) and articles on reward expectations, the labelling of mental illness, and the reduction of gender inequalities.

Morris Zelditch Jr is also Professor of Sociology at Stanford. He received the BA from Oberlin College (1951) and PhD from Harvard (1955). Before joining the faculty at Stanford, he taught at Columbia University (1955–1961). From 1964 to 1968 he was chair of the Department of Sociology at Stanford and from 1975 to 1978 editor of the *American Sociological Review*. In addition to *Status Characteristics and Social Interaction*, *Sociological Theories in Progress*, and *Types of Formalization in Small Groups Research*, all co-authored with Berger and others, he is the author of *A Basic Course in Statistics* (with T. Anderson).